THE PEOPLE'S CO-OP

THE LIFE AND TIMES
OF A NORTH END INSTITUTION

JIM MOCHORUK
WITH NANCY KARDASH

Editing: Doug Smith
Design: Doowah Design Inc.
Printed and bound in Canada by Highnell Printing Limited

A publication of:
Fernwood Publishing
Box 9409, Station A
Halifax, Nova Scotia
B3K 5S3

Fernwood Publishing Company Limited gratefully acknowledges the financial support of the Ministry of Canadian Heritage and the Canada Council for the Arts for our publishing program.

Canadian Cataloguing in Publication Data

Mochoruk, James David, 1957-
      The People's Co-op : the life and times of a north end institution

Includes bibliographical references and index
ISBN 1-55266-018-4

1. People's Co-operative History, I. Kardash, Nancy II. Title.

HD3450.W55M62 2000   334'.5'09712743   C00-901532-2

Photo Credits:

AUUC/WBA	Association of United Ukrainian Canadians / Workers' Benevolent Association Archives
JHS	Jewish Historical Society of Western Canada
MLL	Manitoba Legislative Library
MMMN	Manitoba Museum of Man and Nature
NAC	National Archives of Canada
PAM	Provincial Archives of Manitoba
PCL	People's Co-operative Limited Records
WTPA	Winnipeg Transit Photo Archives

Photo Credits for Chapter Headings

Ch.1:   Dufferin Market, 1916; PAM, Sisler 21, N9633
Ch.2:   May Day Rally, Timmins, Ont., 1923; AUUC/WBA
Ch.3:   Milk Pedlar, c. 1909; PAM, Hall 212
Ch.4:   Unemployed Demonstration, Winnipeg, Man., 1931; AUUC/WBA
Ch.5:   Co-op Milkman, 1936; PCL
Ch.6:   Myron Kostaniuk, 1939; PCL
Ch.7:   Bill Popowich, c. 1941; courtesy Bonnie Skyhar
Ch.8:   Members of the Co-op Board of Directors, 1948; PCL
Ch.9:   Louis Pollack, c. 1950; PCL
Ch.10: Members of the Co-op Board of Directors, Dufferin Employment Co-operative, 1992; PCL
Ch.11: Ernie Krall, 1939; courtesy Beth Krall

DEDICATION

This book is dedicated to the men and women who formed,
worked at and supported the People's Co-op over the course of seven decades.
Their courage to dream of a different world, and to take action to create that world,
is an inspiration to all who believe in the need for positive social change.

ACKNOWLEDGMENTS

A project such as this causes an author to incur innumerable debts of gratitude. As always, the staff at the Provincial Archives of Manitoba, the City of Winnipeg Archives and the Access to Information service at the National Archives of Canada made research more pleasant and fruitful than I had any right to expect. The people at the Workers' Benevolent Association and Association of United Ukrainian Canadians in Winnipeg opened up their records and photo collections – as well as their hearts – which greatly facilitated my research. And the people who still make heavy use of the Ukrainian Labour Temple in Winnipeg's North End, were uncommonly gracious and generous. Although they did not always know it, many of these people were invaluable sources of information to me as I puzzled through the reams of Co-op materials housed in their "Hall." There was always someone amongst the "old-timers" who could answer my questions, or at least set me on a rewarding new track of research. I am also greatly indebted to the former Co-op employees and customers who were willing to be interviewed for this project.

Thanks are also due to Nolan Reilly, a teacher, friend and colleague of long-standing, who leant a keen critical eye to the manuscript on three separate occasions. Wayne Antony, of Fernwood Publishing, gave encouragement, advice and – most importantly – deadlines. Doug Smith, a talented historian in his own right, provided his editing expertise. Tim Dunn's blue pencil finely honed the manuscript. The work of Steven Rosenberg and the staff of Doowah Design is reflected in this book's gorgeous design.

My greatest debt of gratitude, however, is owed to the members of the People's Co-op Wind-Up Committee. It was they who first informed me of the existence of the richly detailed material upon which this book is based, convinced me to take on the project, provided me with complete and unfettered access to these records (in fact, they even gave me keys to the building where the records were housed so that I could work all hours of the day and night) and then helped to underwrite the research costs. Two individuals must, however, be singled out for special thanks: Kosty Kostaniuk and Nancy Kardash. Kosty, despite health problems and a staggering personal loss, was not only the greatest supporter of this project, but also the individual who did most of the translations of Ukrainian documents into English – including five full years' of heavily detailed, and often handwritten, minutes. Nancy, who started out as a self-described "research-assistant" quickly became much more: she aided in archival research, handled all of the paperwork for our access to information requests, acted as an editor through three drafts and then took on the daunting task of locating and choosing the illustrations.

Finally, I must thank my family: Kaitlin, Brendan, and Colleen Mochoruk – who tried to be understanding when Dad was away so much doing research; Mary Mochoruk, who picked up all of the slack at home so that I could research and write this book; Sheila Mochoruk, who put up with her son moving back into her home in Winnipeg for prolonged periods of time; and my father, Zane Mochoruk, who did not live long enough to see this book, but who has always been my inspiration.

Jim Mochoruk

ABOUT THE AUTHORS

Born, raised and educated in Winnipeg, **Jim Mochoruk** earned his Ph. D. in history at the University of Manitoba in 1992. During his years in high school and university, he held many different jobs, but undoubtedly the most interesting was as a milkman for the People's Co-op – the third generation of his family to do so. As a historian his primary research interests are the social and labour history of Western Canada – particularly Winnipeg – and the history of northern development in Manitoba. Since 1993 he has been teaching Canadian, U.S. and British empire history at the University of North Dakota, where he is an Associate Professor of History and Chair of the Canadian Studies Committee. He lives in East Grand Forks, Minnesota, with his partner Mary and their three children, Kaitlin, Brendan and Colleen.

Nancy Kardash was born into a Co-op family and was raised within the Ukrainian community of Winnipeg's North End. She attended the University of Manitoba, the University of Alberta and the International Professional School of Bodywork in San Diego, California. She has had careers in education as a teacher, a curriculum developer and trainer of teachers, and in wholistic health care as a massage and movement therapist and instructor. She has a grown daughter and currently lives and works in Winnipeg.

TABLE OF CONTENTS

Winnipeg, 1928, looking west along Portage Avenue from its famous intersection with Main Street.

CHAPTER ONE
INTRODUCTION

WINNIPEG OF 1928

The Winnipeg of 1928 was a city that few present-day inhabitants would easily recognize. True, many of the major streets and some of the downtown's well-known buildings were already in place, as were some of the city's older residential neighbourhoods. However, none of the skyscrapers were yet built and large portions of present-day Winnipeg were still rural: the Maples, Garden City, Old Kildonan, East and West Kildonan, St. Vital, St. James and several other "suburbs" were still largely occupied by farming families. But perhaps even more notable than these physical differences were those associated with how people lived their lives.

Cars and trucks, although increasing in number, were not as common as other forms of transportation. Most people relied upon walking, bicycles or streetcars for getting around the city. Thousands upon thousands of horse-drawn wagons and sleighs were the backbone of the delivery system for many goods

Horses and wagons were still widely used for everything from hauling and delivery to providing entertainment such as this circus parade on Main Street, 1921.

Corner grocery stores, such as Aaron Grosney's on Selkirk Avenue, dotted Winnipeg's neighbourhoods.

distributed throughout the city. In fact, working people often lived within walking distance of their places of employment – even if that meant a walk of several miles – for a working-class income usually meant that streetcar fare, let alone ownership of a car, was a luxury.

Because of this, it was absolutely essential that people could obtain their food and other goods either very close to home or have them delivered. In heavily populated areas there would be a grocery store, butcher shop or green grocer on almost every street corner supplying a relatively small neighbourhood with its food needs and usually offering home delivery to the customers.

But these stores could not provide for all of the needs of their neighbourhoods. In 1928 refrigeration in homes was virtually unheard of; indeed, in the working-class districts of Winnipeg, even an ice-

Some early Jewish settlers turned to dairy farming in what is now West Kildonan. They peddled their milk directly to Winnipeg households. Shown here is the delivery man from the Chochinov Dairy.

box was deemed a luxury item in most homes and many stores. Home delivery of perishable goods in general and of milk in particular was common. Both milk and bread usually had to be delivered in time to be consumed before people left for work or school in the morning. And there were other goods

This family residence on Selkirk Avenue, which also housed the owner's tinsmith shop, was typical of the small homes owned by the skilled workers of the city's North End. The homes of labourers were just as small but were often shared by two or more families

as well as thousands of other horse-drawn delivery vehicles of retail and wholesale merchants – hit the streets of Winnipeg. Here, the deliverymen would cross paths with the workers either walking to work or walking to the main streets where they could catch the streetcars. The main streets themselves quickly filled up with foot traffic on the sidewalks, while on the roadway itself, streetcars, delivery trucks and the automobiles of the elite had to contend with the slow moving, horse-drawn traffic of the delivery vehicles.

Everywhere one looked, the horse and wagon (or sleigh, depending upon the season) was ubiquitous: stables and barns could be found in every precinct of the city, including the downtown core. However, because of the relative slowness of such methods of delivery, most smaller businesses tended to serve customers only in their own part of the city.

In a very real sense then, Winnipeg was far more a collection of communities than an integrated whole. As has been observed by historians such as Alan Artibise and Ed Rea, Winnipeg was truly a "divided city," and the most profound division was between the region lying north of the Canadian Pacific Railway tracks and those areas south of that line. This was not just a spatial or geographic

that had to be delivered directly to the home. In those days, most buildings were heated by coal and most cooking was still done on wood stoves, so considerable quantities of coal and cordwood had to be delivered to virtually every dwelling in the city. Those lucky enough to possess an icebox also had huge blocks of ice delivered to their homes.

In 1928 a typical day on Winnipeg's streets might look something like this: sometime between 3:00 and 4:00 a.m. hundreds of milkmen would begin their home deliveries from horse-drawn wagons. The uniformed salesmen of City and Crescent Dairies would jostle for customers with a wide array of independent milk peddlers who sold their unpasteurized milk and cream – usually from their own farms – directly from the cans that they hauled into the city every morning. Later in the morning, traffic congestion might develop as the wagons delivering bread, coal, fuel wood, ice and groceries –

The grand homes of Winnipeg's Establishment, such as the residence of timber baron D.C. Cameron on Roslyn Road, were to be found in the south end of Winnipeg.

Many immigrant men took work as labourers, like this street crew paving Magnus Avenue in 1920.

The Dufferin Avenue Market, 1916, already showed the distinct character and flavour that came to typify the North End.

division. The line separating north and south, with a buffer zone in the central core, was a line which encapsulated class, ethnic, political and gender-role differences of staggering proportions.

THE NORTH END

In the North End one could hear what has been called Manitoba's "tower of Babel": Ukrainian, German, Polish, Yiddish, Russian and several other eastern and central European languages seemed to be spoken in virtually every home and shop. Of these, Ukrainian came closest to being the lingua franca of the North End. English was a distant second, the language of school or work, spoken fluently by the children, but usually haltingly, if at all, by the adults. While a quarter of the residents of the North End were of English descent, they tended to live in their own little enclaves surrounding the railway shops and had limited interactions with the immigrants of the surrounding area.

If the North End was divided by language and ethnicity, it was unified and defined by class, for this was a profoundly working-class district. At the

Immigrant women often worked seven days a week in restaurants or earned little pay in the garment district's sweat shops.

It was not uncommon for poor women to walk miles for day work at the market gardens around the city. Here, Ukrainian women pick cabbage in what is now East Kildonan.

upper end of the spectrum there was the "labour aristocracy," the largely English-speaking, skilled workers of the metal and other trades who were employed by the railway at the Weston shops and in the metal shops of the Point Douglas area. The immigrant men worked in a wide variety of semi-

skilled or unskilled jobs, often having only seasonal employment, and just as regularly leaving town to look for work in bush camps, on railway construction projects or on harvest crews. The women, despite the middle-class attitude that "a woman's place was in the home," also tended to be wage earners. They often found work in the "Schmata" trade (garment industry) – either in sewing factories or as sweated labour in their own or a co-worker's home – or as domestic workers in the homes of the middle and upper classes. Indeed, in the North End, it was not uncommon for a woman to be the financial head of the household, often working for low wages, when the men in the family were unable to find work or had been laid off.

The immigrants of the North End and their children not only faced the economic problems common to working-class people, they also faced a vast reservoir of prejudice: the Slavs were the despised "men in sheepskin coats," "dumb hunkies," "bohunks," "garlic-eaters," "Polacks," "drunkards" – and on and on; the Germans were the much hated enemies of the last war; and finally, the Jews faced extreme anti-Semitism, ranging from ethnic slurs, housing covenants which excluded them from certain parts of the city and a quota system which kept their children out of the medical school at University of Manitoba, to actual violence against their persons and property.

Given these factors, it is hardly surprising that many North End residents were more than a bit alienated from the dominant culture of Anglo-Celtic Winnipeg. Some, like the main character in John Marlyn's *Under the Ribs of Death*, tried desperately to assimilate, to rid themselves of all accents, even

going so far as to change their names (although this was usually done to secure jobs reserved for Anglos, rather than to assimilate into the mainstream culture). But for many, this path to "Canadianization" was either impossible to follow or too distasteful to even contemplate. Forced by economic, geographic and cultural considerations to live on the "wrong side of the tracks," in what might be described as a ghetto, these people did not kowtow to their supposed social betters nor try to ape

Members of the Liberty Temple, seen here in 1926 at the Jewish Cultural Centre in the Sholem Aleichem School, were radical activists within the Jewish community.

The Second Congress of the Ukrainian Social Democratic Party of Canada held in Winnipeg, c. 1917. Standing eighth and ninth from left in the second row from the top are Matthew Popowich and William Kolisnyk. Note the presence of women and children in the photo; left-wing politics was clearly a family affair in the Ukrainian community.

The building of the Ukrainian Labour Temple, 1918.

The Ukrainian Labour Temple at the corner of Pritchard and McGregor was built by volunteer labour, reflecting the militancy and commitment of the times. Opened in 1919 and expanded in 1926 to accommodate a school and newspaper, the "Hall", as it came to be known to its members, was the birthplace of the Workers and Farmers Co-operative Association, later known as the People's Co-op.

Ukrainian Dance School of the ULFTA in Winnipeg, 1926. Groups such as this provided cultural and educational opportunities for the growing Eastern European immigrant population.

their mannerisms and values. Instead, they did something quite remarkable: they forged their own community and advanced their own values through a series of cultural and political organizations. In short, they made their own ethnic and class-based culture in the North End of Winnipeg.

They expressed an important part of this culture through their politics. Long before Winnipeg's famous General Strike of 1919, the North End was fertile ground for radical political and industrial organizations. Given their living and working conditions, North Enders did not need a Marx or any other theorist to tell them that the existing economic, political and social system was badly flawed – the harsh reality of inequality was all around them. Thus, it is not all that surprising that several locals of the Socialist Party of Canada, the Social Democratic Party of Canada, the Jewish Arbeiter Ring (or "Workers' Circle" that included separate Anarchist, Marxist and Socialist-Zionist branches) and a whole slew of smaller radical reading circles and dramatic and cultural groups sprang up in the North End during the first two decades of the twentieth century. Nor is it surprising that militant unions such as the Industrial Workers of the World (the Wobblies) and, later, The One Big Union and the Workers Unity League could be found aplenty in

the North End between the turn of the century and the 1930s. What is perhaps surprising though, is that through the financial support and voluntary labour of the truly impoverished people of the North End, the almost unthinkable was accomplished: large and impressive structures were built, owned and maintained by these immigrant workers, both to house their political organizations and, more importantly, to provide space for their printing presses and newspapers and to serve as meeting places for myriad cultural and educational activities.

Of these halls, none was more ambitious or impressive than the Ukrainian Labour Temple, at the corner of Pritchard and McGregor Streets. Completed just in time to serve as a North End headquarters for the 1919 General Strike, it became the political and cultural centre for several generations of left-wing Ukrainian Canadians. Just a few blocks away, at the corner of Pritchard and Salter, stood the equally busy Liberty Temple, which had been opened in 1917 by members of the left-wing Jewish community as a centre for their political, cultural and educational activities. These labour temples and meeting halls, and the activists who made them their homes away from home, inspired other workers to build their own working-class halls and organizations in other parts of Winnipeg and, indeed, all across Canada.

Clearly, the political culture of North End Winnipeg was somewhat different from the norm. For many years after the General Strike it seemed that the essential component of a successful North End political campaign – be it for Parliament, the Provincial Legislature, City Council or the School Board – was a political resume that read "arrested during the General Strike." In later years, that component would be expanded, and including "member of the ILP/CCF" or "member of the Communist Party" at the bottom of a brochure would be the key to success at the ballot box. To the intense frustration of Winnipeg's traditional political elite, North Enders kept on electing socialist and communist representatives to every level of government and played a pivotal role in electing two socialists to the Mayor's office during the 1920s and 30s. And if the election of social democrats such as J.S. Woodsworth, A.A. Heaps, F.J. Dixon, J. Blumberg, Marcus Hyman, Morris A. Gray, William Ivens and many others was frustrating to the elite, the election of Communists like William Kolisnyk, Andrew Bileski, Jim Litterick, Jake Penner, Bill Ross, Joe Forkin, Bill Kardash, Margaret Chunn, Joe Zuken and Mary Kardash was absolutely infuriating.

Still, politics, radical or not, was only one aspect of life in the North End. Far more inclusive than political activities were the cultural and educational programs that operated out of the North End's halls, churches and temples. Musical groups, theatre circles, dance troupes, sports clubs, mutual aid societies, language classes for both children and adults, co-operatives and adult education classes all jostled for time and space with political meetings, press operations and well-attended public meetings and debates. The cultural traditions and languages of eastern and central Europe were kept alive and well in these bastions of multiculturalism at a time when governments sought to suppress, rather than embrace, diversity.

Not everyone in the North End was a left-winger. For every Liberty Temple or Peretz Folk School there was a far more conservative Synagogue or Talmud Torah school and, in between, were organizations representing many shades of political and religious opinion. And for every branch of the Ukrainian Labour Temple Association (later

■ WILLIAM KOLISNYK ■

When **William Kolisnyk**, who became the Co-op's first general manager, was elected as an alderman to the Winnipeg City Council in November, 1926, he had the distinction of being the first Communist to hold public office in North America. His prominence in the ULFTA, along with earlier involvement in the OBU, the 1919 General Strike and the Social Democratic Party provided him with impeccable radical credentials.

According to his daughter, Hilda (one of his four children), Kolisnyk's main interests were "politics and the Co-op." In both areas, he put to good use his organizing and managing skills. He also operated his own bicycle shop on Main and Dufferin, and after leaving the Co-op, managed a co-operative bakery on Selkirk Avenue. His children and the employees who worked with him at the Co-op recalled him as being disciplined, exacting and fair.

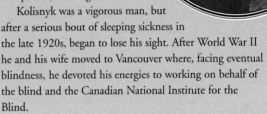

AUUC/WBA

Kolisnyk was a vigorous man, but after a serious bout of sleeping sickness in the late 1920s, began to lose his sight. After World War II he and his wife moved to Vancouver where, facing eventual blindness, he devoted his energies to working on behalf of the blind and the Canadian National Institute for the Blind.

renamed the Ukrainian Labour-Farmer Temple Association and then the Association of United Ukrainian Canadians) there were numerous church-based or nationalist-inclined Ukrainian groups that had their own cultural activities, newspapers and political agendas.

Profoundly divided by politics, religion and, after 1917, by attitudes towards events in eastern Europe, these groups operated in isolation from each other – except when they were in direct conflict – in spite of a shared language and culture. Yet, these groups all imparted their own flavour to the unique community that was the North End. And it was within this unique community that the history of the People's Co-operative would be played out.

The print shop in the basement of the Ukrainian Labour Temple was the heart of left-wing Ukrainian publishing in Canada. In its early years, the Co-op relied on the press for advertising and for reporting its activities to shareholders, customers and supporters.

CHAPTER TWO
BEGINNINGS

A DIFFERENT KIND OF CO-OPERATIVE

I n September of 1928, Joseph Demkiw received the first load of cordwood from Winnipeg's newest fuel yard, the Workers and Farmers Co-operative Association (WFCA), which had just opened for business at the old Robinson yard at the corner of Pritchard and Battery. Joseph Demkiw probably never imagined that his name would be mentioned in any history book. However, as a founding member of the WFCA as well as its first customer, he does have a place in history. He and hundreds of men and women like him in Winnipeg's North End shared an alternative vision of society and worked with phenomenal diligence to realize it. And the co-operative that Demkiw helped found was an integral part of their vision.

WORKERS & FARMERS
ESTABLISHED
1928
CO-OPERATIVE
ASSOCIATION LTD.
HEAD OFFICE: 610 DUFFERIN AVE.

PCL

While most western Canadians are well acquainted with co-operatives, be they wheat pools, grocery stores or gas stations, few know much about the WFCA/People's Co-operative or the handful of other radical co-operatives that once existed in scattered communities across Canada.

And this is a pity, for these co-ops were fascinating both for what they sought to accomplish and in the ways that they differed from other co-operative organizations.

While most co-operatives are either producer or consumer oriented, representing the economic interests of one group or the other, the WFCA/People's Co-op tried to unite producers and consumers within one organization. Hence the significance of its two very inclusive names — the Workers and Farmers Co-operative and then the People's Co-op. But this co-operative was also different because of its political orientation. Co-operatives in Canada have traditionally ranged from fairly

May Day gathering,1923, in Timmins, Ontario, where left-wing Ukrainians and Finns established the Workers' Co-operative of New Ontario in 1926. The Timmins co-operative was a huge success with a turnover of more than $200,000 and a profit of $10,000 in the first six months—impressive sums for that time.

conservative, large-scale producer co-ops to the moderately socialist or reformist consumer co-ops that are most comfortable within either the broad-ranging ideological home of the Co-operative Commonwealth Federation and later the New Democratic Party or an even less focused, anti-big business, small "l" liberalism. From the outset, however, the WFCA/People's Co-op was one of a small group of far more radical co-operatives. Along with the Timmins, Ontario-based Workers' Co-operative of New Ontario, the International Co-operative Stores of the Lakehead region and a few smaller Marxist-oriented co-ops in Toronto, Montreal, Hamilton and in mining towns in Alberta and British Columbia, the WFCA/People's Co-op saw its role as involving far more than saving its members money

or even ameliorating the conditions of workers and farmers under capitalism. Rather, the founders, managers and early workers of the WFCA believed that this co-op was to function as an educational and revolutionary institution, even as it provided service, savings and comfort to its working-class members and patrons.

FOUNDATIONS

The roots of the Workers and Farmers Co-operative extend far beyond its official 1928 start-up date, and go back to the left-wing Ukrainian organizations that had been developing in Winnipeg since the turn of the century. The Ukrainian-language sections of the Socialist Party of Canada, the Federation of Ukrainian Social Democrats, the Ukrainian Social Democratic Party of Canada – as well as Ukrainian supporters of the Socialist Party of North America and a few other U.S.-based Marxist parties – all played a role in supporting a vibrant, Ukrainian-language labour press and a host of left-wing theatrical, musical and literary associations. Collectively the leaders of these political movements, the editors of the labour press and the chief figures within the various cultural societies succeeded in bringing ever more Ukrainian-speakers into a left-wing or "progressive" orbit between the early 1900s and 1919.

Under the leadership of people like Matthew Popowich, John Navis, William Kolisnyk, Dennis Moysiuk and others, these groups coalesced in 1918–19 to form the Ukrainian Labour Temple Association (ULTA). Renamed the Ukrainian Labour-Farmer Temple Association (ULFTA) in 1924, this organization was at the heart of almost every subsequent development among left-wing Ukrainians in Winnipeg and the surrounding area – including the creation of the Workers and Farmers Co-operative Association.

From the outset, the Ukrainian Labour Temple Association was an ambitious undertaking, for it was not just a Winnipeg or even Manitoba-based organization, but a national institution with ties both to Ukraine and to the larger working-class movement. And its self-imposed mandate was broad ranging in more than just a geographic sense. As Matthew Popowich observed, its "activities ... were important not only for the Ukrainian labour-farmer immigrants, but also for the labour movement in Canada as a whole" – particularly through the operation of the ULTA's ten-point plan of educational, cultural and mutual aid activities.[1]

In keeping with this plan of action, in 1922 the ULTA helped to create another national organization, the Workers' Benevolent Association (WBA), a mutual insurance organization for Ukrainian-Canadians, which provided death benefits and a rudimentary form of health insurance for its members. While both the ULTA and the WBA were

The Sixth National Convention of the Ukrainian Labour Farmer Temple Association in Winnipeg, 1925. At its height, the ULFTA had over 350 branches and supported more than 600 cultural groups in approximately 100 halls across Canada.

national organizations, they were firmly rooted in Winnipeg's North End, operating out of the ULTA's main hall at Pritchard and McGregor. They therefore paid particular attention to opportunities for expanding their activities – and their membership – in the Winnipeg area.

Many of the leading members of the ULTA and the WBA had had some experience with co-operatives back in the old country and were keenly aware of the role that co-operatives were playing in the political and economic life of western Europe and in the newly formed Union of Soviet Socialist Republics (USSR). As early as 1925 the executive members of the ULFTA and WBA were discussing the possibility of launching a co-operative that would both serve Winnipeg's Ukrainian working class and bring more workers into contact with the Ukrainian-Canadian left.

Formed in 1922 to provide benefits and assistance to working people when they became ill or injured, the Workers' Benevolent Association often gave loans to the Co-op at crucial moments.

While there was general agreement on the benefits of a co-operative, there were two difficult questions to be resolved: first, were there enough skilled people within the Ukrainian left-wing community to launch and run such a co-operative; and second, what specific type of enterprise should be created? Given that the people involved in these discussions were already running a rapidly expanding mutual benefit/ insurance society, a series of Labour Temples, numerous cultural and educational programs, as well as writing, editing and publishing several Ukrainian-language newspapers and journals, the problem was not lack of expertise, but shortage of time.

The leadership of these organizations was stretched to the breaking point. The few individuals

Some of the newspapers/journals of the ULFTA. At the time of the founding of the Co-op, a single year's circulation of these publications totalled over two million copies.

who had paying positions with the ULFTA, the WBA or the press (poorly paying jobs at that) were incredibly busy. They were expected to be involved with the national and local executives of the ULFTA and WBA, publish *The Ukrainian Labor News* and several other journals, look after all of the business aspects of the various organizations, lead adult education classes, teach the "higher education courses" (designed to provide the next generation of leaders for the organizations) and perform in the various plays and other cultural productions. As guest speakers and organizers they also travelled to any town with a sizable Ukrainian population to help set up branches of the ULFTA and the WBA. Add to all of this their time-consuming commitments to the Social Democratic Party and later to the newly formed Communist Party, Workers' Party and Canadian Labour Party (which many ULFTA and WBA leaders had helped to found, and represented as candidates in various elections throughout the 1920s) and they hardly had time to breathe, let alone create and run another organization.

Nor were matters any better for those who did not work directly for the organizations. Their working days often stretched beyond twelve hours, usually in back-breaking physical labour, for six or six-and-a-half days per week. Very few of these people had any schooling beyond the most rudimentary level (which explains why the ULFTA focused upon adult education classes) and were functionally illiterate in either Ukrainian or English or both. As such, they could not take on a leadership role in an enter-a co-operative coal and wood yard. But this was meant to be only the first step in establishing a diverse set of co-operative enterprises. In fact, the plan ratified at this meeting called for the eventual creation of a grocery store and butcher shop and, space permitting, an information bureau and bookstore.

For the time being, however, it was the coal and wood yard that was to be proceeded with, and a five-member committee was given two weeks to draft a constitution for the new co-opera-

Printed in both Ukrainian and English, the constitution of the Workers' and Farmers' Co-operative was based on one originally drafted in Winnipeg in the early 1920s when a co-operative was first discussed. That draft was used first, however, by the co-operative established in Timmins.

prise that would demand literacy in at least two languages – Ukrainian for dealings with most of the initial customers and English for dealings with government officials and suppliers.

Despite these obstacles, and inspired by the successful establishment of the Workers' Co-operative of New Ontario in Timmins in 1926, the Winnipeg-based leadership of the ULFTA and WBA decided in 1928 to form a "temporary initiating committee" to examine the possibility of creating a co-operative.

On July 25, 1928, Alderman William Kolisnyk, the first Communist ever elected to municipal office in North America, presented the committee's proposal to a special meeting of the ULFTA and WBA executive committees. Kolisnyk's report left the forty-two men and women at this meeting (representing the National, the Winnipeg and the two Women's Section executives of these organizations) with much to consider: it called for the creation of

Original share certificate from 1928. As the minutes of the mass membership meeting of the ULFTA, August 25, 1928, indicated: "Already a number of applications have come from comrades, men and women, who want to become shareholders in their co-operative and are prepared to assist financially to the extent that they can. They are class conscious men and women who believe in the great strength of the working class."

tive. On August 8, the co-op's draft constitution was approved in principle. Funds were to be raised through the sale of $10 shares. Thousands of circulars were distributed to all members of the ULFTA, the WBA and subscribers of the organization's various newspapers and journals, urging attendance at

КООПЕРАТИВА.

Українські робітничі організації у Вінніпегу починають поширювати свою працю на инші галузі діяльности. Вони розпочинають кооперативну діяльність, і в цій справі скликають в суботу, 25. серпня, вечером, в Українськім Робітничім Домі загальний мітінг членства українських робітничих організацій у Вінніпегу.

Що ми називаємо кооперацією? Кооперація — значить співробітничання, співпраця одного великого гурта людей чи цілої громади на певному полі. Кооперативами називаємо інституції, що збудовані громадою на рівних правах і для користи громади. Така громадська кооперативна праця дуже корисна і має величезне економічне та виховавче значіння для працюючих, в першу чергу для тих, що є членами кооперативних інституцій і є їх будівничими.

Великий вчитель трудящих мас Ленін надавав дуже велечезне значіння кооперативному рухові, бачучи в нему школу соціялістичного будівництва в капіталістичних країнах і осн... соціялістичного будівництва в робітничо-селянській кр... В Радянському Союзі нині майже ціле економічне життя кр... збудоване на кооперативних основах.

Кооперативні інституції відограють дещо відмінну р... в капіталістичних країнах, де вони також дуже пошир... Взяти хоч би фармерську пшеничну (гвіт пул) коопер... в Канаді. Капіталісти дуже не люблять, коли працюючі...

This editorial in the August 25, 1928 *Ukrainian Labor News* entitled "A Co-operative" explained the need for such an undertaking and urged readers to attend the mass meeting that day, the first of several to be held. The ad on the right, "Everyone Come to Meetings about the Co-operative," announced a founding meeting on September 1, followed by another gathering on September 3 to sign up new members and get the Co-op off the ground.

a mass meeting to formally launch the co-operative and enroll members in the new Workers and Farmers Co-operative Association. Meanwhile, the search began for a fuel yard location.

The mass meeting on August 25 was a huge success. Over the

course of four hours William Kolisnyk and Matthew Shatulsky, two of the community's best orators, gave rousing speeches in Ukrainian. Both stressed how a co-operative would help the working class to struggle against an oppressive and "unmerciful capitalism" while providing a vital service to the community.[2] They were greeted with prolonged applause, but more importantly, when the clapping stopped, people put their hands in their pockets and took out money to purchase shares.

This meeting also elected a more permanent executive for the WFCA, and charged it with getting the business up and running as quickly as possible. Over the next three weeks, five formal meetings of either the executive or the general membership were held, along with many less formal meetings. Officers were elected; order cards, letterhead and envelopes were ordered from the organization's press; office space at the Labour Temple was rented; cheques and a corporate seal were ordered; ads were placed in the Ukrainian-language *Farmers' Life*, urging farmers to ship cord wood to the WFCA; bank accounts were established; and a part-time general manager, William Kolisnyk, was appointed at the princely salary of $15 per week. After considerable debate over whether to rent or buy their primary business location, the Robinson Yard at Pritchard and Battery was rented for $150 per month. By September 15, less than two months after the start of preliminary discussions, the WFCA was receiving supplies of wood, several carloads of coke and coal were on their way, and North

ПРИХОДІТЬ ВСІ НА МІТІНГИ КООПЕРАТИВИ!

Ініціятивний Комітет українських робітничих організацій при Укр. Роб. Домі у Вінніпегу скликає

В СУБОТУ, 1. ВЕРЕСНЯ 1928 РОКУ

В УКР. РОБІТНИЧІМ ДОМІ У ВІННІПЕГУ

УСТАНОВЧІ ЗБОРИ РОБІТНИЧО-ФАРМЕРСЬКОЇ КООПЕРАТИВИ.

На цих зборах затвердиться статут, членство й виберється заряд кооперативи. Хто бажає ще стати членом кооперативи, того радо вітаємо. ПОЧАТОК ТОЧНО В ГОДИНІ 8.30 ВЕЧЕРОМ.

Ініціятивний Комітет повідомляє українське робітництво у Вінніпегу, що

В ПОНЕДІЛОК, 3. ВЕРЕСНЯ (ЛЕЙБОР ДЕЙ)

— відбудеться —

В УКРАЇНСЬКІМ РОБІТНИЧІМ ДОМІ

МАСОВЕ ВІЧЕ РОБІТНИЧО-ФАРМЕРСЬКОЇ КООПЕРАТИВИ

на яке запрошуємо всіх членів і членкинь робітничих організацій, читачів нашої преси і всіх, хто цікавиться робітничими справами, хто хоче знати, які завдання має кооператива і які користи дає вона робітництву. На цему мітінгу будеться приймати нових членів.

ПОЧАТОК ТОЧНО В ГОДИНІ 8.30 ВЕЧЕРОМ.

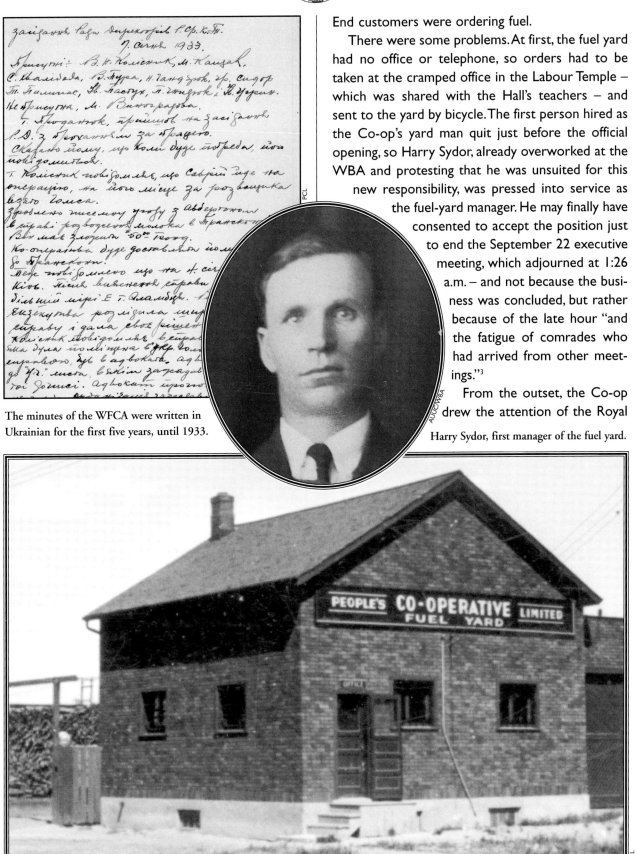

The minutes of the WFCA were written in Ukrainian for the first five years, until 1933.

Harry Sydor, first manager of the fuel yard.

End customers were ordering fuel.

There were some problems. At first, the fuel yard had no office or telephone, so orders had to be taken at the cramped office in the Labour Temple – which was shared with the Hall's teachers – and sent to the yard by bicycle. The first person hired as the Co-op's yard man quit just before the official opening, so Harry Sydor, already overworked at the WBA and protesting that he was unsuited for this new responsibility, was pressed into service as the fuel-yard manager. He may finally have consented to accept the position just to end the September 22 executive meeting, which adjourned at 1:26 a.m. – and not because the business was concluded, but rather because of the late hour "and the fatigue of comrades who had arrived from other meetings."[3]

From the outset, the Co-op drew the attention of the Royal

The Co-op Fuel Yard occupied a square block and included a house for employees. It was bounded on the west by the CPR tracks whose spur lines carried coal cars into the yard. The office stood in one corner of the yard at Pritchard and Battery.

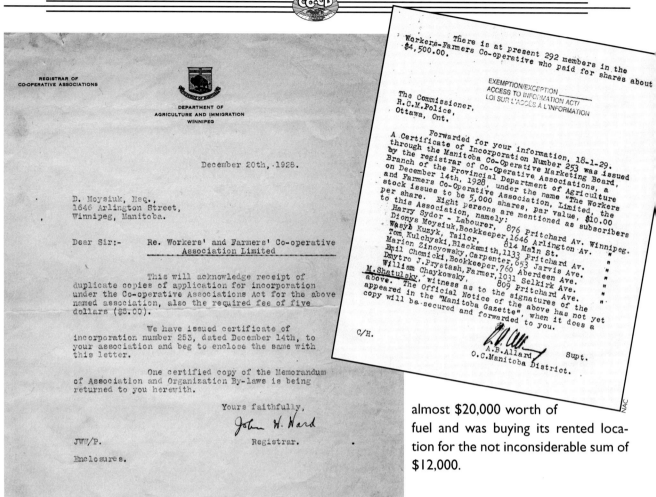

REGISTRAR OF
CO-OPERATIVE ASSOCIATIONS

DEPARTMENT OF
AGRICULTURE AND IMMIGRATION
WINNIPEG

December 20th, 1928.

D. Moysiuk, Esq.,
1646 Arlington Street,
Winnipeg, Manitoba.

Dear Sir:-   Re. Workers' and Farmers' Co-operative
Association Limited

This will acknowledge receipt of
duplicate copies of application for incorporation
under the Co-operative Associations Act for the above
named association, also the required fee of five
dollars ($5.00).

We have issued certificate of
incorporation number 253, dated December 14th, to
your association and beg to enclose the same with
this letter.

One certified copy of the Memorandum
of Association and Organization By-laws is being
returned to you herewith.

Yours faithfully,

John W. Ward

JWW/P.   Registrar.

Enclosures.

Workers-Farmers Co-operative who paid for shares about
$4,500.00. There is at present 292 members in the

EXEMPTION/EXCEPTION
ACCESS TO INFORMATION ACT/
LOI SUR L'ACCÈS À L'INFORMATION

The Commissioner,
R.C.M.Police,
Ottawa, Ont.

Forwarded for your information, 18-1-29.
A Certificate of Incorporation Number 253 was issued
through the Manitoba Co-Operative Marketing Board,
by the registrar of Co-Operative Associations, a
Branch of the Provincial Department of Agriculture
on December 14th, 1928, under the name "The Workers
and Farmers Co-Operative Association, Limited, the
stock issues to be 5,000 shares, par value, $10.00
per share.   Eight persons are mentioned as subscribers
to this Association, namely:
Harry Sydor - Labourer,
Dionys Moysiuk, Bookkeeper, 876 Pritchard Av. Winnipeg.
Wasyl Kuzyk, Tailor, 1646 Arlington Av.   "
Tom Kulchyski, Blacksmith, 814 Main St.   "
Marion Zinoyowsky, Carpenter, 1133 Pritchard Av. "
Emil Chomicki, Bookkeeper, 653 Jarvis Ave. "
Dmytro J.Prystash, Farmer, 760 Aberdeen Ave. "
William Chaykowsky, 1031 Selkirk Ave. "
M.Shatulsky, 809 Pritchard Ave.
above.   The Official Notice of the signatures of the
appeared in the "Manitoba Gazette" when it does a
copy will be secured and forwarded to you.

C/H.

A.B.Allard, Supt.
O.C.Manitoba District.

almost $20,000 worth of
fuel and was buying its rented location for the not inconsiderable sum of
$12,000.

When the Manitoba Department of Agriculture and Immigration issued a certificate
of incorporation to the WFCA late in 1928, the Co-op was already under surveillance
by the RCMP, as shown (right) in this correspondence between the force's commanding officer in Manitoba and his commissioner in Ottawa.

FOR THE CAUSE

Canadian Mounted Police, which had been tracking
the activities of members of the Ukrainian left for
the past decade. In September 1928, just as the Co-
operative was taking delivery of its first supplies,
Superintendent A.B. Allard, the Commanding Officer
of the RCMP for the Manitoba District, predicted in
a report to his superiors that the Co-operative
would soon go out of business because Kolisnyk had
"no business ability."[4]

What is amazing is that despite having no experience in fuel sales, despite several early changes in
the executive and management, and despite the
WFCA's lack of working capital, the venture was a
success within a few months of its September opening. Having begun with only $4000 of shareholders'
capital, by January of 1929 the Co-op had sold

This success would not have been
possible without tremendous dedica-
tion to the cause – and that is precisely what the
WFCA was: a cause, not just a business venture.
Members of the executive served long hours, without pay, in order to organize and help run the Co-
op. Kolisnyk and Sydor held paying management
positions with the WFCA as well as serving on the
executive, but their salaries were minimal: Kolisnyk
made $15 a week while Sydor worked sixty, and
seventy, hour weeks for $27.50. The allied organiza-
tions also played a key role in the WFCA's early success. The ULFTA provided office space for the nom-
inal sum of $10 a month, until the Co-op could
afford to pay more. Meanwhile, when the WFCA's
bank overdraft rose because of the necessity of buying supplies before sales could cover the costs, the
WBA stepped in with a $1,000 loan. When the deci-

ПОТРІБНО ДРОВ НА КООПЕРА-ТИВНИЙ СКЛАД.

Робітничо - Фармерське Ко-оперативне Товариство у Вінніпеґу просить всіх тих фарме-рів, які мають готові і добрі та сухі дрова на продаж, які **зараз** можуть заладовувати в ваґони, щоби зголошувалися на понищу адресу і пода[...] яке число кортів чи ваґонів [...] ни мають, які дрова та по як[...] ціні.

Діставши ці інформації, ко-оператива напише кожному, в кого замовляє дрова, які і по якій ціні, та дасть всі інформа-ції, як висилати. Нам треба дров з білої здорової паплі (трепети), білої здорової оси-ки, темраку, сосни і ялиці або тверде дерево, як дуб і береза.

Зголошуватись можуть лише ті, які не мешкають далі, як **сто миль від Вінніпеґу.** Адрес:

WORKERS & FARMERS COOP-ERATIVE ASSOCIATION,
Cor. Pritchard & McGregor Sts.,
Winnipeg, Man.

Ad in *Ukrainian Labor News*, Sept. 8, 1928 which garnered swift reponse:

WOOD NEEDED TO SUPPY THE CO-OPERATIVE

The Workers and Farmers Co-operative in Winnipeg invites all farmers who have good, dry wood ready for sale, and who can immediately haul it in by wagon, to contact the address below and give the number of cords or wagon loads as well as what kind and for what price. Upon receiving this information, the co-operative will indicate from whom it will order wood, what kind and for what price, and how it is to be delivered. We need white poplar, white pine, tamarack, spruce and fir or hard wood like oak and birch. Only those who live no more than 100 miles from Winnipeg need reply.

sion was made to buy the fuel yard, the WBA loaned the Co-op $2,000 for the down payment.

Membership dedication accounted for much of the Co-op's success. A steady influx of share capital and individual loans got the fuel yard going, provid-ed money for wood purchases when money was scarce, and then allowed for expansion. While the WBA's $3,000 in short-term loans was

More than half the Co-op's start-up capital came from money deposited by members and supporters into loan accounts at the Co-op. Like bank deposits, these Co-op loan accounts earned interest which, in the 1980s reached 18 per cent.

essential, it was the $4,550 of share capital and the $8,000 of member loans that allowed the WFCA to purchase its own premises in January 1929. These loans were a good deal for both the members and the Co-op. The members received 5 percent on the loans they made to their own institution (2 percent more than they would have received from a bank), while the WFCA saved at least 2 percent on the prevailing loan rate. Still, this was an act of faith by those who invested their meagre savings in the Co-op, for any new venture is a risky proposition.

No one could claim, however, that the members of Winnipeg's left-wing Ukrainian community lacked the courage of their convictions. This was, after all, the same community that had erected a $72,000 Labour Temple, formed and sustained a substantial mutual aid society, purchased a $46,000 estate for an orphanage and "Old Folks" home at Parkdale, Manitoba and provided the financial support for a wide variety of publications, political campaigns and educational and cultural programs.

While the members were good to the WFCA, it was undoubtedly a mutually beneficial relationship. Shareholders or their family members were given preference for employment at the fuel yard or as deliverymen, and the Co-op prided itself on paying its yard workers forty cents per hour, making them amongst the best-paid fuel yard workers in Winnipeg. The deliverymen received $1 per ton of coal delivered and

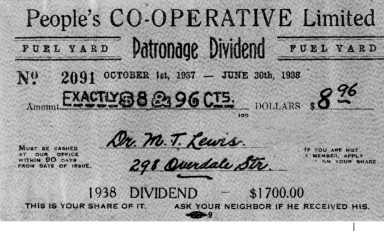

How Much Did You Save on YOUR Fuel Bill Last Season?

How Much Will You Save THIS Winter?

Our Customers saved $1,700 last season on their fuel bill. That saving came back to them as patronage dividends—a photo-copy of which can be seen on the back of this card.

Our Customers expect to realize additional savings this season as a result of their patronage of the People's Co-operative Ltd.

Why don't you make a saving in YOUR fuel bill by also patronizing the People's Co-operative Ltd.?

Your chance to save is as close to you as your nearest telephone. Phone your next fuel order in to us—phone 56 205.

People's CO-OPERATIVE Limited

FUEL YARD   Patronage Dividend   FUEL YARD

Nº 2091   OCTOBER 1st, 1937 — JUNE 30th, 1938

Amount EXACTLY $8 & 96 CTS.   DOLLARS $8 96

Dr. M. T. Lewis.

298 Overdale Str.

MUST BE CASHED AT OUR OFFICE WITHIN 90 DAYS FROM DATE OF ISSUE.

IF YOU ARE NOT A MEMBER, APPLY ON YOUR SHARE.

1938 DIVIDEND — $1700.00

THIS IS YOUR SHARE OF IT.   ASK YOUR NEIGHBOR IF HE RECEIVED HIS.

Patronage dividends were surplus revenues handed back to customers based on a percentage of their purchases. The first year's dividend was three percent; in better years, it was as much as eight percent. Note the name on the cheque – by the late 1930s not all of the Co-op's patrons or members were either Ukrainian or working class.

Workers & Farmers Co-operative Association, Limited

PHONE 56 205

DISTRIBUTORS OF COAL, WOOD AND GENERAL COMMODITIES ON CO-OPERATIVE BASIS

YARD AND OFFICE: COR. PRITCHARD AVE. & BATTERY ST.

Вінніпег, Ман., 20. вересня 1929.

Шановний Товаришу, Приятелю!

З оцим листом посилаємо Вам кредитний нот-чек на суму .... як три відсотки зворотної суми Вашого закупна в Робітничо-Фармерській Кооперативі за час девять і пів місяців, себто від 15. вересня 1928 до 30. червня 1929 року. На річних зборах кооперативи, що відбулися дня 31. серпня 1929 р. члени нашої організації рішили, щоби здобуту надвишку з продажі вугілля і дров розділити рівно для всіх покупців без огляду на те, чи вони є шеровцями кооперативи чи ні.

Загальний звіт з ведення кооперативної продажі вугілля і дров представляється так:

Загальний прихід з продажі палива від 15. вересня 1928 до 30. червня 1929 .. $50,313.10
Заплата за опал включно з фрейтом $46,499.05
Кошти оперування продажі 9,096.25

Разом $55,595.30
Відтягнути товар і приладдя, що є зараз на ярді 7,683.50   47,911.80

Чистий зиск $2,401.30
Відтягнути зниження вартости на приладдю й достaві 129.01

Остає чистого зиску для розподілу $2,272.29

Оставшу суму чистого приходу $2,272.29 після рішення членства кооперативи на річних зборах і після постанов Кооперативного Акту розподіляється так:

Резервовий фонд 227.23
Освітний фонд 227.23
Дивіденди шеровцям від вложених грошей 286.00
Решта для розподілу покупцям 1,531.83

Разом $2,272.29

Бачучи нагоду, кооператива купила для себе за $12,000 ярду, яка складається з 23 лотів, має також заїздну залізничу треку, офіс, вагу, мешкальний будинок і стайню. Суму, за яку куплено ярду, кооператива позичила з членів. Цей крок кооперативи поможе більше розвинутись організації, зменшаться видатки оперовання бизнесом та не буде на майбутнє обави, щоб хто будь підвищив нам рент або сказав випровадитися. З ціни, за яку куплено ярду, всі задоволені.

Це був наш перший рік, в якому ми вели купно й продажу палива на кооперативних основах. Звичайно, з цим були звязані спеціяльні видатки щодо організовання, ознайомлення з потребами і бажаннями наших покупців та трудношами, з якими ми стрічалися в справі задовольнювання цих потреб без проволоки. Ми надіємося, що Ви на майбутнє будете сами кооперувати з нами, як робили ціе в минулому і тоді спільними зусиллями ми зможемо добитися в слідуючому році кращих наслідків для всіх членів і покупців кооперативи.

В додаток вище сказаного ми хочемо звернути Вашу увагу на одну дуже важну річ. Кромі зороту покупцям і членам надвишки кооперативи, кожна особа, яка купує паливо в кооперативі, дістає на сто відсотків справедливу вагу, міру, та якість товару.

Тому надіємося й надалі Вашої щирої кооперації і будемо Вам вдячні за всі вказівки, добрі поради та сугестії, якими можна би попровадити наше спільне кооперативне діло до ще кращих успіхів.

З товариським привітом,

Робітничо-Фармерське Кооперативне Т-во

....

The 1929 Financial Report showed a "clear profit" of $2,401.30. After set-asides for reserve and education funds and a small shareholders' dividend, $1531.83 was distributed as a patronage refund.

seventy-five cents per cord of wood, also the top rate for such work. Better yet, because of the seasonal nature of the fuel trade, the WFCA was able to provide jobs during the winter, precisely when work was most needed in Winnipeg. An effort was also made to provide employment to members physically incapable of heavy work, such as soliciting new customers. When economic times got particularly tough, the Co-op divided up the yard work "to give those without work a chance to earn some money."[5] Finally, while the WFCA charged the prevailing rates for the wood, coal and coke, it was also committed to providing a patronage rebate, which meant that at the close of a successful year, customers would get a refund.

Because of these policies, the WFCA was able to report a surplus to the First Annual General Meeting of Shareholders. In keeping with its role as both a consumers' co-operative and as an educational force in the Ukrainian community, it distributed the surplus in an interesting fashion. After government mandated set-asides for depreciation and general reserve funds, a 5 percent dividend was offered on share capital, a 3 percent patronage dividend was issued to customers and 10 percent went to an education fund to be distributed at the Executive's discretion. This was of considerable importance, for the Co-op's mandate was much wider than that of a simple purveyor of fuel.

THE WFCA MANDATE

Mathew Popowich spelled out this mandate in a speech to the general membership in January of 1929. A driving force behind the ULFTA, the WBA and the Ukrainian-language press, Popowich had also been one of the leading advocates of forming the Co-op. As he saw it on that cold January evening, virtually everything about this co-operative was educational. He hoped that the WFCA's success would not only lead to expansion into many other fields of business in Winnipeg, but would serve as a model and inspire the growth of "this movement to all other parts of Canada among Ukrainian workers on the land and in the factories." Their operation would be part of a broader education for workers and farmers. "The Cooperative teaches people how to allocate products in a community fashion and therefore the community learns how to satisfy its needs..." The WFCA then, was part of an educational effort directed towards the working class, and as such was comparable to "strikes, protests, political struggle etc." in preparing workers and farmers to play their role on the stage of history.[6]

Popowich also suggested that surpluses – the monies saved from the hands of middlemen – could be used for "educational purposes and for our press." Eventually the Co-op might even be in a position to support striking workers, allowing them to win their struggles more quickly. He hoped that the WFCA and other such co-operatives could play an important role in the larger class struggle and would "teach people to work together ... to group into a single large force, a force of workers and poorer farmers that in time will overcome all difficulties and learn to advance to a better future."[7]

DREAMS OF EXPANSION

Expansion was very much on the mind of the WFCA's Executive from the outset. As early as March of 1929, when the first season's business was winding down, there were discussions about a Co-op bakery, a creamery and a store that would sell general merchandise. These suggestions were tem-

Matthew Popowich, seen here with Matthew Shatulsky (foreground), in the editorial offices of *Ukrainian Labor News*. These two men, along with John Navis, are considered to be the founding "fathers" of the Ukrainian labour-farmer movement in Canada.

porarily shelved to deal with the more pressing issue of how to better use the WFCA's existing property. Since the seasonal nature of the fuel business virtually shut down the yard for three months of every year, it was decided to canvass a number of building supply firms. It was hoped they would use the yard on a commission basis as a North End depot for such products as glass, paint, gravel, boards, lime and other such building materials. This would keep people coming to the Co-op and keep two people employed year-round.

By April tentative deals were in the works to handle lumber, doors and windows for one supplier, gravel, sand and cement for another and paint for a third. There was a growing consensus that the WFCA should become a retailer of hardware for a major firm such as Ashdown's or Marshall Wells.

As matters turned out, however, none of these deals were closed in 1929. In some cases, foot-dragging on the part of suppliers was to blame, while in others it was determined that the proposed arrangements would not benefit the WFCA. Thus, by the summer of 1929 expansion plans were deferred, and it was decided that the Co-op should concentrate on becoming better at the fuel business – and paying off the debt owed to its members – before launching any new enterprises.

This decision was probably a wise one, although it is doubtful that Kolisnyk and Sydor really needed much time to perfect their business techniques, as they were proving to be fast learners. They used the press, handbills and word of mouth to spread the news that the WFCA was not only successful, but was saving its customers money on their fuel bills through the patronage dividend. By the start of the 1929–30 heating season, the WFCA had twelve hundred customers placing orders, necessitating the hiring of more workers. Nine men were delivering coal on a regular basis, while the yard and office staff

From the outset, the Co-op realized the value of advertising. Coal was selling at $7-$19 per ton, wood from $7-$10.50 a cord. The ad proclaimed: "By buying from the co-operative—you buy from yourself, because after net profits are determined they are divided among the consumers." (*Ukranian Labor News*, October 11, 1928)

also had to be increased to keep pace with demand. Kolisnyk, meanwhile, was learning how to deal with tough competitors. When some Winnipeg coal dealers threatened the Co-op with a price war in retaliation for the WFCA's payment of the 3 percent patronage dividend, which they viewed as unfair competition, Kolisnyk coolly informed them that the WFCA would be quite happy to see some price-cutting. The Co-op would make sure consumers knew it was the WFCA's competitiveness that was bringing down the price of coal in Winnipeg. When the coal dealers then suggested that they might use their influence with Winnipeg's wholesale coal brokers to cut the Co-op out of the trade, Kolisnyk responded that "we will then obtain the coal [directly] from the mine owners, who themselves are coming to us with ... proposals that we buy the whole mine output."[8] RCMP Superintendent Allard must have wished he could rewrite his first report on the Co-op, which had glibly predicted the Co-op's demise.

Still, while most matters were going well for the WFCA, two serious problems were emerging. Because of the relative poverty and employment problems of many of the Co-op's customers and shareholders, credit was extended from the very outset of operations. At first, only shareholders were eligible. Fuel-yard manager Harry Sydor was to accept personal responsibility for credit extended to non-shareholders. This arrangement soon collapsed; by the end of the WFCA's first year, customers owed somewhere between $2,000 and

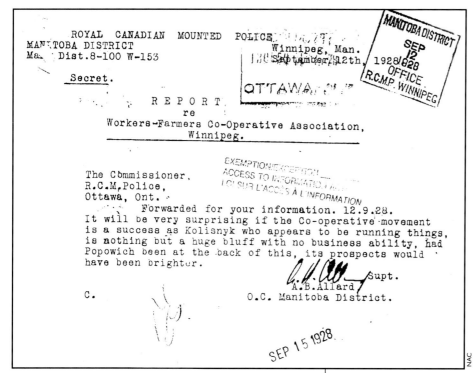

A.B. Allard's correspondence to the RCMP Commissioner in Ottawa. RCMP files were maintained on the Co-op into the 1980s.

$2,500, a large sum to a cash-strapped institution.

Many of the Co-op's shareholders and individual lenders soon found themselves in desperate need of money they had invested in the WFCA. While the Board of Directors discouraged withdrawal of share and loan capital, there was little they could do to prevent it. The loans to the Co-op had been set up as short-term, "on-demand" loans, which meant that people could withdraw these funds at any time. Even refunds of share capital, which involved a formal application and approval, could not be ruled out, given the financial hardships confronting some WFCA members.

Taken together, rising customer debt and the withdrawal of share and loan capital put the WFCA in a state of constant financial crisis. Even when the balance sheet looked good, the Co-op was having serious cash flow problems, necessitating continual appeals to the membership to lend the WFCA money to meet various obligations. Despite this help, loan withdrawals often outstripped incoming loans, so early in 1930 the Board of Directors asked the members to empower the Board to borrow money, issue bonds or to take any other financial

actions necessary to keep the business going without prior approval from the membership. The members not only approved this measure, but also pledged $7,150 for the immediate purchase of more wood. With such support, it is small wonder that the WFCA was able to survive and even thrive.

What needs to be borne in mind is that all of this support was being offered just as the most severe economic crisis to ever hit Winnipeg – and the western world – was beginning to take its toll. Although no one knew it yet, the Great Depression of the 1930s had well and truly begun and it would be in this economic context that the WFCA would have to operate for most of the next decade.

■ ■ ■

1   Matthew Popowich, *Labor-Farmer Calendar*, 1928. (Winnipeg: Labor-Farmer Publishing Association, 1928), p. 330. See also, Peter Krawchuck, *Our History: The Ukrainian Labour-Farmer Movement in Canada, 1907–1991*. (Toronto: Lugus Publications, 1996), p. 34.

2   People's Co-operative Limited, (hereafter PCL) Minute Book 1, "Minutes of the Mass Membership Meeting of all Organizations of the ULFTA, August 25, 1928."

3   Ibid., "Co-operative Executive Meeting, September 22, 1928."

4   National Archives of Canada, Record of the Canadian Security Intelligence Service, RG 146, Vol. 4089, "Report re: Workers-Farmers Co-operative Association, September 12, 1928."

5   PCL, Minute Book 1, "Executive Meeting, December 13, 1929."

6   Ibid., "Minutes of the General Membership Meeting of the WFCA, January 31, 1929."

7   Ibid.

8   Ibid., "Minutes of the General Membership Meeting, September 27, 1929.

The **"Dirty Thirties"** ushered in economic hard times that challenged the ability of millions of families to meet their basic needs. Residents of the North End were particularly hard hit, and they fought back. In the foreground of this picture one can see members of the Women's Section of the ULFTA participating in a demonstration in downtown Winnipeg during the 1930s.

CHAPTER THREE
THE GREAT DEPRESSION AND WINNIPEG'S MILK INDUSTRY

THE EARLY 1930S

As the Great Depression settled over Winnipeg, throwing thousands of people out of work or greatly reducing their wages and hours of employment, some things did not change. Whether working or not, people still needed a home, fuel to heat it, and food and clothing for their family. But neither welfare nor unemployment insurance as we know it today, was available in the early days of the Depression.

What little aid was available – known as "Relief" – was offered in a catch-as-catch-can fashion, with various charitable agencies called in by the City of Winnipeg to help distribute it. Moreover, the City government could not provide for the needs of the underemployed and unemployed. And the provincial and federal governments were slow to help with what was traditionally a municipal responsibility.

This meant that the poorest people in Winnipeg, particularly the North End working class, suffered some very difficult times, especially during the first few years of the Depression. Finding work and providing the basic necessities of life had been difficult enough for working-class families during the late 1920s, but during the Depression it became almost impossible. Because so many North Enders were immigrants, they also faced yet another problem – filing for Relief, and admitting that they had no means of support, could mean deportation to their country of origin. As historians Lyle Dick and Barbara Roberts have observed, the Canadian government turned to "shovelling out" unemployed immigrants as one method of dealing with the mounting economic crisis. At least 28,000 people were deported between 1930 and 1935.

The prospect of being deported to a country that one had left for economic reasons was bad enough, but one can only imagine the terror of those who had fled eastern or central Europe to escape political or religious persecution. Many families and individuals, no matter how dire their straits, never applied for aid once it became known that the government was taking such draconian steps. Since R.B. Bennett's government was particularly anxious to get rid of "dangerous foreigners" such as the left-wing immigrants who were most heavily involved in the ULFTA, the WBA and the Co-op, it would seem that the WFCA faced insurmountable odds. But the Co-op did not die; in fact, it boldly moved into a new venture just as the economic world was crashing down around everyone's feet.

> Comrade Yurechko came to the Board asking for work. He said that right now he is in dire financial straits, does not receive Relief because he was told he could be served deportation papers. He has been in Canada for 3 1/2 years. It was decided to take up this matter with Comrade Sydor to acquaint him with this situation; and after that, he would be given a few days' work at the wood yard.
>
> (Minutes, WFCA Board of Directors' Meeting, Nov. 27, 1932)
>
> Comrade Koshowski came to the meeting with a request for employment. He says that he cannot get Relief and was to be deported, and at present has no means of livelihood. He was told that when we will be installing the boiler that he will be taken on for a couple of days' work.
>
> (Minutes, WFCA Board of Directors' Meeting, April 30, 1933)

THE DESIRE FOR EXPANSION

The 148 shareholders at the August 1930 general membership meeting were keenly aware of the mounting economic crisis. As the minutes show, some people at this meeting had already lost their jobs, while others had withdrawn their shares because "they were forced by the crisis to the point where they could not make ends meet." If individual members were suffering, the Co-op was doing very well. Business had grown considerably. There were

now over 2,500 customers, and once again the WFCA had a healthy surplus for the year. As general manager William Kolisnyk reported, this customer base now included "even people who do not sympathize with our movement," but who were drawn to the Co-op because of its quality products and fair business practices.[1]

Emboldened by this success, several shareholders called for an immediate expansion of the Co-op's activities. Some focused upon practical reasons for expansion with one member observing that since the Co-op had to pay taxes year-round, it should make better use of its property by entering into year-round fields of endeavour. Others argued that expansion should take place for political reasons. Kolisnyk's report had stressed that by expanding operations and attracting new members and customers, the Co-op would be bringing new people "into our class organizations," and that the larger movement would benefit as people moved from "economic interests to political" ones.[2] Kolisnyk struck a cautionary note, though, for while he wanted to branch out into new enterprises eventually, he felt that the WFCA did not yet have the necessary funds or qualified people to start new businesses.

But the manager's caution was lost on many. As one speaker argued, there was a need to "start something new," for people would see such forward motion as "a great moral victory."[3] Following this comment many ideas for new ventures were presented: the construction of warehousing facilities at the fuel yard, the wholesaling of a broad range of farm products, the purchase of an existing small bakery, the construction of a new bakery and the construction of a milk and butter plant – all over the objections of those who insisted that the WFCA should pay off its debts before starting anything new.

Despite the reservations of some of the shareholders and Kolisnyk, a special meeting was scheduled for later in the month to consider expansion. In the interim, the Co-op's executive made preliminary investigations into the bakery and dairy proposals. Both involved products which were necessities and for which there was a strong daily demand on a year-round basis. Moreover, both were cash businesses that would generate immediate cash flows, enabling the Co-op to pay down the upfront

Small-scale milk suppliers such as the Belot sisters were common throughout Winnipeg. At the time that the Co-op was considering expansion into the creamery business, 109 small-scale milk producers accounted for approximately 40 percent of all dairy sales.

costs of establishing a new plant as quickly as possible.

By the end of August 1930 it was clear that the Executive was leaning towards a milk and butter plant, because a creamery was about to become available in the North End, but also because many Ukrainian dairy farmers just north of Winnipeg had expressed a willingness to supply the milk and cream. (In the language of the dairy industry, a creamery is the generic term for a plant that processes fresh milk and/or cream, usually for a variety of dairy products. A plant which handles only cream, for use in butter making, could be referred to as either a butter plant or a creamery.) After a flurry of investigations into potential creamery locations, the project was put on hold.

The reasons for this were clear: fall and winter were the Co-op's busy seasons and the leadership had little time left over from the fuel yard operations; as well, the mounting problems of running a business in the midst of a depression made them

increasingly cautious. The Co-op's expenses were rising quickly. To keep up with demand at the fuel yard it was necessary to buy a new truck, purchase more horses and sleighs, improve the yard, build a garage and order far more coal and wood than in the previous two years of operations.

While this should have been good news, indicating increased sales, these rising expenditures came at a time when fewer of the WFCA's customers were able to pay for their purchases immediately, or in some cases, to pay at all. By December of 1930 the Co-op was still carrying $1,800 worth of customer debt from the previous year and $15,000 more from 1930. Several customers who had no hope of paying off their debt in any other way were given temporary employment in the yard to reduce their fuel accounts, while several others cashed in their shares in order to pay all or part of their bill. Worse yet, while the price of wood in Winnipeg was dropping because of increasing competition from small-scale wood peddlers (primarily farmers who

By 1931 the city's two largest distributors, City Dairy and Crescent Creamery cornered 60 percent of the market.

were trying to survive by selling the wood they cut from their own or government land), the Co-op was bound by contracts with its suppliers to pay the price for wood agreed to earlier in the season. Thus, there were several instances when the WFCA sold its wood for less than cost in 1930–31.

When the membership pressed the executive to explain its lack of activity concerning new enterprises early in 1931, Kolisnyk argued that this was no time to consider new expenditures of $32,000–35,000: not when the Co-op's debts were mounting and its loan capital evaporating. Still, the idea of expansion simply would not go away, and by the spring and summer of 1931 a series of factors propelled the WFCA into one of the most highly competitive and closely scrutinized industries in Winnipeg.

THE DAIRY TRADE

Until the late 1920s, the people of Winnipeg satisfied their milk requirements in two ways: they either had raw, unpasteurized milk delivered to their doors by independent peddler/producers, or they had pasteurized milk delivered by a creamery. And

during the 1920s, Crescent Creamery and City Dairy controlled all of the production and distribution of pasteurized milk in Greater Winnipeg. Together they constituted an oligopoly that set the price of milk in the city and established the price paid to milk producers in the region surrounding the city, what the creameries referred to as the "Winnipeg milk shed."

By not competing with each other, these two creameries maintained a highly profitable spread between what they paid their milk shippers and the retail, or home-delivery price. A study conducted by Professor H.C. Grant of the University of Manitoba in the mid-1920s showed that Winnipeg's two major dairies enjoyed one of the highest price spreads in the country. That same study also reprinted a remarkably frank speech given by a representative of Crescent Creamery, which explained in some detail how Crescent used ethnic divisions, economic pressure, anti-co-operative propaganda, red-baiting, contracts that prohibited workers from joining unions and political influence to keep milk producers under the company's thumb during the 1910s and 1920s.

Given the level of control that the major creameries exerted over the local dairy trade, it might have seemed foolhardy for any competitor to enter the

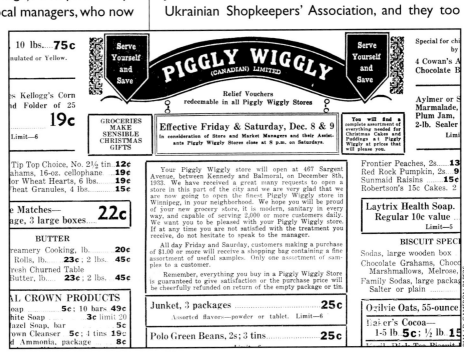

milk distribution field. But, by 1931 the situation in Winnipeg's milk industry had changed dramatically.

To begin with, Winnipeg's major creameries had been caught up in the merger madness of the 1920s. In 1927, Eastern (later Dominion) Dairies paid double the book value of the Crescent Creamery to make this firm its new Winnipeg subsidiary, while, in the fall of 1929, the Toronto-based Dairy Corporation of Canada made an even more generous offer to purchase the debt-ridden City Dairy. The combination of rapid physical expansion during the 1920s (when land, equipment, construction and other costs were relatively high), overpriced buy-outs and the frustration of local managers, who now had to answer to head offices in the east before they could act, would greatly destabilize the industry.

Beyond this, Crescent and City were no longer the only players in Winnipeg's milk market. Early in the 1920s several small operations had opened on the outskirts of Winnipeg: Charles Gaudette established the St. Boniface Creamery Company; Albert Paquin founded St. Andrews Dairies; and in 1929 another St. Boniface operation, Modern Dairies, was built by Mr. A. DeCruyneare. Of greater significance though, in May of 1931, J. W. Speirs, a longtime executive with Crescent Creamery, put together a locally funded company and bought out Modern Dairies plus two smaller plants. In a matter of months Speirs used his experience, his contacts with milk producers and his ownership of the newest, most efficient milk plant in Winnipeg to transform Modern Dairies into a company capable of taking over approximately a quarter of the Winnipeg milk market.

Another important development was taking place – the entry of stores into the field of milk sales. Prior to 1929 it was almost unheard of for

consumers to purchase milk from stores, primarily because people needed their milk early in the morning, before the stores opened. This began to change in 1929 when the U.S.-based Piggly Wiggly chain came to Winnipeg and began selling milk, often as a loss-leader, to get people into its stores. Soon after Piggly Wiggly's arrival, Safeway also began opening stores, and it too sold milk. To meet the challenge of these chains, a number of local stores banded together into co-operative purchasing and advertising units, such as the Associated Retail Grocery (ARG) chain, the Red and White stores, Jewel stores and merchants associations such as the Ukrainian Shopkeepers' Association, and they too

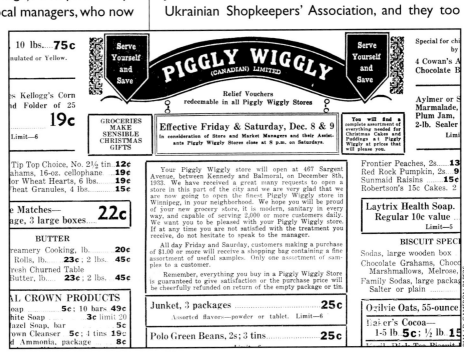

The face of the retail grocery trade began to change when Piggly Wiggly and Safeway stores arrived in Winnipeg in the late 1920s. They ushered in the trend toward the foreign-owned supermarket chain store.

began selling milk.

In 1931 Piggly Wiggly purchased the Sundale Creamery and provided all of its Winnipeg stores from this one location. Because it had no distribution costs, it could sell milk at far lower prices than the home-delivery dairies. Even with its own plant, Piggly Wiggly could not supply more than 3 to 4 percent of Winnipeg's milk needs. Because most people did not have refrigeration or vehicles, they continued to rely upon home delivery. Still, Piggly Wiggly's widely advertised low prices and its public position on the milk-pricing question during the early 1930s would give it a very loud voice in the milk industry.

It was not only the merger movement, the establishment of new competitors and the coming of chain stores that reshaped Winnipeg's milk industry from the late 1920s to the early 1930s. The Depression itself also had a major impact.

Even after the Depression began to settle in and the price of many consumer goods fell, milk prices changed very little, largely because the big dairies controlled prices. The typical cost of a quart of milk in Winnipeg had ranged from twelve cents in the summer to thirteen cents in the winter from 1921 to 1929. In 1930 it dropped one cent and held at this rate into the summer of 1931. Considering the drop in value of most farm products (50 percent on grain alone), milk was one product that still brought farmers a good price, so those who had kept some cows for family use, now turned to the production of milk for commercial purposes.

This quickly led to overproduction, and when combined with the declining incomes of Winnipeg's consumers, it was inevitable that prices paid to farmers would fall, particularly when the big creameries had no intention of cutting into their price spread. The average price of $2.20 to $2.41 per hundredweight of milk, which had been fairly constant in the 1920s, began falling slowly in 1930 and then plummeted. By early 1932 the price paid to milk producers was under $1 per hundredweight, a 60 percent drop over a two-year period.

The long tradition of milk peddlers who ladled unpasteurized milk from their milk cans into the customers' containers dated back to the city's inception. Their days were numbered, however, as health concerns caused city officials to consider a ban on the sale of unpasteurized milk.

Some milk producers sought to avoid this creamery-imposed pricing system by acting as independent retailers. Close to a hundred producers peddled their own raw milk door-to-door, ladling it directly from milk cans into the customers' containers. Some producers preferred this method of doing business, and a few larger dairy farmers had employees peddling for them, or subcontractors who purchased their milk to peddle in the city. However, with mounting fears about the safety of unpasteurized milk, even the lower price the peddlers offered did not always guarantee that they could hang on to their market share. Between 1928 and 1931 unpasteurized milk sales in Winnipeg fell from a 40 percent market share to 32 percent, and many on City Council were in favour of passing a bylaw that would allow only pasteurized milk to be sold in Winnipeg.

By 1931 the creamery business was ripe for new entrants, particularly those willing to establish a pasteurization plant. Milk was a basic product for which there was always a strong demand, and there were enough dissatisfied, even desperate, producers to provide a large pool of potential suppliers. Consumers who wanted pasteurized milk, but who were unwilling or unable to pay the higher prices demanded by the existing companies, provided a natural market. Finally, startup costs had not been lower since before the First World War, as real-estate values, construction materials, wages and interest rates had all fallen dramatically. For those bold enough to start a new enterprise, a creamery operation seemed a good bet.

THE LITTLE RED DAIRY

In the case of the WFCA, the final push to get into the creamery business came from shareholders who were engaged in small-scale dairying just beyond the city limits. One such man, named Karpishyn, came to an executive meeting early in April 1931 and reported that a number of local dairymen had already gotten together and pledged a small amount of money to help the Co-op launch a creamery. On May 12 twenty Ukrainian-speaking milk producers, most of whom were independent peddlers, met with the Co-op's general manager to explore the idea more fully. Kolisnyk proposed a mutual-aid package to them. The Co-op's aim, he said, was to "supply milk products to workers in the city" at a reasonable cost, but certainly not at the expense of the producers. Rather than exploiting the producers, as the big companies did, the Co-op would help them. As Kolisnyk saw it, the small producer/peddler was in direct competition with "those companies that exploit customers." By working with the WFCA, producers would save time and money and have access to the growing group of customers who wanted pasteurized milk. Moreover, the profits from such an operation would be "distributed among producers and consumers."[4]

The WFCA was willing to go into such a venture on an almost altruistic basis because it was committed to demonstrating that working people and poor farmers could get together and challenge the way things were done in a capitalist society. This is not to say that Kolisnyk or other leaders of the Co-op thought that their operation, or even those of all co-operatives combined, would overthrow the existing order. Rather, they were concerned with the educational value of such co-operation. The more that people saw of production for use, rather than profit, and the more that people banded together in a struggle against the existing system, the more likely they were to take part in the larger class struggle. As the Co-op's amended constitution of 1931 put it: "The Workers and Farmers Co-operative Association sets as its objective the rallying of workers and poor farmers into consumers co-operatives for the support of the liberation struggle of the working class in all its forms, from the minor, everyday struggle to the ultimate one for the establishment of proletarian power."[5] Thus, the milk business, just like the fuel business, was a means to a revolutionary end, not an end in and of itself.

However, dedication to a revolutionary ideal was not enough.

The Preamble to the amended constitution of the Co-op, 1931.

For the Co-op to have any impact upon the consciousness of the workers and farmers it would have to be successful, and that meant that it would have to be set up and run on a solid business basis. From the outset, the intention was to run this new venture as well as, and more frugally than, any capitalist enterprise.

The Co-op leaders took their next steps with considerable care. Following the May 12 meeting a subcommittee of area milk producers was formed. Its task was to recruit even more dairy farmers who would be willing to commit to this project, both by supplying milk and by taking out shares or making cash loans to the Co-op. Over the next two weeks 143 new shareholders were signed up from the ranks of local producers, generating over $2,000 of start-up capital. A second meeting of milk producers was convened at the end of May, at which time

market price established by the big creameries was falling rapidly, they wanted assurances that the Co-op would pay them a higher price. They also wanted guarantees that once the creamery was established and they signed up as milk shippers, the Co-op would not turn around and start buying milk from producers willing to sell at lower prices.

Kolisnyk did not please everyone when he told them that the Co-op would not be paying over the market price. He did, however, assure them that the WFCA would not turn to cut-rate milk suppliers,

The Co-op Creamery, 610 Dufferin Avenue at McGregor Street. Besides installation of equipment, much repair and conversion work had to be done on this former bakery before the creamery could open for business.

Kolisnyk explained that selling unpasteurized milk was becoming a thing of the past. He pointed out that 109 independent producer/peddlers were supplying less than 40 percent of Winnipeg's milk while the big companies, like Crescent and City Dairy, had over 60 percent of the market. The only way to avoid being cut out of the Winnipeg market was to switch to pasteurization.

The questions these farmers put to Kolisnyk indicated that while they were interested in the project, they were concerned about how much the WFCA would pay them for milk. Keenly aware that the

and would always give first preference to buying at the prevailing market price from its own members. To pay anything over the established price meant that "the Co-op would not make ends meet and would have to charge its customers more and this, from a business point of view, is not good."[6]

While not everyone was happy with these answers, there was enough support for Kolisnyk and other members of the Co-op to feel that they could go ahead with the new project. As a brief report to the Executive early in June of 1931 noted, "there is quite a good profit [to be made] on the sale of milk and besides that, milk peddlers are demanding to start something with a dairy."[7] As a result, the final decision to start up a milk plant was made and the search for a suitable creamery location was launched in earnest.

After rejecting an existing creamery on McPhillips Street, because it was too small for the operation that was being planned, the executive opened negotiations to purchase a former bakery on the corner of Dufferin and McGregor. Several North End building lots were also examined, with an eye towards constructing a new plant. However, it was decided that buying the building on Dufferin and converting it would be more economical if it could be obtained for somewhere between $8,000 and $9,000. This was an exceptionally low price given that the same building had been valued at over $13,000 just one year earlier, but this was how the real estate market worked during the Depression.

After rejecting an offer of $8,500, the building's owners accepted a bid of $9,000 early in July – based on a $4,000 down payment, five annual payments of $1,000 and a 7 percent interest rate. To cut costs and provide employment to Co-op members, most of the conversion work was done by shareholders such as Marion Zmiyowsky, who was in charge of all repair work. He was told to use "as many comrades from the organization" as possible, particularly those who owed the WFCA money for fuel supplies. The wage rate for most work was to be a very respectable eighty-five or seventy-five cents per hour, "unless of course the workers themselves agree to work for less."[8]

Financing this project was no easy matter, as the surplus from fuel sales was insufficient to cover even the down payment on the building, let alone pay for $9,000 of equipment and $6,000 worth of repair and conversion work. And even though the Co-op had demonstrated its credit-worthiness over three years of operation, a left-wing co-operative was not

Ad in *Ukrainian Labor News,* October 31, 1931:

INVEST YOUR SAVINGS WITH WFCA

The Workers and Farmers Co-operative is accepting loans refundable on request and earning a higher interest rate. The Cooperative has opened a creamery and in its first weeks since opening, it has met with extraordinary success. It needs to expand its machinery and delivery equipment in order to provide dairy products. These can be obtained on credit but in that event the cost and interest would be higher. Every cent invested in WFCA is guaranteed 100% because the funds are invested in worthwhile necessities. WFCA is truly a worker-farmer organization serving the interests of the working class and deserving of the support and confidence of workers and farmers.

likely to qualify for a large bank loan. More to the point, this was not the way the Co-op did things. As much as possible, the money was to come from within the family of left-wing organizations and the membership.

Over the years, shipments of milk to distributors in the city grew from single cans sent by train to large loads hauled in by truck. Seen here, a family hauling milk to the railway station at Malonton, Manitoba.

percent over typical interest rates.

These share and loan campaigns, plus loans from the WBA and the liberal use of a bank overdraft were the primary methods of financing the move into the milk business. By the close of 1931 there was $47,376 on loan to the Co-op: $18,840 was from the main branch of the WBA, but the remaining $28,536 came from eighty-four individuals whose loans ranged from $30 to $2,100. Only five of these loans were for $1,000 or more, but, large or small, these sums often represented the life savings of entire families. In several cases

Appeals for loans and new share capital were made in the *Ukrainian Labor News*, the various journals published out of the Labour Temple and at the August General Membership Meeting. Shares were reduced in price from $10 to $2 to allow "poorer workers to become members of the Co-operative."[9] Time after time it was explained how such share purchases, and especially loans made to the Co-op, were the best way for members to utilize their savings, as the banks would only give them 3 percent on their deposits while the Co-op paid 5 percent interest. Such interest-bearing loans would allow the Co-op to pay cash for more of its upfront costs, and even after paying interest to its member-lenders, it would be saving 2 percent to 3

■ JOHN KRALL ■

By the time **John Krall** retired from the Co-op in 1949, he was regarded as Winnipeg's longest-serving veteran of milk production. His career in the city dairy trade had begun in 1909 as a pasteurizer with Crescent creamery, but it would be fair to say that he was born into the industry.

His father was a milk distributor in Switzerland, and, as a boy, John ladled out milk to the customers in their village. While still in his teens, he moved to Germany where he opened a pasteurizing plant and learned the art of cheese-making. Before the age of 20, he was overseeing a large dairy herd on the estate of a German baron in southern Russia.

By the time John came to the Co-op in 1931 as plant superintendent for the newly opened dairy, he had worked in every phase of the creamery business. A hard-working, unassuming, and, by nature, jovial man, his most famous legacy was the development of the formula for the Co-op's popular cream cheese.

every family member, including children as young as nine, had a loan account at the WFCA, which clearly represented every penny that their parents had been able to accumulate for themselves and their children. Thirty dollars per child may not sound like much money, but when a family of four was living in rented rooms shared with another poor family on Manitoba Avenue, it is a certainty that this was every last dollar they had – and certainly more than they could afford to lose if the Co-op failed. This only underlines the commitment of these poverty-stricken immigrants to an alternative vision of society.

The money thus raised was invested in the mounting costs of the milk plant. The roof of the building had to be redone, the boiler for the furnace had to be replaced, the entire floor had to be covered in concrete to meet City health codes and machinery costs – even for used equipment – were rising far beyond initial expectations. Add to this the cost of wagons (seven were ordered at prices ranging from $332 to $420), horses, a truck, a car for Co-op business, $5,000 to construct a barn and garage, and such prosaic but essential supplies as a carload of glass milk bottles, and one can see why expenditures had risen to $35,000 by the end of August. Still the plant would not be ready to sell milk and earn revenue until the middle of September.

Another problem came up late in August. At a meeting of the milk producers who had first encouraged the Co-op to enter the creamery business, it became obvious that these farmers had lost interest in dealing with the Co-op and intended to continue peddling their own milk. The Executive would have to move quickly "to obtain milk from farmers who do not do their own delivery."[10] This news was taken calmly; after all many farmers were desperate to find an outlet for their milk. The Executive had other problems to deal with, such as staffing their new operation.

Jacob Penner, the Creamery's first bookkeeper, went on to become one of North Winnipeg's longest serving aldermen.
PHOTO COURTESY ROLAND PENNER

Some staffing choices were easy to make. The first three employees, a shipper and two drivers, were very active members of the organizations affiliated with the Co-op and were apparently losing their current jobs because of that involvement. Next, John Krall, an experienced dairyman, was hired as the plant superintendent, a position which, like his recipe for cream cheese, would be handed down to two more generations of Kralls. Another fifteen men and women were chosen from a fairly long list of applicants to serve as drivers, plant workers and office help, virtually all of whom had long records of involvement with the Co-op, the ULFTA or the WBA. Finally, just before operations commenced on September 15, 1931, Jacob Penner, already one of the leaders of Winnipeg's radical community and

РОБІТНИЧО-ФАРМЕРСЬКА КООПЕРАТИВНА
МОЛОЧАРНЯ У ВІННІПЕГУ
ДОСТАВЛЯЄ
ПОЧАВШИ СЬОГОДНЯ, 15-ГО ВЕРЕСНЯ
МОЛОКО, СМЕТАНУ і МАСЛО
ДО ВСІХ СВОЇХ КОСТУМЕРІВ, ЩО ДОТЕПЕР
ДАЛИ СВОЄ ЗАМОВЛЕННЯ.
Ті, що ще не дали свого замовлення, хай
передадуть його нашому розвощикові, або **56926**
хай телефонують — — — —
АДРЕСА: РІГ ВУЛ. МЕКГРЕГОР І ДОФРІН

The Workers and Farmers Co-operative Creamery in Winnipeg is supplying, starting today, September 15, milk, cream and butter to all its customers who have already put in an order. All those who still haven't given in their order can give one to their deliveryman or can phone 56926. (*Ukrainian Labor News,* Sept. 15, 1931)

soon to become its most successful elected official, was hired as the creamery's bookkeeper. The WFCA was not only looking after its own members, but

was also assuring itself of a highly motivated and dedicated work force, a combination that was essential to survival in the difficult days ahead.

The last few days leading up to September 15 were consumed by a whirlwind of activity. Contracts with milk suppliers were signed, and North End neighbourhoods were canvassed for customers by the seven recently hired drivers, their helpers, the Executive and three special canvassers. And as the first shipments of milk began to arrive, Krall fine-tuned plant operations with his growing staff. The fuel yard was also heading into its busy season. All in all, it was both an exciting and somewhat frightening time for the Co-op. No one, however, could have predicted just how tumultuous the future would be.

■ ■ ■

1 PCL, Minute Book 1, "Minutes of General Membership Meeting, August 14, 1930."

2 Ibid.

3 Ibid.

4 Ibid., "Minutes of Meeting with Milk Producers, May 12, 1931."

5 PCL, Constitution and Bylaws of the Workers and Farmers Co-operative Ass'n Limited, 1931. P. 27.

6 PCL, Minute Book 1, "Minutes of a Meeting of the Milk Producers, May 23, 1931."

7 Ibid., "Minutes of the Special Executive Meeting, June 7, 1931."

8 Ibid., "Minutes of the Executive, July 4, 1931."

9 Ibid., "Minutes of the General Membership Meeting, August 15, 1931."

10 Ibid., "Minutes of the Meeting of the Executive, August 25, 1931."

This full page ad, surrounded by congratulations from other businesses appeared in the *Ukrainian Labor News*, September 12, 1931. The WFCA announced the creamery as "Yet another great achievement," and adopted the slogan "From producer to consumer at cost." It kicked off the venture with an open house. The fleet of delivery vehicles consisted of seven wagons and one truck.

Children line up in front of the Ukrainian Labour Temple as they prepare to participate in a peace march, c. 1936. Demonstrations about unemployment, working conditions, human rights, and war and peace were common throughout the 1930s, as hard times at home and a drift to war abroad prompted growing public concern – and militancy.

CHAPTER FOUR
THE HEROIC PERIOD

DIFFICULT TIMES

W hen the first seven Co-op milkmen took to the streets of Winnipeg in September 1931, there was no question in their minds that these were hard times. The Great Depression was entering its worst phase and the winters of 1931–32 and 1932–33 would be the most devastating seasons in that decade-long tragedy. Annual unemployment rates for non-agricultural workers rose to over 26 percent nationally, while in Western Canadian cities like Winnipeg official unemployment rates hit peaks of 33 percent during the winter. Not the perfect time to be launching a new venture – especially one which relied upon the patronage of those living in the North End, the part of the city hardest hit by unemployment.

But when the Co-op's drivers started delivering milk at ten cents per quart, a penny less than the major dairies' prices, they soon found customers. Between September 15 and the end of October

1931, the Co-op doubled its number of routes from seven to fourteen and this soon increased to nineteen. The volume of sales was rising, yet unfortunately, according to some handwritten notes tucked into one of the Co-op's financial reports, the creamery was losing money on every quart of milk it sold. The first six weeks of operation saw operating losses of $64 per day. The debt on the creamery had now risen to $45,000, and even worse, the competition for customers was about to get far more intense.

THE ORIGINS OF THE MILK PRICE WAR

The opening salvo in what came to be known as the "Milk Price War of 1932" was actually fired just before the Co-op's creamery commenced operations. In the summer of 1931, when the big dairies – Crescent, City and Modern – were still selling milk "off the wagon" for eleven cents per quart, Piggly

"MAY DAY" DEMONSTRATION 1932

(above) A May Day demonstration at Market Square. Scenes such as this were common throughout the 1930s when, at times, one in three workers was without a job.

(left) With the opening of the creamery, the Co-op began issuing information bulletins about the price of milk, the activities of the Co-op and, in keeping with its aim of educating the public, about "the co-operative way."

Head Office & Creamery:
Cor. Dufferin & McGregor Sts.
Phone 56 926

Coal & Wood Yard:
Cor. Pritchard & Battery Cts.
Phone 56 205

WORKERS & FARMERS
ESTABLISHED 1928
CO-OPERATIVE
ASSOCIATION LTD.
CREAMERY BRANCH
Fuel, Creamery Products and Other Commodities
Bought and Sold on Purely Co-operative Basis

Bulletin No. 3   Winnipeg, Man.   October 30th, 1931

THIS is our third Bulletin since the opening of our Creamery Branch. Two former Bulletins have been distributed to the consumers of our Creamery products, and this one is being sent out to all that may be interested in the Co-operative — together with a handy pocket card, containing our address for both the Creamery and the Fuel Yard, prices of coals and coke and a calendar, which you may hold and call us up when in need of commodities we handle on purely Co-operative basis.

The Workers & Farmers Co-operative Association, Limited, was organized in 1928 and has since refunded to its customers the sum of $7,104.00, being the net profit in the operation of the Fuel Yard during the last three years. Have you ever received any portion of profit from private concerns?

The Co-operative, after three years of successful operation of a Coal and Wood Yard, has branched out into Creamery business. This and in six weeks we have doubled our delivery equipment. This shows what support we are getting from those who are acquainted with the service of the Co-operative.

The Workers & Farmers Co-operative Ass'n, Ltd., has been instrumental in reducing the cost of milk and other Creamery products. The Co-operative delivers to the homes in Winnipeg a **pure, fresh, clean, rich, pasteurized** milk in bottles at 10 cents per quart, and other products at proportionately lower prices. At no time before has such a high grade of milk ever been sold in the City of Winnipeg at such low prices. We buy our milk from well chosen milk producers, and pay them a fair price for it. Do you know how this is done?

We have bought a large modern brick building at a very low price, had it altered to suit a creamery plant by day labor, thus eliminating the contractor's profit. Our staff, while organized, are 100% behind the welfare of the Co-operative. We have no high-salaried officials, but their devotion, ability and efficiency is proven by the success and progress of the Co-operative. We manage to get our money to conduct business, from the members and friends of the Co-operative at a low rate of interest. We sell no bonds to guarantee a high rate of interest and have no "watered" stock that requires high dividends. Our dividend on shares is limited, and we, therefore, can operate very economically so that after our low operating expenses are paid, we are able to give a refund of profit to our consumers, which we do.

Won't you participate in this? Start buying your fuel and Creamery products from the Co-operative now. Increase the volume of business and reduce the cost. It is to your advantage.

Workers & Farmers Co-operative Ass'n, Ltd.

Wiggly, Winnipeg's biggest chain store, began selling milk on a cash-and-carry basis for eight cents per quart. Although this chain only accounted for a tiny percentage of Winnipeg milk sales, its heavy advertising of these lower milk prices had caused an immediate reaction. The city's other grocery store owners feared that they would lose business to Piggly Wiggly on all goods if they did not match prices on milk. However, because the big three dairies were unwilling to lower their prices to storekeepers, raw milk was all they could buy at a price low enough for them to compete with Piggly Wiggly.

In July of 1931 the three major creameries attempted to shut down this source of cheap milk by lobbying the City government to enact stricter health codes and to license and inspect all stores handling milk. This would have effectively driven most stores out of the milk business. This lobbying effort failed, however, and by the fall of 1931 the small creameries established in the 1920s, the new ones such as the Co-op and its North End competitor, St. Joseph's Dairy, and the independent peddler/producers were all willing to sell milk

to stores for eight cents per quart or less. Small stores could then resell it for nine cents, making them at least somewhat competitive with Piggly Wiggly.

The big three now had to sell milk to stores at eight cents per quart to keep this part of their business. However, this price-cutting to stores meant that the dairies were potentially cutting their own throats. For a difference of two or three cents per quart many Winnipeggers were willing to abandon home delivery and find some way to buy their milk from stores. Thus, the big three dropped their wagon price to ten cents per quart late in the fall of 1931 so that home-delivery prices would only be one cent higher than in most stores.

Formal price-cutting was only the tip of the iceberg because individual milkmen soon began making side deals with customers. They would sell milk at lower prices either as an "introductory price" to recruit new customers or to prevent existing customers from buying elsewhere. While it may seem strange that milkmen would get involved in price-cutting, they had a powerful incentive to offer rebates. At the larger dairies (and the Co-op) most milkmen were paid on a sliding scale. Typically a milkman with one thousand "units" (a quart of milk or its equivalent in other dairy products) would earn $20 per week, while twelve hundred units paid $24 and fourteen hundred units $29. Everything above this would earn a milkman an additional $1 per one hundred units. Simple arithmetic dictated that between the $20 and $29 level a delivery man could cut one cent per quart out of his own pocket and still earn an extra $5 per week.

The nastier implication of "milkman calculus" was that anyone who was not "pulling" enough units could be let go, since there were countless people looking for work. If holding on to customers, and therefore one's job, came down to offering discounts that cut into take-home pay, that was the price many milkmen were willing to pay. Information collected by government agencies during the 1930s, shows that few milkmen took home their full base pay. Between privately offered rebates, responsibility for customers who failed to pay their accounts and charges for breakage and the like, most milkmen earned far below their supposed wage level, while working a six- or, at companies such as St. Joseph's, a seven-day week of ten to thirteen hours per day.

THE CO-OP'S RESPONSE

The Co-op could not afford a milk price war, especially in 1931–32 when its fuel yard was also having a bad year. Mild weather, rising unemployment and the City's policy that Relief recipients cut their own wood at the City wood yard as proof of their willingness to work, were all lowering the demand for fuel.

Rather than cut its losses and get out of the milk business, the WFCA launched into the increased competition with a renewed sense of purpose. WBA

Wood yards, which had been operated by the city for many years, became "relief wood yards" during the Depression. Here, poor families could cut their own wood to "prove" that they were willing to work, and thus qualify for Relief.

and member loans, the financial lifeblood of the Co-op, increased from $47,376 in December of 1931 to $79,388 in March of 1932, largely because of relentless campaigning in Winnipeg, and eastern Canadian centres of left-wing activity such as Timmins, Kirkland Lake, Rouyn, Fort William and Port Arthur.

No stone was left unturned as the Co-op struggled for survival. If a customer left the Co-op, both milkmen and members of the Board of Directors went to see why they had quit. And their reports of such visits offer a vivid picture of life in the North End during the Depression. The most common reasons given for not taking milk from the Co-op were the hard times: lower prices at the store, lower prices from independent peddlers, people moving away suddenly (usually without paying their milk bill) and people losing their jobs. But there were other reasons as well. Some customers had returned to Europe (some were even deported), one couple was angered because their son had not been hired by the Co-op, and a few families were frustrated because the Co-op driver would not extend credit for two weeks. And political schisms were also a constant part of the Co-op's life: one family did not want Co-op milk because "they were Catholics," while in another case a woman "was afraid of the church organization to which she belongs and doesn't buy [from the Co-op] for that reason."[1] Then there was even a family on Magnus Avenue who didn't take Co-op milk because they had their own cow!

Personal visits from Board members restored some customers, and new ones joined thanks to pressure on people associated with the Labour Temple and the WBA and to canvassing in working-class districts beyond the North End, such as Transcona, Elmwood and East Kildonan. But it was clear that if the Co-op was to remain in business it needed to increase its sales volume even more, and to do this it would have to lower its price to nine cents per quart, the typical store price.

The big three dairies had already come to the same conclusion. Late in October of 1931 they told their milk shippers that instead of the usual winter price increase, they would be paying producers twenty-one cents less per hundredweight of milk so that the dairies could reduce the price to the consumer. The Co-op, which saw itself as serving both the producers and its working-class patrons, wanted to avoid following suit for as long as possible, but the Board knew that eventually it might have to.

By December of 1931, the Co-op's Board made preparations to lower the wagon price to nine cents per quart and to begin a major customer recruiting campaign. A first step was to meet with the Co-op's milk shippers and explain why prices had to be lowered.

The January 2, 1932, meeting was a surprisingly positive one, given the topic under consideration. The only major problem brought up by the producers was that some shippers who had been dealing both with the Co-op and other dairies had found that the big dairies stopped taking milk from anyone who dealt with the WFCA. In response, Co-op manager William Kolisnyk promised to take as much milk as possible from anyone who had been cut off from the other dairies. At the same time, he pointed out that the Co-op would like to see its loyalty to the farmers rewarded through share purchases and loans. The Co-op, Kolisnyk promised, would not lower the price paid to its shippers until absolutely forced to do so. As a stop-gap measure he proposed paying the same prices, but increasing the percentage of milk that was bought at the lower, "surplus milk" price (dairies received anywhere from 10 to 20 percent of a shipper's usual quota at a special surplus rate). This meant that the shippers' next milk cheques would "be somewhat less."[2] This price reduction by indirect means was seen as a reasonable compromise. None of the shippers complained and several purchased Co-op shares. The meeting also agreed that eventually a lower price for all milk was unavoidable, as the big dairies had just announced they would lower the price paid to producers by another nineteen cents per hundredweight, effective January 1, 1932.

The Co-op's deliverymen immediately started recruiting new customers with promises of nine-cent milk, while storekeepers were offered a rate of seven cents per quart so that they could resell at eight cents. Handbills listing the new prices were circulated throughout every working-class district. But these were not simple price lists; they were

political and educational statements as well, proclaiming that this price reduction was achieved through careful management and increased distribution, not through wage cuts to employees or price reductions to producers. It was stressed that only co-operation, not the profit motive, could yield such results.

This handbill appealed to the family's budget as well as to its social conscience. Effective advertising like this helped vault the Co-op into the ranks of the top five dairies in the early months of 1932.

This mixture of lower prices and class-conscious advertising soon bore fruit. In less than two weeks the Co-op gained over 220 customers, with the total rising daily. Deliveries were also increasing in areas such as Transcona and Elmwood, as the Co-op expanded its customer base from an almost strictly Ukrainian and Jewish one into much more ethnically diverse areas. Inroads were also made in East Kildonan, in the primarily English-speaking areas north of Mountain Avenue, and in the central core of Winnipeg. And store sales of Co-op products were increasing, particularly in the small stores of the North End.

Although the Co-op was still losing money on both the fuel yard and the creamery in the first months of 1932, the rate of loss was declining. Member loans were continuing to rise, so the creamery was able to establish itself more firmly. Beyond this, everyone was getting better at what they did: deliverymen were getting to know their customers and routes better; plant workers were becoming more experienced; inefficient or inadequate equipment was being replaced; and even the bookkeeping was becoming more streamlined.

Buoyed by this success, the creamery's product line was expanded to include cottage cheese and buttermilk, and in April the Co-op attempted to win the largest milk contract in Winnipeg, the Social Welfare Department's "Relief milk" contract. Even though its bid of nine cents per quart, less a 10 percent rebate, was a full penny lower than that of its competitors, the Co-op's bid was rejected. The Board suspected a political motivation in this decision, and even Kolisnyk's direct appeal to his former colleagues on City Council had no effect. Soon after, however, the Co-op was awarded a smaller, yet important, contract to supply milk to the City's municipal hospitals.

In slightly over half a year the Co-op had emerged as a significant player in Winnipeg's milk industry. By March 1932, it was becoming the fourth or fifth largest creamery in Winnipeg (it was in a dead heat with St. Boniface Creamery in terms of milk sold), providing approximately 6 percent of the city's pasteurized milk, and its percentage was rising faster than that of any other dairy.

Because of this new status, Kolisnyk was invited to meetings of the leading dairies to discuss matters such as establishing a set price for milk in Winnipeg, negotiating a new price to milk shippers and encouraging increased consumption of milk products through a "Milk Week" public relations campaign. Kolisnyk's first reports of these meetings to his colleagues at the Co-op were sketchy and optimistic, suggesting that he might not have fully appreciated the level of panic amongst his capitalist competitors. They were worried about the state of their industry, and not just because of new creameries like the Co-op, St. Joseph's and a few other small milk plants. The North End market was important enough that Crescent was willing to work with Abe Greenberg, another veteran of the Winnipeg milk industry, to establish its own North End subsidiary, Home Dairy, early in 1932, while the other large dairies tried to regain lost customers in the area. However, their greatest concern in the spring of 1932 was Piggly Wiggly.

This American-based chain store (with its own milk plant, whose capacity had just been doubled) made it policy to sell milk for less than any other retailer. It also made it clear that it would not par-ticipate in any attempt to stabilize milk prices unless it was guaranteed the right to offer its milk for at least one cent, but preferably two cents, less per quart than any competitor. And Piggly Wiggly's regional manager let everyone in Winnipeg know that he would maintain this price differential no matter how low milk prices might go. A spectre was haunting the Winnipeg dairy industry, and it wasn't communism, but a very aggressive brand of U.S. corporate capitalism.

THE WAR HEATS UP

In March Piggly Wiggly dropped its milk price to seven cents per quart, which triggered price reductions all across Winnipeg. The Co-op, for example, had to lower the price it charged stores to six cents per quart at the beginning of May. With the store price falling, home-delivery prices were also forced downwards, as few people would pay nine cents to a milkman when they could get milk for seven cents at the corner store. The Co-op reduced its home-delivery price to eight cents per quart, which forced it to lower the price paid to its milk shippers, although not as much as the big dairies had. Piggly Wiggly responded by reducing its price to six cents per quart.

While consumers were reaping the benefits of reduced milk prices (in a few cases prices even fell to five cents per quart for "Grand Opening" sales or "two for one" sales where a quart of milk and a half pint of cream were sold for ten cents), there was concern that these prices would not only bankrupt some creamery companies, but might cause a public health crisis. As early as March of 1932, *The North Ender*, a small local newspaper, had warned that falling prices would lead to a situation where sanitary standards both for creameries and dairy farms would be abandoned in the quest to protect the bottom line. There was a very real possibility that the price paid to milk producers would fall so low that dairy farmers would not only lose money (most producers claimed they had been losing money since early in 1931) but would begin selling off their herds in desperation. Government officials worried

The Winnipeg Evening Tribune

5 O'CLOCK FINAL EDITION

VOL. XLII.   WINNIPEG, FRIDAY, SEPTEMBER 2, 1932   26 PAGES   Price 5 cents; With Comics, 10 cents.   No. 211

The Weather

Forecast: Fair and cool.

Temperature at 7 a.m. today was +82‡
noon, +78. Tribune thermometer,
Thurs. max., +77; min. today, +49.

Sun Above Horizon—13 hours, 27 mins.
Sunrise, 5.44; sunset, 7.11. Moonrise,
8.6; moonset, 19.45.

*Detailed Weather Report on Page 19

CITY MILK PRICES FIXED

Average Rate For Producers Is $1.53 Per Hundred Pounds

Ending a dispute between milk producers and distributors in Greater Winnipeg district, the Municipal and Public Utility board, today made an interim order fixing milk prices, to become effective Sept. 12. The scale agreed upon is as follows:

Producers will receive $1.62 per 100 pounds for 80 percent of the milk they deliver. The remaining 20 percent will be paid for at the rate of $1.17 per 100 pounds, or an average of $1.53. These prices are based on a content of 3.5 percent butterfat.

The settlement of the Milk Price War was clearly headline news in Winnipeg in 1932. Although the Co-op finally agreed to the PUB's settlement, it had initially refused to sign the consent order because the prices to consumers were "too high ... in proportion to the prices that were suggested to be paid to the producers." (PCL, Circular, "Position of the Workers and Farmers Co-operative Association Ltd., On the Increase of Milk Prices" undated, probably September 2-4, 1932)

that this would create a "milk famine" in Winnipeg by driving the existing creameries out of business. In this worst-case scenario, the city would be left without an adequate milk supply or distribution system, thousands of workers would be unemployed and Manitoba's milk producers would join the West's grain farmers as the newest victims of the Depression.

Nor was this fear unwarranted. On June 16, 1932, the big dairies again dropped the price they paid to milk producers, this time to $1 per hundredweight for 80 percent of the milk and sixty-five cents for the remaining 20 percent. Milk shippers would now receive ninety-three cents per hundredweight (2.4 cents per quart) for milk delivered to the city. This was ruinous, for as a later study demonstrated, most farmers needed $1.65 per hundredweight just to break even. Even the big dairies were suffering. Crescent and City Dairy claimed that after getting their milk for 2.4 cents per quart and with overhead costs of slightly over six cents per quart, they had to charge eight-and-a-half cents per quart to break even — and they were already selling it for less.

The Co-op was also in a difficult situation. Gradual improvements in plant efficiency and lower overhead costs than the big dairies had brought the creamery to the break-even point. The Co-op's May 1932 financial statement even showed a small operating surplus at the creamery. Because the Co-op was committed to paying its milk producers as

much as it could, it continued to pay them $1.30 per hundredweight at a time when other dairies were cutting their prices. This meant that the WFCA was playing very close to the margin, and any slip could be disastrous. This point was borne out in June, when a simple accounting mistake led the Co-op to

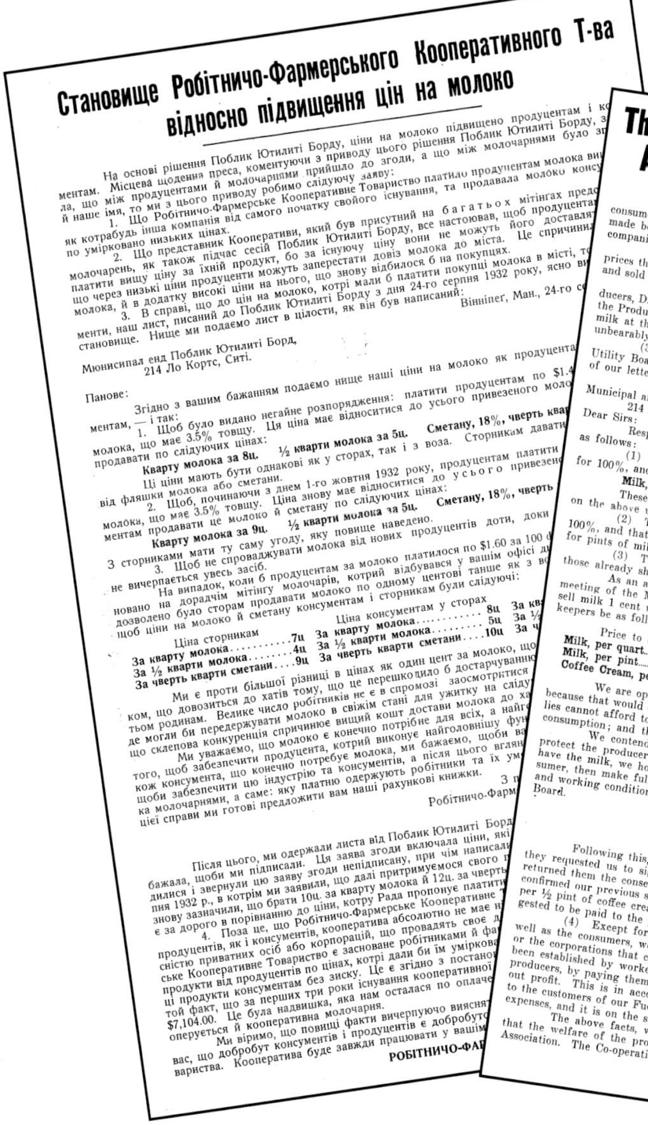

Становище Робітничо-Фармерського Кооперативного Т-ва відносно підвищення цін на молоко

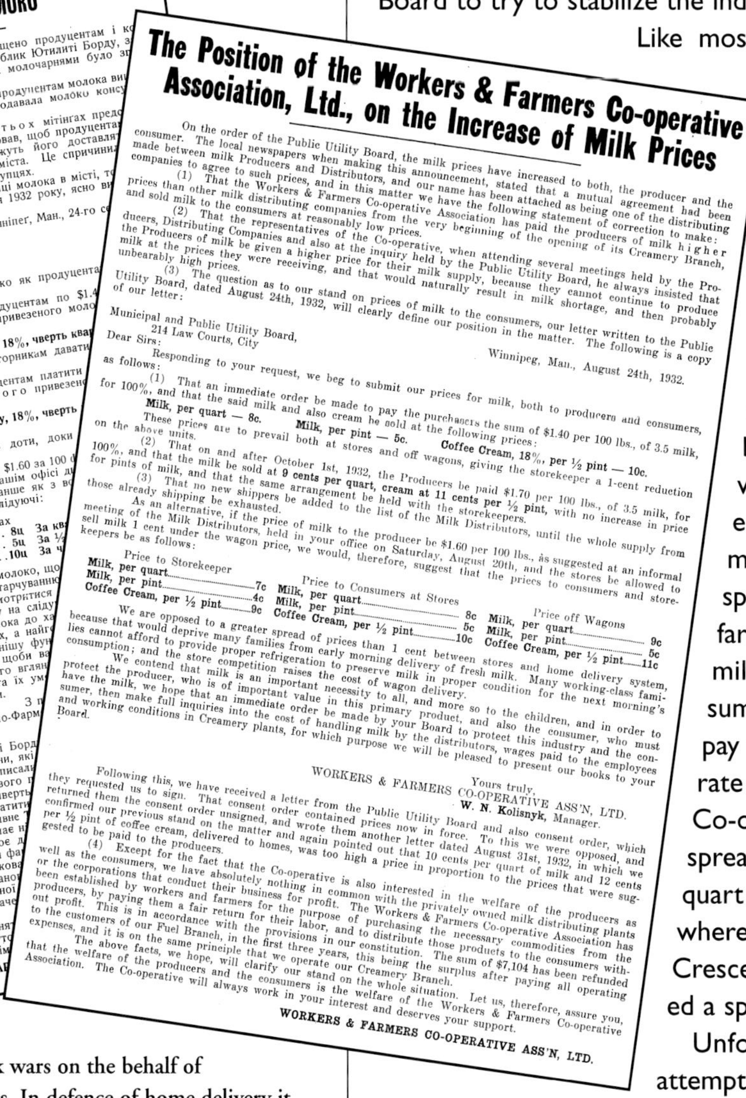

На основі рішення Поблик Ютиліті Борду, ціни на молоко підвищено продуцентам і консументам. Місцева щоденна преса, коментуючи з приводу цього рішення Поблик Ютиліті Борду, заявила, що між продуцентами й молочарнями прийшло до згоди, а що між молочарнями молока включаючи й наше ім'я, що ми з цього приводу робимо слідуюче заяву:

1. Що Робітничо-Фармерське Кооперативне Товариство платило продуцентам молока вищі ціни, як котрабудь інша компанія від самого початку свойого істнування, та продавало молоко консументам по умірковано низьких цінах.

2. Що представник Кооперативи, який був присутній на багатьох мітінґах предсставники молочарень, як також підчас сесії Поблик Ютиліті Борду, все настоював, щоб продуцентам платити вищу ціну за їхній продукт, бо за існуючу ціну вони не можуть далі продукувати молоко, що через низькі ціни продуцентам можуть запрестати довіз молока в місто, та викликати недостачу молока, й в додатку високі ціни на молоко, котрі мали б платити покупці молока 1932 року, ясно виставлено.

3. В справі, що до цін на молоко, що звому навязалося б на покупців менти, наш лист, писаний до Поблик Ютиліті Борду з дня 24-го серпня 1932 року, ясно вистановище. Нижче ми подаємо лист в цілости, як він був написаний:

Вінніпеґ, Ман., 24-го серпня 1932 р.

Мюніципал енд Поблик Ютиліті Борд,
214 Ло Кортс, Сіті.

Панове:

Згідно з вашим бажанням подаємо нижче наші ціни на молоко як продуцентам і консументам, — і так:

1. Щоб було видано негайне розпорядження: платити продуцентам по $1.40 за 100 фунтів молока, що має 3.5% товчу. Ця ціна має молока за 5ц. Сметану, 18%, чверть кварти давати продавати по 8ц.

Ці ціни мають бути однакові як у сторах, так і з воза. Сторінкам давати по 1ц. меньше від фляшки молока або сметани.

2. Що, починаючи з днем 1-го жовтня 1932 року, продуцентам платити по $1.70 за 100 фунтів молока, що має 3.5% товчу. Ця знову має відноситися до усього привезеного молока.

Кварту молока за 9ц. ½ кварти молока за 5ц. Сметану, 18%, чверть кварти молока за 5ц.

3. Щоб не спроваджувати молока від нових продуцентів доти, доки з сторінками мати ту саму угоду, яку повище наведено.

На випадок, коли б продуцентам за молоко платилося по $1.60 за 100 фунтів не вистачить на наш засіб. На зарадчім мітінгу молочарів, котрий відбувався в вашім офісі дня 20-го серпня, дозволено було сторам продавати молоко по одному центі таньше як з воза, щоб ціни на молоко й сметану консументам і сторінкам були слідуючі:

Ціна сторінкам		Ціна консументам у сторах		
За кварту молока.........7ц	За кварту молока.........8ц		За кварту молока.........9ц
За ½ кварти молока 4ц	За ½ кварти молока 5ц		За ½ кварти молока 5ц
За чверть кварти сметани...9ц	За чверть кварти сметани..10ц		За чверть кварти сметани..11ц

Ми є проти більшої різниці в цінах як один цент за молоко, що перешкоджало б доставленню свіжого молока ранком, що довозиться до хатів тому, що це перешкодило б достарчуванню свіжого молока до багатьох родинам. Велике число робітників не є в спромозі заосмотритися в лідницю, де могли б переховувати молоко в свіжім стані для ужитку на слідуючий день. Кошт доставка молока до хатів, що скоріше конкуренція між молоко в конечні потрібне для всіх, а найгірше дітей, котрим необхідно потрібне молоко...

Після цього, ми одержали листа від Поблик Ютиліті Борд, а також консент ордер, якого бажали, щоби ми підписали. Цей консент ордер завіряв згоду включав у собі ціни, які є тепер у силі. Ми були проти цего, і відіслали назад неподписаний, пишучи при тім дальший лист з дня 31-го серпня 1932 р., в котрім ми знову затримували свого попереднього погляду на справі, і знову зазначили, що брати 10ц. за кварту молока й 12ц. за чверть кварти сметани, доставлюваної до хатів, є за дорого в порівнанню до цін, котру Рада пропонує платити продуцентам.

4. Поза ся цент, що Кооператива цікавиться також добробутом продуцентів, як і консументів, кооперацію провадять абсолютно свою діяльність привативні особі або корпорації, що провадять робітництво. Робітничо-Фармерське Кооперативне Товариство установлено робітниками й фармерами в ціли закупна потрібних продуктів від продуцентів по цінах, котрі дали б їм умірковану заплату за їхню працю, і щоб ці продукти продуцентів без зиску. Це є згідно з постановами нашої конституції. Сума від перших трьох років істнування кооперативної вуглярні в $7,104.00 була повернена. Це була кооперативна молочарня.

Ми віримо, що повищі факти вичеркнуть в добробут провас, що добробут продуцентів і консументів в добробутом Робітничо-Фармерства. Кооператива буде завжди працювати у вашім інтересі.

РОБІТНИЧО-ФАРМ...

The Position of the Workers & Farmers Co-operative Association, Ltd., on the Increase of Milk Prices

On the order of the Public Utility Board, the milk prices have increased to both, the producer and the consumer. The local newspapers when making this announcement, stated that a mutual agreement had been made between milk Producers and Distributors, and our name has been attached as being one of the distributing companies to agree to such prices, and in this matter we have the following statement of correction to make:

(1) That the Workers & Farmers Co-operative Association has paid the producers of milk higher prices than other milk distributing companies from the very beginning of the opening of its Creamery Branch, and sold milk to the consumers at reasonably low prices.

(2) That the representatives of the Co-operative, when attending several meetings held by the Producers, Distributing Companies and also at the inquiry held by the Public Utility Board, has always insisted that the Producers of milk be given a higher price for their milk supply, because they cannot continue to produce milk at the prices they were receiving, and that would naturally result in milk shortage, and then probably unbearably high prices.

(3) The question as to our stand on prices of milk to the consumers, our letter written to the Public Utility Board, dated August 24th, 1932, will clearly define our position in the matter. The following is a copy of our letter:

Municipal and Public Utility Board,
214 Law Courts, City
Dear Sirs:

Winnipeg, Man., August 24th, 1932.

Responding to your request, we beg to submit our prices for milk, both to producers and consumers, as follows:

(1) That an immediate order be made to pay the purchasers for milk, both to producers and consumers, for 100%, and that the said milk and also cream be sold at the following prices: the sum of $1.40 per 100 lbs., of 3.5 milk,

Milk, per quart — 8c.
Milk, per pint — 5c.
Coffee Cream, 18%, per ½ pint — 10c.

These prices are to prevail both at stores and off wagons, giving the storekeeper a 1-cent reduction on the above units.

(2) That on and after October 1st, 1932, the Producers be paid $1.70 per 100 lbs., of 3.5 milk, for 100%, and that the milk be sold at 9 cents per quart, cream at 11 cents per ½ pint, with no increase in price for pints of milk, and that the same arrangement be held with the storekeepers.

(3) That no new shippers be added to the list of the Milk Distributors, until the whole supply from those already shipping be exhausted.

As an alternative, if the price of milk to the producer be $1.60 per 100 lbs., as suggested at an informal meeting of the Milk Distributors, held in your office on Saturday, August 20th, and the stores be allowed to sell milk 1 cent under the wagon price, we would, therefore, suggest that the prices to consumers and storekeepers be as follows:

Price to Storekeeper	Price to Consumers at Stores	Price off Wagons
Milk, per quart 7c	Milk, per quart 8c	Milk, per quart 9c
Milk, per pint 4c	Milk, per pint 5c	Milk, per pint 5c
Coffee Cream, per ½ pint ...9c	Coffee Cream, per ½ pint ...10c	Coffee Cream, per ½ pint ...11c

We are opposed to a greater spread of prices than 1 cent between stores and home delivery system, because that would deprive many families from early morning delivery of fresh milk. Many working-class families cannot afford to provide proper refrigeration to preserve milk in proper condition for the next morning's consumption; and the store competition raises the cost of wagon delivery.

We contend that milk is an important necessity to all, and more so to the children, and in order to protect the producer, who is of important value to all, and also the consumer, who must have the milk, we hope that an immediate order be made by your Board to protect this industry and the consumer, then make full inquiries into the cost of handling milk by the distributors, wages paid to the employees and working conditions in Creamery plants, for which purpose we will be pleased to present our books to your Board.

Yours truly,
WORKERS & FARMERS CO-OPERATIVE ASS'N, LTD.
W. N. Kolisnyk, Manager.

Following this, we have received a letter from the Public Utility Board and also consent order, which they requested us to sign. That consent order contained prices now in force. To this we were opposed, and returned them the consent order unsigned, and wrote them another letter dated August 31st, 1932, in which we confirmed our previous stand on the matter and again pointed out that 10 cents per quart of milk and 12 cents per ½ pint of coffee cream, delivered to homes, was too high a price in proportion to the prices that were suggested to be paid to the producers.

(4) Except for the fact that the Co-operative is also interested in the welfare of the producers as well as the consumers, and the corporations that conduct their business for profit. The Workers & Farmers Co-operative Association has have absolutely nothing in common with the privately owned milk distributing plants been established by workers and farmers for the purpose of purchasing the necessary commodities from the producers, by paying them a fair return for their labor, and distribute those products to the consumers without profit. This is in accordance with the provisions in our constitution. The sum of $7,104 has been refunded to the customers of our Fuel Branch, in the first three years, this being the surplus after paying all operating expenses, and is on the same principle that we operate our Creamery Branch.

The above facts, we hope, will clarify our stand on the whole situation. Let us, therefore, assure you, that the welfare of the producers and the consumers is the welfare of the Workers & Farmers Co-operative Association. The Co-operative will always work in your interest and deserves your support.

WORKERS & FARMERS CO-OPERATIVE ASS'N, LTD.

---

ticipated in the June conferences hosted by this Board to try to stabilize the industry.

Like most of the creamery managers, storeowners, milk producers and government officials who attended these meetings, Kolisnyk was committed to working out a livable compromise but since the Co-op was not profit-oriented, he proposed a much smaller price spread between what farmers were paid for milk and what consumers would have to pay than did his corporate counterparts. The Co-op maintained that a spread of four cents per quart would be sufficient, whereas City Dairy and Crescent Creamery wanted a spread of 6.25 cents.

Unfortunately, all attempts to reach a truce in the price war were continually frustrated by Piggly Wiggly's Winnipeg manager. His insistence that the chain be guaranteed the right to sell milk for at least one cent less than any other cash-and-carry store and two cents less than stores offering credit accounts and home delivery (the most common form of grocery store business at the time) defeated all attempts at compromise.

The Municipal and Public Utility Board, unable to negotiate a settlement, launched a formal inquiry into Winnipeg's milk industry which dragged on throughout the summer. While the inquiry provided reams of testimony and documentary evidence, the price war intensified: milk producers began threatening to halt all shipments to Winnipeg; cut-throat competition between individual milkmen and various mer-

---

The Co-op fought the milk wars on the behalf of both consumers and producers. In defence of home delivery it distributed thousands of flyers that argued: "We are opposed to a greater spread of prices than 1 cent between stores and home delivery system, because that would deprive many families from early morning delivery of fresh milk. Many working-class families cannot afford to provide proper refrigeration to preserve milk in proper condition for the next morning's consumption; and the store competition raises the cost of wagon delivery."

assume that it was still showing an operating profit when in fact it had fallen into a deficit position.

Keenly aware that it could not go on losing money forever, the WFCA supported Premier John Bracken's announcement that the government was preparing legislation to bring Winnipeg's milk industry under the partial control of the Municipal and Public Utility Board late in the spring of 1932. Kolisnyk, as the Co-op's representative, avidly par-

Translation of an ad in *Ukrainian Labor News*, Sept. 15, 1932:

ONLY ONE YEAR AGO...THAT IS, SEPT. 15, 1931

The Workers and Farmers Co-operative Association opened a branch with the aim of providing the richest quality milk, cream and other dairy products to consumers in the city of Winnipeg and its suburbs.

In this short time we've grown from a relatively small dairy enterprise to an important provider of these products to the whole city including Transcona and St. Boniface.

The successful growth of this worthy undertaking is due to the quality of products and delivery and also to the fact that customers want to support the co-operative system of distribution.

Our milk, cream and other dairy products are of the Highest Quality and once you try them, we're certain that you'll accept no substitutes.

Current increases in the price of milk to producers and consumers which came into effect following the order of the Public Utility Board help us continue to improve the quality of our products and when we will have any profit after paying all necessary expenses connected to the operation of our enterprise, we will return it to producers and consumers, proportional to their purchases and sales.

May this year and the coming ones be mutually successful for us. This great cause of co-operation deserves your support.

chant groups raged on unchecked; and Piggly Wiggly spent huge sums of money on advertisements lashing out at what it saw as the big, inefficient dairies and the Municipal and Public Utility Board. It was an unpleasant situation for everyone but the consumer, and several creameries and most milk producers tottered on the edge of financial ruin.

Throughout all of this, the Co-op took the high road, maintaining that the producers deserved far more money than they were getting. The WFCA put its money where its mouth was, paying its milk shippers more than the ninety-three cents the big dairies were offering. At the same time, the Co-op kept arguing for reasonable consumer prices. While it could not afford the full- and half-page ads that Piggly Wiggly took out in the daily papers, Kolisnyk, the Board, and the deliverymen all made certain the public knew that the Co-op stood four-square behind low consumer prices. When the Public Utility Board finally worked out an agreement on milk prices in September of 1932, the Co-op made it clear that although it would abide by the agreement, it did not support it entirely, primarily because the negotiated price to consumers was too high and the price paid to producers was too low.

A flyer, in both English and Ukrainian, was distributed to all Co-op customers and to most of Winnipeg's working-class homes in September of 1932, reprinting the WFCA's submission to the Board which called for a two-step price increment to both producers and consumers. The Co-op's rationale was class- not profit-based. As it said in its submission, "Many working-class families cannot afford to provide proper refrigeration for the next morning's consumption; and the store competition raises the cost of wagon delivery."[3]

While the Co-op was less than enthusiastic about the terms that ended the price war, it was nevertheless glad the war was over. Thanks in large part to the financial and moral support of its North End constituency, it had survived, and the creamery had even earned a small profit during July and August. Better yet, the Co-op emerged as a champion of poor farmers and the working class. Finally, although it disapproved of the new price spread, the Co-op could benefit from this spread, if it could keep its home-delivery sales growing.

"Our achievements during the first year" read the signs on the Co-op's black, white and red wagons and trucks. The creamery's first anniversary was celebrated with a parade from Dufferin and McGregor to the corner of Portage and Main and back to the creamery.

THE NEW COMPETITION

But the Co-op was not out of the woods yet. There would be several more outbreaks of cutthroat competition during the 1930s, most notably in 1933, 1936–37 and 1939, when even more competitors entered the milk business. Standard Dairies, the Associated Retail Grocers (ARG), Royal Dairy, and Central Dairies all established milk plants in Winnipeg between 1933 and 1939. Meanwhile, J.W. Spiers of Modern Dairies, the most aggressive player in the Winnipeg milk market, was always ready to step in and buy out the plants and delivery routes of any company that faltered. He bought St. Boniface Creamery and Standard Dairies in 1935–36 and

Central Dairies during World War Two. Companies from out of town were also moving into Winnipeg. In 1941 Calgary-based Palm Dairies set up shop in Winnipeg, while in 1943 Silverwoods, the large London, Ontario-based dairy corporation added City Dairy to its Western Canadian division. But the most frightening competitive development of all took place in 1936 when Safeway took over Piggly Wiggly's Sundale milk plant on Henry Avenue. Safeway expanded its production and began supplying both of these American-based chain stores with dairy products from one location – in effect establishing the precursor to Safeway's famous Lucerne Dairy.

Competition was not, however, the Co-op's only problem during the 1930s and 1940s. It also faced difficulties more related to politics than to the milk business.

PCL

THE TWO-EDGED
SWORD OF POLITICS

■

From its founding to its closure the Co-op was led by high profile members of the Communist Party. In and of itself this was not a problem. No leader of the Co-op ever tried to hide his political affiliations and over the years many of its managers and workers stood for election on the Communist Party ticket – with considerable success, as witnessed by the electoral records of William Kolisnyk, Jake Penner, Andrew Bileski and Bill Kardash. Although most members of the Co-op were not Communists themselves, they tended to support the political ideals of its leaders.

Still, the politics of the Co-op's leaders did have repercussions for the WFCA. Whenever a con-

tentious issue involving the Co-op arose, there were bound to be political overtones. Even if there was no political aspect to an issue, those who disliked the Co-op's politics would often create one by engaging in generalized red-baiting. On the other hand though, the leaders of the Co-op sometimes ascribed political motives to valid criticisms.

An example of the leaders' defensiveness arose in the fall of 1932. At the Annual Meeting one member, J. Kozlowski, made a startling charge: he claimed to have proof that the 1929 purchase of the Co-op's wood yard had been manipulated for private gain by a number of individuals. He produced a letter from a lawyer showing that the agents who conducted the land deal on the Co-op's behalf had bought the property for $8,800 and resold it to the WFCA for $12,000. When nothing that Kolisnyk or Harry Sydor (the Co-op officials most closely associated with the purchase of the yard) said about the purchase satisfied Kozlowski, Sydor demanded a special commission to investigate the claim. Sydor's remarks left no doubt as to what he expected from this commission. He wanted it to "investigate the given matter and give its report to the press in which all the slanders of the yellow-blue [a reference to Ukrainian nationalist organizations] on the workers' co-operative and its workers" would be disproved.[4] With this mandate, passed unanimously, the inquiry's result was never in doubt.

This fight spread into the wider Ukrainian community. An article in the *Ukrainian Voice*, a paper allied with the Ukrainian Greek Orthodox Church and the Ukrainian Self-Reliance League, attacked the Co-op leaders so harshly that the Co-op's lawyer recommended Kolisnyk and Sydor sue the newspaper for libel. And Kozlowski took his fight to the streets, apparently telling people all over the North End that there must be "some kind of machination between the Board of Directors and the [real estate] agency regarding the purchase of the yard."[5]

In December 1932 the five-man commission reported that it had found absolutely no evidence of wrong-doing on the part of anyone associated with the Co-op. Moreover, all statements made by "Kozlowski and other enemies of the association" were labelled as false.[6] In actuality, Kozlowski was correct in many of the particulars he had brought to the members' attention. Whatever his political motivation and whatever political use others made of his accusations, the truth was that the real estate agent had flipped the property for a quick profit of $3,200 in 1929. And early in 1936 the Co-op acknowledged this, launched a lawsuit, and later accepted an out-of-court settlement from the real estate agents for the exact amount specified by Kozlowski. There was no direct evidence linking Kolisnyk or Sydor to this deal but this affair coloured Kolisnyk's remaining years with the Co-op. In December of 1935 Kolisnyk tendered his resignation as general manager. Clearly, then, the Co-op should have treated the whole matter more seriously at the outset instead of dismissing it as mere political manipulation.

While it is easy to be critical of this blindness, the Co-op had reason to be defensive; its critics and enemies were legion. The Ukrainian-speaking community had long been split along ideological lines

and the high-profile Co-op was an obvious target for those who wanted to strike at the leadership of the Ukrainian left. Like other organizations on the political left, the Co-op was constantly spied upon and harassed by the RCMP and other state agencies. It was not surprising that a type of bunker-mentality developed: criticisms were almost automatically perceived as political attacks and any problems within the ranks of the leadership were dealt with behind closed doors so as not to expose any schisms to its enemies.

No matter how understandable, this political rigidity was a weakness. Conflicts over political matters became so intense that the stability of the WFCA was threatened, even when the issue in question had no direct bearing on the Co-op. And this is exactly what happened in 1935–36 when one of the most divisive issues ever to confront the Ukrainian left erupted. It caused a wholesale realignment of the Co-op's Board of Directors, led to withdrawals of loan capital and brought forth a new group of critics of the Co-op – including some people who had been involved with the WFCA since its inception.

Beginning in 1933 reports of famine in the Soviet Ukraine, enforced collectivization and the repression of the Ukrainian intelligentsia, began to be circulated in the nationalist Ukrainian-Canadian press. The majority of those on the political left could not bring themselves to believe that these conditions were being perpetrated by a socialist government and dismissed such reports as anti-Soviet propaganda. This changed, though, when two left-wing intellectuals, Myroslav Irchan and Ivan Sembay, were arrested in the Soviet Ukraine in 1934. Both men had lived and worked in Canada for several years before returning to Ukraine and had been important figures in several left-wing Ukrainian-Canadian organizations during the 1920s and early 1930s. Their arrest led some prominent members of the Ukrainian-Canadian left to raise difficult questions.

The most persistent and high profile questioner was Daniel Lobay. He touched off a storm of controversy in 1935 when he insisted upon a full investigation of what was taking place in the Soviet Ukraine and used his position as a senior editor of the *Ukrainian Labor News* to broadcast his doubts to the entire Ukrainian-Canadian left-wing community. Those who agreed with Lobay included several influential members of the ULFTA and the WBA, among them, some of the board members and founders of the Co-op. A bitter struggle with their former friends and political associates ensued: a struggle for the very heart and soul of the Ukrainian left-wing community.

Although today it is clear that Irchan and Sembay were innocent and Lobay's demand for a more critical attitude towards the Soviet Union well-founded, the leaders of the Ukrainian left put aside their own doubts and accepted the explanations coming from Kiev and Moscow. They rallied their supporters and succeeded in expelling Lobay and his followers from all of the Ukrainian left-wing organizations late in 1935 and early in 1936.

In the tight-knit left-wing community of North End Winnipeg the fallout from this rift was impossible to avoid, and it affected the WFCA significantly. It too expelled its "Lobay faction," which included some directors. As a result, for quite some time they denounced each other in the pages of the various Ukrainian-language papers, including a 1936 letter from the Co-op's workers denouncing the "Lobayists." There was even talk that members of the Lobay group might try to take control of the Co-op and some of the other organizations they had helped to found and lead.

Coming at roughly the same time as Kolisnyk's resignation, this rift created an unhealthy situation for the Co-op. Indeed, the sudden withdrawal of $4,000 of loan capital by members of the Lobay faction, with more withdrawals soon to come, briefly threatened it with financial ruin.

Still, if political disagreements sometimes weakened the Co-op, political commitment was often its greatest strength. The people who led the Co-op, as well as many of its first generation of rank-and-file workers, had a dedication at which one can only marvel. They believed that they could change the world and make it a better place for everyone. Moreover, they were convinced that the success of the Co-op would play a role – albeit a small one – in that change. On the strength of those convictions they were willing to loan money to the Co-op, buy

■ MYRON KOSTANIUK ■

Myron "Mike" Kostaniuk came to Canada in 1909, a powerfully built seventeen-year-old. He worked his way around the country, labouring on the railroad extra-gangs, the West Coast docks and the barges that plied Lake Winnipeg to the Nelson River.

Kostaniuk called himself "tough guy from storage" because of his ability to stack heavy milk cases ceiling-high. The name—and the attitude—helped him handle the hardships he faced, such as being jailed for leading workers' demonstrations, wartime internment and, later in his life, the amputation of both legs.

Long remembered for his sense of humour, Kostaniuk was known for being practical and fair. In his memoirs, he wrote: "In the first place one has to try a thing to determine if it is possible or not. Then you can be sure when you ask others to do it. Here's how I studied these problems [at the Fuel Yard]. On Sunday when no one was at work I would take the scraper and unload 40 tons of coal. I then knew how long it would take to unload that coal. Then I would be competent to tell someone else to do his quota conscientiously."

its shares and work incredibly hard to assure the success and survival of this unique institution.

There is perhaps no better example of this dedication than Myron (Mike) Kostaniuk. He came to the Co-op in 1932 directly from a cell at Burwash Penitentiary in Ontario where he was doing hard labour for his role in leading a 1932 May Day demonstration in Sudbury, a demonstration which had been violently broken up by the police. The Canadian Labour Defence League (CLDL) was able to secure Kostaniuk's early release, provided that there was a

The fuel yard meant strenuous physical labour for the yardmen and manager Myron Kostaniuk, and never-ending coal dust for his wife who kept the couple's home (its roof can be seen near the top left corner). But it was a great playground for Kostaniuk's young grand-children who, he said, left no corner unexplored!

job waiting for him. It was the Co-op that respond-ed to the CLDL's appeal for a suitable job.

A long-time railway worker, smelter worker and labour organizer, Kostaniuk became a legendary fig-ure at the Co-op. He embodied a work ethic that, even by the standards of the Co-op's hard-working milkmen, plant workers and managers, was remark-able. During the mid-1930s, when he was a shipper inside the milk plant, Kostaniuk put in sixteen-hour days on split shifts for six and sometimes, seven days per week. Later, when he became the fuel yard man-ager, passers-by were amazed to see this fifty-year-old man unloading box cars of cordwood or coal –

all by himself – on Sundays. He did this backbreak-ing work in order to save the Co-op the "demur-rage" or storage costs that the railway companies charged. No detail was too large or small for his attention. Whether it was unloading coal or wood on a Sunday, studying the fuel delivery routes so that they could be replanned to save an extra block's gas consumption, or instituting a regime of cost-cutting and recycling in the yard office, Kostaniuk would do almost anything to ensure that the Co-op could save time, money and other resources in order to pass on those savings to its patrons. And he did all of this while remaining incredibly active within a

52

broad range of the Ukrainian left's cultural and political activities and serving on the Co-op's board.

But, if Myron Kostaniuk's dedication was remarkable, it was part of a larger pattern of dedication and commitment at the Co-op. The workers not only laboured long and hard for the Co-op but often helped it deal with ongoing financial problems. In 1933, when the Co-op had to mortgage its buildings and postpone its move into butter production, the workers each contributed seven weeks' salary to help cover the operating deficit between 1933 and 1934. In 1936–37, when it looked as if the Co-op would show a surplus, the Board of Directors offered the employees a special bonus to repay them for these contributions. But at a meeting of the thirty-three workers eligible for this offer, twenty-six voted to turn it down and have the surplus reinvested in the Co-op, while the seven who voted to keep the money suggested that it be transferred to Co-op shares in their names.

Clearly, the Co-op's political orientation was a two-edged sword, being both its greatest strength and at times its greatest weakness; but it was what made the Co-op so unique. A different type of co-operative, indeed!

■ ■ ■

1   PCL, Minute Book 1 "Minutes of the Executive Meeting, December 27, 1931 and January 3, 1932."

2   Ibid., "Minutes of the Executive Meeting, January 3, 1932."

3   PCL, Flyer, "The Position of the Workers and Farmers Co-operative Assoc., Limited on the Increase of Milk Prices." nd.

4   PCL, Minute Book 1 "Minutes of Shareholders' Meeting, October 4, 1932."

5   Ibid., "Minutes of the Board of Directors Meeting, December 3, 1932."

6   Ibid, "Report of the Special Commission Elected at the General Membership Meeting ... in the matter of accusations made by J. Kozlowski, December 3, 1932."

The blacksmith shop. From the time that the fuel yard opened in 1928 until the 1950s, the Co-op used horses, wagons and sleighs for delivering first coal and wood, then its dairy products.

CHAPTER FIVE
EVERYDAY LIFE AND BUILDING THE CO-OP

A COMMUNITY INSTITUTION

While it is easy to focus upon the "great events" of the Co-op's history – the struggle to get into a new business, the political schisms, the milk price war and some of the leadership shake-ups – this also gives a misleading impression of what the Co-op was becoming. There is another way of looking at what made this institution unique: that is, by examining its day-to-day struggle to survive and to serve. And this successful struggle was embodied in small details – details that never made headlines.

The Co-op was always intimately involved in the everyday struggle of working-class people to survive: it was, after all, the purveyor of some of the most important products that people needed. The Co-op often extended credit to many of these people for as long as it could, longer than was probably wise from a strictly business standpoint, so that these working-class families could have milk for

their children and heating fuel for their homes during difficult financial times.

This day-to-day contact – not just at moments of dramatic confrontation, as in a strike or a political battle – gave the Co-op an interesting perspective on class struggle. There was nothing theoretical or abstract about its involvement in this working-class community, nor could it just pick up and move on to the next hot spot on the "road to revolution" when the situation changed for either the better or the worse. The Co-op was both in and of the North End's working class, and could never afford the luxury of simply accepting the worsening condition of these people in the hopes that they would be stirred to greater levels of political militancy. Rather, the Co-op's leaders felt duty-bound to find some way of helping the people of the North End cope with the crises in their lives. On many occasions, when someone was facing deportation because of unemployment, a job, no matter how temporary, was found for him in the fuel yard. When a fuel or milk bill had risen to the point that it simply could not be paid, the Co-op was committed to giving a

The Co-op stable, with stable man **Theodore Gordienko** on the left. Working with horses was never predictable. Veteran milkman **Peter Kochan** recalled that shortly after he started with the Co-op he had to make a delivery to a new customer on Main Street. "I didn't tie up my horse. I figured I would do it rather fast. I came out and the horse is gone. No horse, no load. The horse went from City Hall, Main Street up to Aberdeen, turned down Aberdeen to the creamery. I'm looking for the horse and I can't find it. The horse came to the front door of the stable and it was closed. The horse couldn't open the door and it went back where the hay was, stopped there in the corner and put his head down. And we were looking, had it on the radio all over, that someone had stolen a horse. Later, the stable man came and heard the horse snorting."

family member the chance to work off that debt at regular Co-op wages, whenever possible, allowing the person to work a day or two longer so they could have a few extra dollars.

The Co-op was providing an ever-increasing number of jobs for the people of the North End. Decent-paying employment for over fifty men and women by 1934 and for over one hundred by the close of the decade was of considerable significance in the 1930s, particularly for immigrants who were

so often the last hired, the first fired and the easiest to deport when unemployed. The Co-op's management and workers were very much committed to staying in business and expanding, not only to keep these existing jobs going, but also in the hope that more good jobs could be created. This was a responsibility that an ideologue might not have fully appreciated, but one which hands-on managers could never escape. To these leaders there was nothing abstract about the Co-op, its work force, or its customers; all three had to be protected, expanded and cherished in any way possible.

THE PEOPLE'S BANK

The Co-op not only provided dairy products, heating fuel and employment opportunities, it also became a bank of sorts. This came about almost accidentally as a result of the Co-op's need for loans from the members and friends of the WFCA. Then, because these loans earned depositors an average of

Translation of an ad in *Ukrainian Labor News*, June 25, 1932:

YOUR MONEY--

WILL GIVE YOU TWO-FOLD BENEFITS WHEN
YOU INVEST IT IN THE WORKERS AND
FARMERS CO-OPERATIVE IN WINNIPEG

When you invest money in the Workers and Farmers Co-operative you are helping it to carry on its business successfully and a
successful Co-op brings benefits to the working class, and at the
same time to you. Moreover, the Co-op pays 5% interest on all
loan capital and will refund it whenever requested.

The co-operative in Winnipeg is meeting with unanticipated
success and the expansion of its business requires more capital,
therefore, don't delay, but invest your savings in...

The Workers And Farmers Cooperative Association

2 percent more than the banks were paying and because the Co-op never missed an interest payment, considerable confidence developed in this unusual financial institution. Beginning in the early 1930s, the Co-op issued its own pass books for depositors and, according to some of its critics, was willing to provide anonymity for depositors so that they would not be disqualified from Relief just because they had their meagre life savings invested in the Co-op. This was an unproved allegation, repeated by some provincial, city and RCMP investigators during the 1930s and early 1940s, but it does raise the fascinating image of the Co-op offering the equivalent of Swiss bank accounts for the working class!

From beginning to end, the Co-op took good care of its investors' money. Most was invested in its fuel yard and creamery operations, which became increasingly successful in the 1930s, but the Co-op also put money back into the community. Loans were made to local stores and restaurants so that they could purchase refrigeration equipment, to area farmers so that they could purchase feed for their herds and to truckers who hauled milk on contract for the Co-op, so that they could purchase the necessary vehicles, licenses and insurance for this work. Even some simple small loans were provided for Co-op members who were in need, while larger loans were made to co-op stores in parts of rural Manitoba where the Co-op had large numbers of milk and cream shippers and cordwood suppliers, such as at Broad Valley and Fisher Branch. Co-op employees were also fairly regular borrowers, including loans of several hundreds of dollars for the purchase of homes. Later, the Co-op would even offer mortgages on homes that it helped to build. Thus, for many people in the North End, and beyond, the Co-op became a full-service financial institution.

CHARITY BEGINS IN THE NEIGHBOURHOOD

The Co-op also started, very early in its life, to take on a role as a charitable institution. Striking workers and unemployed workers' associations could always count on a steady supply of dairy products or fuel from the Co-op, as well as the occasional $10 or $25 cash contribution. And most left-wing groups in the North End received some sort of Co-op sponsorship, either in products for a raffle (a ton of coal, a cord of wood, or milk tickets were common prizes), a paid advertisement in the program for their latest play or performance, dairy products or ice cream for their picnics or a small cash contribution for a special cause. Beyond this, the English- and especially the Ukrainian-language radical press got much of the Co-op's small advertising budget, as well as regular contributions to the various "press fund campaigns" that were always

Such contributions were obviously consistent with the intentions of the Co-op's founders. The Co-op was the child of the Ukrainian left and tried to support the left's causes, papers, cultural activities and political campaigns whenever it could, even when it had little surplus to donate. What is surprising, however, is this: by 1933 and 1934 the Co-op was making small contributions to a broad array of decidedly non-left-wing groups. The St. Joseph Society, the St. John Cantius Society, the Sts. Vladimir and Olga Parish Association, the Sir Isaac Newton School Association and innumerable

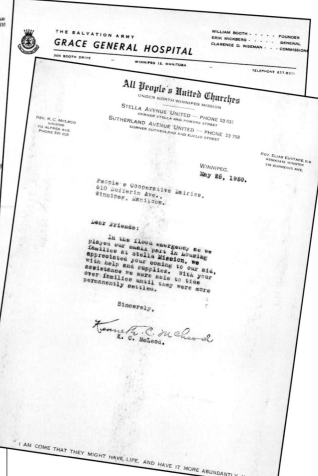

For as long as it existed, the Co-op responded to appeals from various community groups by donating money, products, services and equipment.

being mounted to keep these papers afloat. But the Co-op also made it a point to put some advertising money into the left-wing papers of the Jewish, Polish, Russian and German communities. Numerous North End sports clubs and youth groups affiliated with the Labour Temple or other such institutions also benefited from the Co-op's largesse – including entire baseball and basketball teams sponsored by the Co-op, both of which played their games with the trademark logo of the Workers and Farmers Co-operative Association prominently displayed on their uniforms.

church bazaars, regardless of religious denomination, suddenly start showing up in the Co-op's books as recipients of donations, usually in the form of free products from the creamery. And even more donations never officially recorded in the Co-op's books are attested to by a voluminous file of thank-you notes sent over several decades from every conceivable church group, synagogue, Hadassah Association, parochial school, Ladies

A milkman's day began at the loading docks sometimes as early as 3:00 a.m.

Loading up...

...Heading out...

Aid society, YMCA, Cub Scout troop and the like in areas the Co-op served. These were not exactly the sort of donations expected from a left-wing co-op but they certainly were good for community relations and they were a way of re-paying a constituency that had steadily grown beyond the limits of the Ukrainian-speaking left-wing community.

In the process of running a commercial enterprise and responding to real-life situations, the Co-op was taking on an institutional life of its own. While always mindful of its political orientation, the Co-op was reaching out to various parts of the working class in practical, humane and sometimes quite non-ideological ways. Both the leaders and workers were shaping the Co-op into a North End and even a Winnipeg-wide community institution. This was a very gradual process – at times imperceptible and very often unintentional – and one that usually came from the ground up. The drivers, for example, were very much aware that once they pulled away from the creamery's loading dock or from the fuel yard, politics had little to do with their jobs. True, they knew that many of their customers were fellow members of the Labour Temple, the WBA, the Co-op or other such organizations, but early on it had become clear that the Co-op was growing precisely because it had gone beyond this initial pool of patrons. For both ideological and practical purposes this expansion into the broader community had to be continued.

THE MILKMEN

Because the milkmen were the Co-op's most visible representatives, it is important to understand the role that they played in making the Co-op into a community institution. To begin with, the life of a milkman was not for the faint of heart. In a few cases there were drivers who would show up for work at 1:00 a.m. – so that they could catch the last street car of the day to get to work – nap for a while, start loading at 3:00 a.m. and then not get back to the creamery until well into the afternoon. Even then they still weren't done for the day, for there was still the part of the job that almost every milkman hated – cashing out and balancing the route book. In fact, this was a job that many milk-

59

...Making deliveries...

A milkman's
order book.
COURTESY PETER KOCHAN

men reserved for home so that wives and older children could lend a hand with this last, and some-times frightening (if your debt load was getting too high) part of a very long day's work.

Of course, not everything was drudgery. The sto-ries of drivers who stopped too long to chat or for coffee on a cold morning – or for a drink or two or more during the holiday season – only to find that their horse and

Walter Kochan helped his father deliver milk when he was a boy. "He had an open wagon, one horse. There was a case for milk on both sides of the wagon and there was no seat, you stood all the time. It was fine on a nice day, but during the winter or if it was raining, it made for miserable conditions to work in. In the winter, you couldn't deliver too early because the milk would freeze if you would leave it between the doors. Eventually, the wagon was covered. The milk was in a metal basket and the basket was heavy, and it was all bottles. The cus-tomers usually left a note; if they wanted something other than their usual, maybe you'd have to go back to the wagon."

wagon had abandoned them, are legion. What makes these stories so funny is that the unattended hors-es were busy pulling milk wagons from home to home, stopping dutifully in front of each resi-dence where a delivery should have been made, and then proceeding back to the barn. In retro-spect, these stories are delightful, as one pictures the bewilderment of the stable worker confronted by a driver-less rig or bemused spectators watching a horse and wagon stopping every few houses for no apparent reason.

These, however, were fairly rare occurrences – they only seem common because the stories were repeated so often. For the most part the Co-op's deliverymen were extremely conscientious. Their livelihood and the survival of their employer depend-ed upon offering exactly what the customers want-ed, exactly when they wanted it and at a price that was reasonable every day of the week, regardless of the weather. In Winnipeg this last factor was a huge consideration, especially when one considers that for many years the Co-op's wagons and sleighs offered some protection for the milk, but not for the

...Heading back...

lishing close personal ties with customers, which built up loyalties that could survive price wars and political differences. Many of the early Co-op drivers were well known for their affability and their ability to get and keep customers. This could include giving someone a little more credit than they should have had, shaving the occasional penny off the price of a quart of milk or pound of butter, keeping quiet when someone tried to provoke a political fight, or patiently explaining for the hundredth time that the latest price increase was mandated by the Municipal and Public Utility Board and was not the fault of the driver or the Co-op.

driver. Like it or not, milk had to be delivered every day of the year, even when it was forty below zero or when there was a blizzard raging – which made a deliveryman's life both difficult and dangerous.

Success as a Co-op deliveryman, however, went far beyond a capacity for hard work and a weather-resistant constitution. It also came down to estab-

Many of these deliverymen became integral parts of the neighbourhoods they served and a surprisingly large number of the Co-op's early drivers served the same route for many years, even decades. However, if a driver did not fit into a certain district or could not act as an effective salesman, then he was shifted around or removed from the route altogether. And the Co-op was always very sensitive to issues of ethnicity; it was a point of

...To the wagon yard on McGregor and Dufferin, across from the creamery.

Peter Kochan, on the right, started working for the Co-op as a milkman just one month after the creamery opened. When he first started as a Co-op delivery man, his work day began at one in the morning. "If you got there early, you had a better chance to understand what to do. It took eight or ten hours, there was no punching a clock."

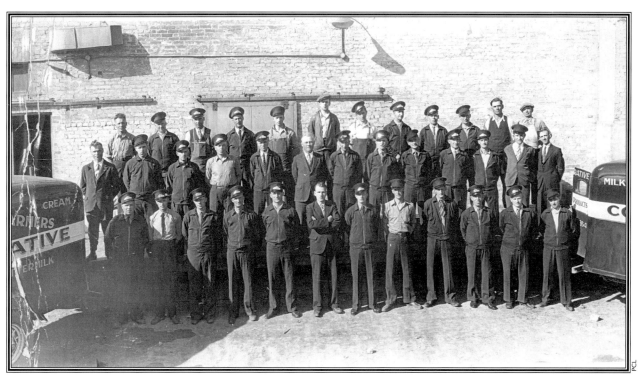

The drivers, seen here with general manager **Andrew Bileski** (front row centre), did more than just deliver dairy products. Their daily interaction with the public was crucial in maintaining and building the number of customers. Long-time milk delivery man **Murphy Dola**, who worked during a later period, recalled, "I was a go-getter. I always enjoyed canvassing. Canvassing was part of my day, each and every day. Several times I built a route up to capacity and then I'd give it away to other drivers. They said I was the best one they ever had. Sometimes my commission was double my salary."

pride that their milkmen could serve their customers in most of the languages of the North End, not just in English as was the case with some of the larger dairies. Ukrainian was the most common language, but from the outset there were Co-op milkmen who could speak Yiddish and German and many of these deliverymen had more than a smattering of Polish and Russian along with English to offer their customers.

Then, as the Co-op expanded into other areas such as St. Boniface, or into a heavily Icelandic-speaking portion of the city, French, Icelandic and Belgian drivers, as well as a few Anglo-Saxons, were added to the sales force. In the context of 1930s' Winnipeg, the milkman's linguistic facility was a true asset for the Co-op and its customers – as the bond of language and ethnicity could be very powerful.

Regardless of ethnic background or political affiliation, the Co-op's driver-salesmen – and the managers back at the creamery – wanted everyone in the vicinity of their route to become Co-op customers and they continually canvassed their territory for new customers. At times they were aided by large-scale recruitment campaigns, where additional canvassers would be put into their districts or radio advertisements would be used. But more often than

---

THE CO-OP AND ITS EARLY UNIONS

When the Co-op established its creamery branch in 1931, greatly increasing the size of its labour-force, it was clear that the time had come for unionization – hardly a surprising conclusion given the trade union experience of almost everyone involved with the Co-op. Nor was it surprising that the preferred labour organization was Canada's most radical union movement of the early 1930's, the Workers' Unity League (WUL).

This overtly revolutionary union shared many of the goals and ideals of the WFCA. In fact, it viewed "Co-operatives organized on class principles and accordingly conducted" as "part of the general labor movement..." not as a typical business operation. This being the case, the first contract signed between the WUL and the Co-op had some clauses not found in other, more traditional, union agreements. For example, a provision that allowed for the Co-op and its workers to join forces in its battle against capitalist firms was built right into the contract. Clause 22 noted that, "In the event of serious competition against the Association in either of its branches, that may be caused by private concerns at the expense of the employees, the question of wages and working conditions in the Co-operative may be re-opened during the life of this Agreement, but only with the consent of the Union ..."[1]

Signed on December 31, 1931, this contract stipulated a six day work week for all Co-op employees, one week's paid vacation after a full year of service, and a wage scale ranging from a low of $20.00 per week for deliverymen whose "load" was 1000 units or less, up to $32.00 per week for the spare route driver, who had to function as a route supervisor and be able to handle each and every route on the drivers' days off or when they were ill. Meanwhile, inside plant workers were to earn between $20.00 and $25.00 for their six day week, "averaging 8 hours per day," although the contract also noted that "no employee shall leave the plant until all work is completed ..."[2] And finally, fuel yard employees were to be paid a minimum of 40 cents per hour.

By the standards of the 1930s this agreement was quite progressive in terms of wages and benefits; indeed for the deliverymen it mirrored and even bettered the conditions of unionized drivers at other Winnipeg creameries. But it also reflected the spirit of mutuality, self-sacrifice, and militancy that was such a hallmark of the WFCA in its early days. And, as discussed elsewhere in this book, when times got difficult for the WFCA the workers and their union did in fact make sacrifices which allowed the Co-op to survive.

The Workers' Unity League continued to represent the Co-op's workers until 1935–36 when the WUL was disbanded – a move that was related to a change in the tactics of pro-communist organizations all around the globe. In Canada the various union locals that had been formed under the umbrella of the WUL now sought to join or re-join the mainstream labour movement. Thus, in 1937 the Co-op's workers entered Local 119 of the International Teamsters Union, the union which then represented the majority of Winnipeg's organized creamery workers. Unfortunately, membership in this rather conservative trade union would ultimately cause the Co-op's workers and the Co-op itself considerable grief in 1940.

not, it was the drivers' responsibility to increase and maintain their own customer base and, whenever possible, to convince these customers to become Co-op shareholders and depositors as well.

The interactions of the drivers with customers – be they Relief milk recipients (at one point during the Depression, 35 percent of the Co-op's customers were on Relief), small storekeepers, or "regular" customers – were absolutely critical to the Co-op's success. The managers understood this and listened to them when it came to finding ways to improve sales or to discover what it was that the customers wanted most.

THE MANAGERS

Like the milkmen, the Co-op's management collective – consisting of the Board of Directors and the senior managers – understood that the practical aspects of running a business had to be attended to. No matter what they may have thought about their competitors in political terms, the Co-op's leaders had no problem sitting down with their capitalist counterparts in efforts to avoid the ruinous competition of milk price wars. They also became active members in the various trade associations

related to the milk and fuel businesses such as the Dairyman's Association, the Greater Winnipeg Bottle Exchange, the Winnipeg Coal Dealers Association and the Winnipeg Wood Dealers Association. Moreover, the leadership's relations with government agencies were remarkably good. For example, a letter written by the Secretary of the Municipal and Public Utility Board indicated that by the time Kolisnyk resigned as general manager in 1935, he had earned the respect of everyone involved with the Board, despite their distaste for his politics. And if anything, his successor, Andrew Bileski, earned an even better reputation among government and dairy industry officials.

STOREKEEPERS AND THE CO-OP

Both Kolisnyk and Bileski understood that the small storekeepers of the North End and other working-class districts were an important patronage group. Thus, even though the Co-op usually wanted store and home delivery prices to be the same – which was a sore point to store owners – the Co-op attempted to find other issues where they could be more supportive. In 1933, for example, the Co-op sided with the storekeepers of the North End in

Some of the office staff and management, 1936: left to right, Winnie Bindas (Harrison), Walter Sawiak, Eloise Maksymchuk (Popiel), Andrew Bileski, Hilda Kolisnyk (Stevenson), Abe Greenberg and Goldie Sandler (Phomin).

AUUC/WBA

■ ANDREW BILESKI ■

Andrew Bileski's political education began the day the raw, young farm boy from Saskatchewan started work at the Cominco Smelter in Trail, British Columbia. After a few days of backbreaking work for Cominco, Bileski could see the value of a union.

He was soon playing an active role in the Ukrainian left. A man of initiative, energy, talent and organizing ability, he was only thirty-two when he was appointed Co-op general manager in 1935.

During the 1930s, he formed the Workers' Sports Club, organized neighbourhood councils of the unemployed and helped build the Canadian Labour Defense League and the Committee to Aid Spain—all while managing the Co-op and serving as a school trustee and alderman.

Within the Ukrainian community, Bileski organized and participated in cultural groups, directed fundraising campaigns for the Ukrainian press and, later, spearheaded the development of activities and facilities for its senior members. Both he and his wife Mary sang in local choirs throughout their lives. He was a physically active man, an avid curler, golfer and gardener. He was a great baseball fan and also an accomplished chess player. Even when delivering a hard-hitting speech, Bileski projected a dignified presence.

After Bileski retired in 1972, he continued to be involved in cultural activities, the Manitoba Peace Council and the Age and Opportunity Centre. He sat on the Civic Charities Bureau and was recognized by the mayor for his years of community service. During his retirement he continued to serve on the Co-op's Board of Directors.

their fight against the imposition of a new bylaw which would have stopped milk sales in stores that did not have full refrigeration. This was a very serious issue for the corner stores, as many of these small businesses could not afford such equipment. Later, when it became clear that this was a losing battle, the Co-op began a program of lending money or actual refrigeration units to these storekeepers so that they could remain in the milk-selling business. In the interim, though, the Co-op was willing to continue supplying these small stores in almost all circumstances, which was not always easy or profitable. As one 1933 investigation showed, the Co-op had the highest "return rate" of milk from stores of any dairy in Winnipeg, largely because its clients usually had the least efficient storage facilities.

When some stores refused to take milk from the "red dairy" on ideological grounds, or because drivers from other dairies told them that it was risky doing business with "those communists" or that Co-op products were sub-standard, members of the Co-op developed some interesting tactics. This included having Co-op supporters launch small-scale and highly informal boycotts of stores that did not carry Co-op products. If these mini-boycotts and repeated requests for Co-op milk did not have the desired result, local Co-op supporters would go into the store, put together a big grocery order and then, just before paying, would ask for milk – Co-op milk. When the storeowners said that they didn't carry it, the customer would say "too bad" and leave all of their purchases behind. Apparently, this worked well, and usually resulted in yet another store customer for the Co-op, as no one wanted to lose any big orders in the 1930s.

The Co-op also found itself subsidizing the activities of the Ukrainian Storekeepers Association, helping cover the costs of its organizer in 1935. This was an act of enlightened self-interest, for the Co-op recognized that members of this Association constituted a large part of its store clientele, particularly in the North End. Moreover, the Co-op's $30 per month "donation" did have strings attached: the Association would have to agree to "push Co-op products" and if there was no subsequent rise in sales, the donation would be discontinued.[3]

Part of the daily office work involved tallying cream shipments and drivers' sales to calculate cream cheques and drivers' commissions. **Beth Krall**, recalls the long hours she put in at the Co-op offices during the 1930s. "I used to do what they called 'rebates' for the drivers. They got a certain amount of commission after every week or two weeks. On those occasions, we had to have those ready by the time the drivers came to work next morning. Eloise [Popiel] and I used to stay to 11, 12 o'clock at night. The police used to come and pick us up and take us home—they used to drop in to the dairy for chocolate milk or buttermilk and they'd give us a ride home."

CO-OP PRODUCTS

The Co-op had to make the highest quality products possible and as many different dairy products as consumers and storeowners wanted, for if the Co-op did not provide these products, consumers and storeowners might turn to another creamery for their dairy needs. Thus, although the Co-op had started out by making and selling nothing but pasteurized milk and cream, it moved into every other form of dairy production as soon as was possible. In the first year of operation, buttermilk, sour cream and cottage cheese (all-important products for Eastern European consumers) were added to the Co-op's product line. Butter, which called for more expensive processing equipment, was still being bought from other plants and then cut and wrapped with a Co-op mark. This meant that the Co-op did not have full control over the quality of the product. The Co-op's management also noted that while all increases in the price of butter were passed along very quickly to the Co-op, price cuts could take weeks to filter through. Given this, and the simple fact that butter was often a major money-maker for

Ice boxes, referred to as ice refrigerators in this billboard from 1937, were still widely used in the 1930s. Cooling was provided by large blocks of ice that had to be delivered regularly by an iceman. Keeping milk and other foods from spoiling was a major concern not only for householders but also for small storekeepers who made up most of the Co-op's store trade.

The staff in the creamery worked at everything from butter- and cheese-making, milk processing and bottling, to stocking the cold storage and maintaining the plant. They had to contend with wet concrete floors and wildly differing temperatures in the various parts of the plant. Back row, left to right: M. Biniowski, Fred Pankiw, unknown, Bill Hryciuk, John Krall, Henry Stein, Tony Boychuk, Myron Kostaniuk. Front row: unknown, Deyholos, Henry Paskiewich, John Prossack, Hamil Chopp, James Semeniuk, Ernie Krall.

the creameries, the Co-op desperately wanted to begin making its own butter as soon as possible.

It was not until 1934 that it finally was able to purchase butter making equipment; but once Plant Superintendent John Krall got this equipment, he and his staff began producing some of the highest-quality butter in Canada, as proven by many national and provincial awards. This move into butter production symbolized a greater financial stability for the Co-op (butter in cold storage was quite literally like money in the bank, as the Co-op often used its stored butter as security for short-term bank loans), but it also signalled its determination to become a full-service dairy. For the remainder of the 1930s, the Co-op's product line was continually expanded so that by 1936 it was producing what would become its most famous product, the cream cheese that was based upon a recipe and technique that Krall had brought with him from Switzerland. And by the close of the decade the Co-op was producing such "luxury" products as ice cream and ice cream novelties – product additions that called for considerable rebuilding and expansion of the Dufferin Avenue plant.

In the plant: Ernie Krall seen here receiving cream...

The Co-op took great pride not only in the expansion implied by all of these product additions, but also in the quality of the products themselves. Every award and blue ribbon and every positive comment from a government inspector made its way into the Annual Reports, the minute books and

...Weighing in...

...Processing...

...Testing...

Peter Stastook, plant supervisor: "In the lab, the butter maker would pour eight grams of cream into the testing bottles and put them all in order, up to twenty-four bottles. You would take samples from cream, twenty-four samples to test. Once you'd put the cream in there, you'd add about the same amount of sulphuric acid, then you'd stir them up and as soon as they got dark, brown to black, you had to check them and add hot water to each one. Then you had to put them into the centrifugal machine for so many minutes. All the butterfat would come to the top."

...Bottling (seen here, **Fred Pankiw**).

Bob Pawlyk, plant worker, milkman: "I even worked on the milk line packing the milk in the boxes which was very hard because you have to pick up four cartons at a time off the conveyor belt, then the jugs and the cream cheese. It was fast. I found that the harder people worked, the bond was closer because they would rely so much on each other."

of course, into the Co-op's advertising. The Co-op even used pictures of Winnipeg's "beautiful baby" photo contest winner in its advertising , after it was discovered that the baby in question had been fed nothing but Co-op milk.

CONTEST FOR A NAME

"Here is your chance to get that Spring Outfit that you've wanted!"

Suggest a Worthy Name for a Worthy Product

We Want You to Help Us Name

– OUR NEW – CREAM CHEESE

"You'd Be Contented, Too!"

One-year-old Marjorie Cole seems to say in this attractive picture, "if you were a winner in the Free Press Children's Photo Contest, and if you picked a winner like I have—

Co-op Milk

Yes sir-ee, its the tops in its field, just like our other creamery products!

And if YOU want to pick a winner, just choose the co-operative brand of creamery products!

Our products are RICH, HEALTHY, PURE and RE-FRESHING. Buy them!

Rush your entry in to our office. In addition to our big prize money, we will pay $5.00 every week in milk tickets for the three best entries received starting April 22nd.

Final $50 Prize

(Contest closes May 20th)

LISTEN IN ON STATION C.J.R.C. FOR OUR ANNOUNCEMENTS OF THE WEEK'S WINNERS

Mail all suggestions to the
WORKERS & FARMERS CO-OPERATIVE ASS'N LIMITED
Creamery Branch: 610 Dufferin Avenue   Phone 57 354

RULES

1. This contest is open to anybody wishing to take part in it, with the exception of our creamery employees and their families.

2. Every entree must be accompanied by a milk, cream cap or butter wrapper panel.
3. The decision of the judges will be final.

It'll be The BIG Cheese on the Market!

With this 1936 flyer, the Co-op turned to its customers for a name for its newest product, cream cheese. The winning entry: "Velva-pac." The Co-op also used the opportunity to boast that the winner of Winnipeg's "Beautiful Baby" photo contest had been fed nothing but Co-op milk her entire life.

Many of these products were of excellent quality and were in considerable demand throughout the North End and in several other parts of the city. Co-op butter, sour cream, ice cream and cream cheese became particularly popular, and by the close of the 1930s and early 1940s could be found in stores in virtually every part of Winnipeg.

The Co-op's production and heavy sales of certain items was closely related to the ethnic composition of its eastern and central European clientele. Sour cream was sold in the North End – not just by the pint, but by the quart and gallon – as the natural condiment for perogies, as a dressing for salad and as the final touch for borsch. And much of the

Co-op's whipping cream was sold, not so much for whipping, but as an important component of the thick, dark purple borsch that was a staple of the eastern European dinner table. The cream cheese, of course, was used for spreading on bagels – preferably from the North End's famous Gunn's bakery – and for making cheese cake, a delicacy that the Co-op's advertising stressed should only be made with Co-op cream cheese, following the Co-op's own widely publicized recipe. And during the Jewish High Holidays and Passover there was probably no dairy in Winnipeg that sold a higher percentage of kosher milk, bottled especially for these occasions, than the Co-op. No dairy whose primary business was in the North End

■ ELOISE POPIEL ■

Eloise Maksymchuk (later **Eloise Popiel**) was just seventeen years old when she began working in the office at the Co-op in 1932. Throughout her sixty years with the Co-op she was active in the union and instrumental in administering both the employees' mutual aid sick fund and the Co-op pension. If you needed to find out something, you'd "Ask Eloise".

"When John Fedirchyk joined the Air Force, Andrew called me and asked me to be the office manager. I almost fainted. I took over, and I called all the girls in and I told them, 'I don't know very much about what John did and I'll have to study everything.' I used to come in evenings and peer through his books and I didn't think I was good enough, but they seemed to think I was okay. The girls co-operated and it turned out okay."

She was proud of the benefits that the union and the Co-op were able to provide the Co-op employees. "When people came to work for us and we said, 'You get Blue Cross partly paid and medical partly paid,' then they'd see that the company is very good to the employees. Anytime we got a new person and they found out that we had all these different things and they could become a shareholder and we had a banking account and we paid interest on it, we got a lot of nice people working for us. I had money in the Co-op right up to the time that I left, all those years I was saving money."

could ever afford to run short of these essential components of eastern European cuisine, and the Co-op became particularly adept at meeting the requirements and high standards of its customers.

THE CO-OP RECIPE FOR SUCCESS

By any standard, the Co-op did exceedingly well in the 1930s. Against considerable odds it had survived the typical problems associated with starting up a new business, a brutal milk price war, some major internal problems and the Depression itself. But it had also survived some of the most intense competition imaginable as new dairies entered into the Winnipeg milk market and vied for their share

One of the managers, George Paulowich, came up with the idea of naming the Co-op's ice cream "Carmichael" after a polar bear at the Winnipeg zoo.

of it. This competition included not only price-cutting and politically motivated rumour-mongering, but also several attempts to recruit Co-op route supervisors and drivers (and their customers) to other dairies.

In spite of all this competition, the Co-op had continued to grow and to cut into the market share both of the larger creameries and the independent peddlers. To a very large extent this was a result of all the factors mentioned above – hard work, dedication, knowledge of its customers' needs and desires, quality products and good salesmanship. There were also times when this success came down to some very astute management decisions, a willingness to go beyond typical business practises and good timing.

When the Co-op started producing butter in 1934, it needed steady shipments of already sepa-

rated cream. As this was quite different from the regular supply of whole milk, cream shippers had to be recruited from much further afield. Then, because butter production was so successful, both in terms of the quality of the product and the surplus that butter sales generated, only one year later it was decided that production should be doubled. With the rising profitability of butter, however, came intense competition for cream supplies. The larger dairies had already established butter-making plants in the countryside and a whole series of cream depots where local farmers could deliver their cream. This was too expensive for the Co-op, which opted for a simpler solution – the profit motive. It began giving a cash bonus to every shipper who had sent in more than $25 worth of cream in the past year – a bonus that became a regular feature of Co-op cream purchases for the remainder of the 1930s.

But it was never the Co-op way to stop with only a financial incentive. Because an important part of its mandate was educational and cultural, the Co-op would encourage potential cream shippers and patrons to develop a much closer relationship with their co-operative. Thus, in areas where there was both cream available and a large Ukrainian population, the Co-op would host picnics, put on small concerts featuring Ukrainian ensembles from Winnipeg and send out speakers to talk to local farmers about the Co-op and its goals. In fact, this coupling of cultural, educational and social events with the more practical aspects of running a co-operative became quite common. In the 1930s and 1940s, the Co-op took on an increasingly important role in promoting Ukrainian music and culture. It sponsored Ukrainian music programs on the radio and plays at the Labour Temple and hosted massive picnics for the Co-op, featuring the various musical ensembles of the ULFTA and the talents of many other North End performers. By the late 1940s these picnics were turned into huge events that became, in essence, North End "block parties."

In many of these initiatives, the new general manager, Andrew Bileski, was clearly a driving force. But he had considerable support from the Board and, after 1936, from the Co-op's newly hired director of education and publicity, Mitch Sago. Together, from the mid-1930s to the early 1950s, they created a

Fussy Winnipeg cooks maintained that, to make the best cheesecake, they needed Co-op's old-fashioned block of cream cheese which was wrapped in parchment and moistened with its own whey. **Arthur Gunn**, of Gunn's Bakery, another North End institution, said "the cheese and the cream cheese were, in my estimation, unsurpassed anywhere and I've looked at dairy products all over the place. We used the cream cheese in our cheesecake and it was absolutely the best. It was always nice and smooth and it didn't have lumps. It was a wonderful, wonderful product."

regular program of membership and customer recruiting campaigns, educational campaigns for the work force and membership, and several large-scale advertising campaigns. However, it was Bileski who was instrumental in the Co-op's decision to take advantage of one of the most unique opportunities ever to afford itself to the creamery branch.

THE HOME DAIRY

In the spring of 1936 rumours were swirling in the dairy industry that Crescent Creamery was

planning to shut down its North End subsidiary, Home Dairy, in order to consolidate operations in its under-utilized main plant. Several of the Home Dairy drivers were convinced that this consolidation would eventually cost them their jobs. Even before the plant was closed, first one driver, then, an entire delegation approached Bileski asking for jobs with the Co-op, promising to bring enough customers with them to make viable routes. Bileski also discovered that Abe Greenberg, the manager and former part-owner of Home Dairy, was very disappointed with Crescent's decision to close his shop. After several discussions, and despite being offered a job at Crescent's main plant, Greenberg told Bileski that he would be willing to bring over as many drivers and customers to the Co-op as he could if the Co-op would guarantee jobs for his drivers and for himself as Sales Manager.

This was a ticklish proposition. It would mean the shifting around of several existing North End routes and potentially ruffling the feathers of some existing employees and customers. Beyond this, such a takeover could be costly, as the addition of new routes would mean thousands of dollars in start-up costs for horses, wagons, salaries and increased production – a worthwhile expenditure if this "merger" worked, but ruinous if the men from Home Dairy could not hold onto their customers. Finally, Bileski and the Board knew that this was not the way the Co-op typically did business. It always hired people from within its own organizations, people who the Board and the members felt could be trusted. Considering the recent internal problems at the Co-op, the idea of bringing in a whole group of outsiders, including a man who would automatically be elevated to a senior management position with considerably higher pay than that of the general manager (Greenberg was asking for $55 at a time when Bileski was only making $35 a week), might be worrisome to Co-op members.

Bileski and the Board, however, felt it was worth the risk. Greenberg had over sixteen years' experience in the dairy industry, not only as a manager but also as a butter-maker. His connections with cream shippers all over the province were impeccable – a significant consideration as the Co-op sought to expand its butter production. Greenberg also had excellent connections in the Jewish community, an already important part of the Co-op's customer base that Bileski hoped to tap into even more effectively. And Abe Greenberg had one other qualification that set the Board's mind at ease about bringing him into the Co-op's leadership structure. Although not particularly active in any of the left's political or cultural organizations (a prerequisite for a Co-op manager), Greenberg was sympathetic to the working-class movement. And the Greenberg name was well-known in left-wing political circles, for Abe Greenberg's brother Saul was not only the Co-op's lawyer, but was also one of the country's most highly regarded radical lawyers.

On the basis of all of this, the Co-op went ahead with its incorporation of Home Dairy staff. In May of 1936, Greenberg, five drivers and later, a clerk, came over to the Co-op from Home Dairy, bringing six hundred customers with them. For Bileski this was clearly a gamble. The ongoing fight with the Lobay faction and the exodus of its members from the Co-op had caused a serious cash drain. And Bileski had only taken over from Kolisnyk as general manager five months earlier. Any failure associated with this move could be disastrous for the Co-

op and would reflect badly upon his leadership abilities. He also knew that because it was a controversial decision, everyone – friend and foe alike – would be watching very carefully.

As matters turned out, the move soon seemed like a stroke of genius. At a special meeting of the Co-op's membership in June, Bileski was able to report that after only three weeks on the job, the former Home Dairy employees were pulling their own weight and paying for themselves. Hiring Greenberg seemed particularly astute: he immediately donated a week's salary to the Co-op as a sign of his commitment to helping strengthen the organization and he had already used his contacts and expertise to increase both cream receipts and butter production. Indeed, between a recruiting campaign that Bileski had just launched and the arrival of the Home Dairy drivers, Bileski was able to announce to this meeting that the Co-op's customer base had grown by over one thousand in a matter of a few weeks and was still rising.

A BOLD APPROACH

It was this willingness to take chances that would be one of the Co-op's hallmarks for the next few years. Advertising and recruitment campaigns became regular features of life at the Co-op, making it a much better-known institution throughout the city. The Co-op was even willing to try and reach out to a broader audience in 1938 by changing its name from the now familiar Workers and Farmers Co-operative Association to the broader and more inclusive, "People's Co-operative." This may not seem like all that bold a move, but considering the years of effort that went into building the Co-op's reputation, a name change could have been risky. Once again, though, this was a calculated risk that worked well.

The 1938 name change from "Workers and Farmers" to "People's" Co-operative was part of a move to broaden the Co-op's appeal to customers and supporters.

Bileski pushed the Co-op further into the limelight, addressing some controversial questions about the creamery industry during the late 1930s and 40s. On several different occasions Bileski called for the creation of a municipally run milk plant in order to protect consumer interests. He also raised the ire of milk producers when he publicly pointed out how inefficiently many of them ran their farms. At the same time Bileski also raised the hackles of those running the large creameries, by criticizing them both for inefficiency and for not supporting full unionization of workers within the dairy industry. He also criticized the Milk Control Board of Manitoba itself when, after the Inquiry of 1937–38 ended, it raised consumer prices. Bileski argued that this sacrificed the interests of working people so that the for-profit dairies could pay dividends to shareholders.

This angered the profit-oriented creameries, more than a few of the milk producers and several members of the Milk Control Board-groups, with which the Co-op had always tried to get along. Bileski, however, was consciously expanding the Co-op's role as a champion for the interests of the urban working-class consumer. Immediately after the Second World War, Bileski and others at the Co-op would push the People's Co-op to the forefront of the fight to retain government subsidies on milk so that consumer prices could remain low. Only through subsidies, they argued, could the dual goals of livable prices for milk producers and low prices to consumers for "milk, the perfect food" be guaranteed. This position would be held consistently for the remainder of the Co-op's life.

There was certainly no other dairy in Winnipeg which fought so hard to protect and educate the consumer. Circulars, fliers, bulletins and other informational packages were distributed as a matter of course by the People's Co-op. Bileski and the Board

thought nothing of printing twenty to thirty thousand copies of his sixteen-page briefs to the Milk Control Board or printing even lengthier presentations to other inquiries so that working-class consumers could get the Co-op view on the "milk question" along with their morning's milk.

The Co-op was also exposing itself to more scrutiny from both its competitors and its political opponents. But this was a risk that was well worth the taking, for consumers rewarded the Co-op with increased patronage for its tough stand on their behalf. Although this was never its intention, the Co-op's well-considered stand on consumer issues became an incredibly effective form of advertising. In modern marketing language, the Co-op had established a unique brand identity.

However, while much of the Co-op's success came from hard work, it also benefited from some developments over which it had little control. The decisions of the Municipal and Public

CITY MAY OPPOSE PROPOSED BOOST IN PRICE OF MILK

Application Made to Utility Board Not ...

Price Boost Confuses

Confusion and uncertainty reigned among 1,000 storekeepers licensed to sell milk in Greater Winnipeg, Saturday, regarding order of the Milk Control board effective Oct. 1, increasing price of milk from nine to ... cents. Most of them, lacking ... cial confirmation of the ... were uncertain as to wheth ... is yet enforceable.

The degree to which the ... keepers may oppose the ... probably will be settled to ... extent at meetings of the R ... White group and United ... called through the Retail ... ants' association for Monda ... G. R. Cormack, secretary

Grocers To Battle Milk Cost

Housewives and anyone else feeling the pocketbook-pinching effects of the milk control board's order raising the price of milk in stores by one cent a quart will be able to register their protests within a few days.

It will be possible to go into a store, buy a quart of milk and then express the indignation that extra cent stirs up by signing a petition of protest.

Petitions will be on the counters of hundreds of stores throughout Greater Winnipeg as soon as forms can be obtained. The decision to place the petitions at the disposal of customers was made Monday night when retail grocery store owners met to consider what action to take on the order of the board ...

The Co-op argued that working people were the big losers and for-profit dairies the winners when the Milk Control Board increased prices after public hearings.

Utility Board and the Milk Control Board are certainly a case in point.

When, in the aftermath of the milk price war, the Municipal and Public Utility Board had established a two-cent price differential between wagon and store prices, the Co-op had faced a serious decline in revenues. While its store sales increased, it made virtually no money on these and was losing home delivery sales which had generated revenue. This was why the Co-op had had to solicit a donation from its workers in 1933 just to stay in business. Owing to pressure from the big three dairies, in

the City of Winnipeg in 1938 put an end to the independent peddling of raw milk. This allowed the Co-op to pick up hundreds of new customers, particularly in the North End where peddlers from the Kildonans had always had a strong presence. The advent of milk control in Winnipeg, so shortly after the WFCA entered the industry, was very good for the Co-op.

Similarly, the City of Winnipeg's policy of allowing Relief recipients to receive their milk from home delivery wagons — although hotly contested by Piggly Wiggly, Safeway and the ARG creamery — also aided the Co-op. The city government paid the dairies slightly less than the usual price for this Relief milk, but this was a very important part of the milk business for a creamery that was located in the area of the city with the highest unemployment rate. Beyond

> The final observation that I want to make is that while we agree with public hearings in principle, I wish to state that most of the time spent at this hearing was a waste of money. By a public hearing I understand a hearing where the public would come down and be heard. What did we have here—a battery of lawyers milking the milk industry for the last two months, at an approximate cost of $1000.00 per day, if the Free Press calculation is correct. If anything, the public would like to know who is going to foot the bill. The answer is obvious—the public.
>
> Printed copies of this brief could be obtained
> on application from the
> Workers & Farmers
> Co-operative Ass'n Ltd.,
> 610 Dufferin Ave., Winnipeg.
> --Phone 57354--

Andrew Bileski concluded the Co-op's submission to the 1937–38 Milk Control Board hearings with a fiery statement, indicating the Co-op's on-going commitment to the public interest.

1933 the Board lowered the price differential to one cent per quart. This created a much better situation for the Co-op, for, while consumers might have been willing to go out of their way to buy milk at the store if they could save two cents, they were far less likely to do so if there was only a penny difference. In October of 1937, the newly created Milk Control Board briefly did away with any differential whatsoever — and what a boon this was for home delivery dairies like the Co-op. Beyond this, the much closer inspection of the industry provided by these Boards gradually did away with much of the "chiselling" (secret rebates) on store prices and forced everyone in the industry — including the Co-op — to do away with some of the worst forms of rebating and price-cutting. These Boards also did much to regularize the milk supply with the introduction of the quota system for milk shippers. Finally, pressure from the Milk Control Board and

this, there was no such thing as a bad debt on Relief milk sales: the City always paid. Even if the profits on these sales was smaller, they were usually a paying proposition.

The combination of aggressive management, hard work, quality products, attention to its constituency, employee dedication and a bit of good timing conspired to make the Co-op the most unique and successful of all the small dairies in Winnipeg, and a very successful fuel yard as well. By the end of the Depression the People's Co-op had emerged as a half-million dollar a year business operation that could boast almost fifty delivery routes, over one hundred employees, a high public profile and most impressively, several new additions to its physical plant. Beginning with the 1939 move into ice cream production, and the subsequent enlargement of the Dufferin Avenue plant, the People's Co-op had moved into a period of substantial physical growth:

in 1939 alone, it built a new state-of-the-art butter plant at Glenella, Manitoba, purchased another butter plant at Minnedosa and opened one of the North End's larger grocery stores on Selkirk Avenue – the first of several that were being planned. The future could not have looked very much better. It seemed almost inevitable that 1940 would be the beginning of the Co-op's Golden Age.

■ ■ ■

1   PCL, Box 4, "Creamery Workers' Union, Pre-1970"

2   Ibid.

3   PCL, "Minutes of the Board of Directors Meeting, May 17, 1935."

Winnipeg, c. 1939. Both the city and the Co-op had changed since the opening of the fuel yard a decade earlier.

CHAPTER SIX
THE AGE OF CRISIS

THE NEED FOR EXPANSION

By the second half of the 1930s, steadily increasing sales had pushed the capacity of the Co-op's plant to its limits and beyond. The 1939 move into ice-cream production meant building an addition to the Dufferin Avenue plant to house the specialized equipment. And even though butter production had been increasing steadily since 1934, the Co-op had never been able to keep up with demand, due to both the shortage of cream and limited production capacity. Thus, the Co-op had to buy as much as 50 percent of its butter from other plants. By late 1938 there was considerable talk among Board members that a Co-op butter plant should be established in rural Manitoba.

Such an operation would produce enough butter for the Co-op's growing market and it would ease the pressure on its overburdened Winnipeg plant. Production and storage space were already at a premium, and machinery was being constantly replaced, upgraded or repaired. More routes were always

being established, so more trucks and horse-drawn rigs were needed, and garage and stabling facilities had to be expanded. At loading time the plant was a madhouse as shippers struggled to fill all of the drivers' orders, and horses and trucks vied for position in the yard, which shrank as the plant, stable and garage facilities expanded.

To get more cream to churn into butter—which was becoming a hot commodity—the Co-op offered bonuses to its shippers. Later, the Co-op's butter supplies served as collateral for much-needed loans. Says Arthur Gunn of Gunn's Bakery, "You could feel the difference between the Co-op butter and the stuff you got elsewhere. The Co-op butter was like an old-fashioned, really hearty type of butter and it really worked out well in our recipes."

As delivery routes increased, more milk trucks like these were added to the Co-op's fleet.

Conditions were similar at the fuel yard, where business had also grown. In 1931 the entire Co-op had only twenty-three full-time workers, but by the fall of 1939 the fuel yard alone had eighteen employees — twenty-two including the part-time helpers that the commission drivers paid for out of their own pockets. Besides handling several different grades of wood, coal and coke, the fuel yard was now selling paint, animal feed, gasoline and the occasional load of lumber. With three Co-op fuel trucks and four owner-operated commission trucks, it was sometimes more than the yard workers, shipper and yard man could do to keep them filled, while also unloading the rail cars full of coal and wood as quickly as possible. Add to this the increasing demand for gasoline at the Co-op's pump, the steady traffic of the Co-op's cream trucks pulling up to take on loads of feed for its rural cream shippers and the fuel yard was as congested as the creamery yard, particularly during the fall and winter.

Small wonder that many felt the time had come for real expansion — a new butter plant in rural Manitoba, new fields of enterprise and maybe even

building a brand new creamery in the North End. Just as the 1920s had closed with calls for a bakery, a store, a creamery and year-round use of the fuel yard, the 1930s closed with even more grandiose plans hatching in the minds of the Co-op's most active members.

There was, however, one drawback. While growth made expansion necessary, expansion could not be financed out of existing revenues. For the financial year ending June 30, 1939, the People's Co-op had done a very respectable $629,850.50 worth of business in its two branches. However, after setting aside the 10 percent for depreciation mandated by law, the surplus was only $2,830.85 — most of which went back to fuel yard customers as patronage dividends, to cream shippers as cream bonuses and to the nearly two thousand shareholders as dividend payments. And this had been a good year, one of the few in the 1930s when both branches produced a surplus. As in the past, the Co-op would have to secure loans if it hoped to expand.

Still, the allure of more butter production was considerable, as the butter department was already earning a disproportionate share of the creamery's surplus. Building a new plant with borrowed money might very well be worth the risk, particularly now that the Depression was over.

EXPANSION BEGINS

Early in 1939 the Board was making preliminary plans for a rural butter plant when a delegation of farmers from Glenella, Manitoba asked the Co-op for its help in establishing a creamery. Two Board members who were also Co-op employees, Jim Larkin and Mike Kostaniuk, met with farmers to determine how broad the support for a butter plant was. What they heard convinced the Board that Glenella would be a good location. Larkin, who had some experience as a farm organizer with the

Building the butter plant at Glenella. Some of the labour was done by Co-op employees, and the work crew included one woman.

Farmers' Unity League and the ULFTA, was sent to start building a foundation for a co-operative movement.

As these plans were being developed, John Wagner, another member of the Co-op's Board of Directors and its in-house auditor, did an appraisal of the Co-op's finances. He thought the project worthwhile, but was worried about what it might

do to the Co-op's debt load. Between WBA loans, member loans of over $100,000 and a bank overdraft of almost $10,000, the debt consisted almost entirely of demand loans that could be called in on very short notice. As Wagner pointed out, even without spending the estimated $20,000 for a butter plant, the Co-op needed to restructure its debt in order to put itself on firmer financial ground.

Despite this cautionary note, though, everyone on the Board, including Wagner, thought that the time had come to expand. With more loans from the WBA and an extension of its credit line at the bank, the Co-op went ahead with the Glenella venture in the summer of 1939, ultimately investing $25,000. No sooner had the Glenella plant celebrated its opening with a picnic and concert attended by two thousand area farmers on August 13, than new plans were unveiled for even more expansion.

In his report to the September 19 Annual General Membership Meeting, Andrew Bileski urged the incoming Board to extend the Co-op into the Winnipeg grocery trade. He and the Co-op's Director of Education and Publicity (and the temporary fuel yard manager), Mitch Sago, had already started preparations for such a move. And plans were already in the works to acquire another butter-making plant, this time in Minnedosa.

The minutes of the new Board's September 21 meeting show that the previous Board had initiated talks with Mr. Anderson, the owner of the Minnedosa plant, and authorized a purchase offer. Bileski and Kostaniuk had gone to Minnedosa and negotiated a price of "$5,000 for the plant and three trucks."[1] Apparently though, this was only for the equipment, as another $1,800 had to be paid for the building. It was also deemed advisable to purchase the adjoining house and lots for $700 and another truck for $750. The building also needed repairs estimated at $1,400, making a grand total of $9,650 for this second butter plant. Buying this

THE GLENELLA CREAMERY. Many left-leaning Ukrainian farmers lived in the area and would lend support as well as ship milk and cream. **Harry Stefaniuk**, later an office and creamery manager at the Co-op, recalled:

"We came from Ukraine in 1938, and we settled on the farm near the town of Glenella. Shortly after that, Co-op was building a creamery at Glenella and I recall, after the creamery was completed, there was a big, massive picnic that was put on in Glenella. The cultural forces here in Winnipeg – the orchestra, the gymnasts, the choirs – participated. For me, it was very, very impressive. My father, being a progressive person, right from the beginning, we knew what the Co-op stands for.

For the farming community in Glenella, it was very beneficial, because prior to that they had to ship their milk to Neepawa or Gladstone. They had to take it to the station and ship it by train. But when Co-op came in, everybody was very glad that Co-op was able to provide them with such a service right in town and would serve all the district. And it provided jobs, building the creamery."

The Minnedosa creamery (above) was purchased in 1939. Over the years, it was guided by managers like John Kosmolak and John Wityshyn and became an important part of the Minnedosa community.

The interior of the Minnedosa creamery, c. 1939 (right). To serve the local community, new milk processing equipment was installed, but it had to be sold in 1941. Thereafter, the creamery made local deliveries of dairy products supplied by the Winnipeg plant and, in return, shipped top quality butter to the Winnipeg creamery. The milk processing equipment was reinstituted later in the decade, only to be removed again in the early 1960s.

to supply the local market and several other major alterations, the Minnedosa branch would cost the Co-op $27,005 over the next eight months.

The Co-op's new Board of Directors was a very active one. Within two days of being elected, it was not only heavily involved in the Minnedosa purchase, but its members were looking for suitable grocery store locations in "Point Douglas and other parts of the North End."[2] By November of 1939 the People's Co-op had fulfilled two of the earliest goals of its founders by opening up a sizable grocery store with a butcher shop on the North End's real main street, Selkirk Avenue. And this was just the start of a much larger move into the grocery trade, for as Bileski told a member of the Milk Control Board late in October of 1939, the Co-op was about to "enter upon the establishment of groceterias throughout strategic points in the city."[3] The plan was to estab-

plant, however, would soon cost the Co-op much more than anticipated. A provincial auditor's report later showed that between these initial costs, new refrigeration equipment, a milk pasteurization plant

lish a chain of stores throughout Winnipeg, much like their comrades in Timmins and at the Lakehead (Thunder Bay) had already done.

The grocery trade seemed to offer the Co-op certain advantages. Start-up costs were fairly low because so many former stores were available at reasonable rents. Sales were to be carried out on a strictly cash-and-carry basis, which might help the Co-op's cash flow. Finally, it was not uncommon for grocery store suppliers to offer certain goods on thirty-, sixty- or even ninety-day terms. After an initial outlay for rent and store fixtures, the Co-op could start generating revenues immediately.

While there were many good business reasons for entering the retail trade and the opportunity to become an even more active co-operative force in several Winnipeg neighbourhoods, there was perhaps something unwise about the haste of this move. Almost $3,000 was spent on equipment for the Selkirk Avenue store and another $3,500 to equip other stores before locations had even been rented – a large sum considering the cost of the Glenella and Minnedosa plants. More to the point, the Co-op did not have any real experience in this business, and it probably would have been smarter to learn the trade in one store before opening others. Sending Sago and bookkeeper Walter Sawiak to Timmins to study how the Worker's Co-operative of New Ontario ran their stores was a good idea, but it was no substitute for a lengthier apprenticeship in the retail trade. But Sago, who more than anyone else had pressed for this rapid expansion and was responsible for purchasing the store fixtures in advance, was impatient. He meant to open up no fewer than five stores before the start of 1940.

In the best of times, the Co-op's move into the retail grocery trade and its simultaneous expansion into two butter-making plants would have been difficult, but these were not to be the best of times. Although no one could have known it in the sum-

■ MITCH SAGO ■

When the twenty-two year old **Mitch Sago** became the Co-op's first Director of Education and Publicity in 1936 he was already a labour-movement veteran, having cut his teeth organizing miners in Flin Flon and heading up the Manitoba contingent of the On-to-Ottawa Trek in 1935. His talent as a writer, speaker and artist, coupled with his ability to think big, made him a natural for the role he played at the Co-op.

Like many other leaders of the Ukrainian left he was interned by the Canadian government during the early years of the Second World War. While interned he designed posters supporting the war effort. These so impressed the camp commander that he sent them on to Ottawa. Following his release, Sago discovered that the government had made use of his poster ideas.

Sago wrote for political publications throughout his life, starting his career with the *Mid-West Clarion* and later, the *Westerner*. Following a move to Toronto, he edited the *Ukrainian Canadian* magazine for twenty-six years. Sago loved the performing arts and was, at various times, playwright, music producer, concert promoter and songwriter. He remained a forceful and outspoken social activist, particularly in the area of citizenship rights.

PCL

mer or early fall of 1939 when these plans to invest $57,000 were being made, the Co-op's impeccable sense of timing had finally failed.

THE GATHERING STORM

———— ■ ————

The old axiom, "it never rains, but it pours" would be an enormous understatement in reference to the events of the year following September 1939. There were, of course, some ominous signs on the horizon which, in retrospect, might have tipped off the Co-op that its enthusiasm for expansion should have been reined in. The first was the precariousness of world affairs. The Peoples' Co-op, like every other part of the left, was well aware of the threat that Fascism and Nazism posed. One would have been hard-pressed to find people in Winnipeg who were more certain that Hitler would start a war in the very near future than those working at the Co-op in the summer of 1939. But, even this politically aware group would be stunned by the toll this looming war would take on the Co-op.

Closer to home, there were two other unsettling developments confronting the Co-op. Late in the summer of 1939 word began circulating in the North End that a new creamery with Ukrainian managers and workers was about to be opened in the Home Dairy's old plant, Central Dairy. As troublesome as this was, the Co-op had survived local competition before. But Andrew Bileski and others at People's Co-op were convinced that this new dairy would try to use its ties to the Ukrainian-speaking community to destroy the Co-op.

The second problem was even greater. Earlier in 1939 the Milk Control Board (MCB) had set prices for the entire year, both for milk producers and for the Winnipeg market. As was normal, there was to be a price increase for the winter months; commencing on September 1, 1939, the cost to consumers was to rise from ten to eleven cents per quart and the price paid producers from $1.80 per hundredweight to $2.10. However, Modern Dairies, without any advance warning, decided unilaterally not to increase the price to consumers. The Co-op and the other creameries complained to the MCB, which prepared to fine Modern for violating a board order. However, Modern's manager, J.W. Spiers, was not intimidated and said that with war looming in Europe this was not the right time to change prices. Before the MCB took any action, all of the creameries met Modern's price. The MCB then made a most unusual ruling: it endorsed Modern's pricing decision and left the ten-cent per quart price in effect, while enforcing the higher price that was to be paid to the milk producers.

Modern Dairies, the city's largest distributor, demonstrated its clout by defying the Milk Control Board's ruling on the price of milk and entrenching a price spread that was devastating for the Co-op. While J.W. Spiers, Modern's manager, (inset) touted the move as a patriotic gesture, the Co-op saw it as an attempt to drive it and several small dairies out of business.

For the Co-op this ruling was disastrous. Wages for its plant workers and deliverymen had been increasing slowly but steadily since 1936–37, as had other costs. This had increased the Co-op's per unit production costs considerably. It could no longer survive on a price spread of four cents per quart as it had done in 1932, but that was approximately what the Board's price order allowed. None of the other major unionized dairies could make any money at this price either, but they had deeper pockets than the Co-op and might be able to hold on longer at these money-losing prices.

Bileski was convinced that this price war was begun by Modern to drive the Co-op and other small creameries out of business. He also believed that the newly opened Central Dairy – which, like Modern, was non-unionized – and some of the other creameries were targeting the Co-op's store trade by undercutting the Co-op with offers of secret rebates.

Members of the MCB, who thought that Bileski was being paranoid and overly pessimistic, looked askance at his charges, particularly those concerning the upstart Central Dairy. But there was no denying that the new price spread caused a dramatic fall in Co-op milk sales and an even greater fall in revenues in September 1939. Milk sales were almost 11 percent lower than for September 1938. Even worse, the quota system in effect for purchasing milk from farmers forced the Co-op to buy more milk than it could use.

From September 1 to December 2, 1939, when the MCB finally relented and enforced the original eleven-cent per quart price, the creamery branch lost approximately $7,500 of revenue. This was a staggering loss for the Co-op given the way money was flowing out of the treasury. Start-up expenses for Glenella were still coming in, as the new plant ironed out its operations, hired staff and began purchasing cream, while the expenses associated with buying the Minnedosa plant were just beginning. Add to this the start-up costs and the price of equipment for the Selkirk Avenue store, as well as the equipment for other stores that never opened (a second store location was chosen at the corner of Salter and Redwood, but was never rented, while the other hoped-for stores never got beyond the planning stage) and it is easy to see how serious the cash flow problem had become.

The management dealt with the immediate crisis in the milk business as well as it could. Bileski went to the MCB on several occasions asking for permission to transfer thirteen of his milk shippers to other companies, or failing that, to be allowed to reduce the quota of milk the Co-op bought from each shipper. He also lobbied hard to have the price of milk pushed up to eleven cents as soon as possible. By December, when the MCB raised the price of milk and allowed the Co-op to transfer seven of its shippers to other companies, four North End routes had already been taken off, with plans for four more route consolidations. As well, five horses were sold, expenditures on everything from milk, to fuel and plant supplies were slashed and managers were asked to take paycuts, the most dramatic of which was Abe Greenberg's salary reduction of $20 per week.

These steps, however, would at best only slow the flow of red ink. Indeed, given that the Co-op was in the midst of contract negotiations with Local 119 of the Teamsters – which was looking for a 10 percent wage increase for all milk plant and delivery employees – it seemed likely that things would get much worse before they got better.

It was assumed that, as in the past, the Co-op would be able to turn to the membership and to the WBA for loans, and that, again, the local manager of the Bank of Commerce, would allow the Co-op's overdraft to grow. It was hoped that this would be enough to keep the expansion on track. However, appeals for new share and loan funds were not going as well as expected: Glenella and Minnedosa were providing some new shareholders, but nowhere near enough loan capital was coming into the treasury to keep expansion on track.

By November and December, the Co-op had to turn to its bank and the WBA for funds to cover both operating losses and expansion costs. By the close of November, the Co-op's bank overdraft stood at $10,500 and the bank then wanted security over and above the butter that the Co-op had in cold storage before it would extend the Co-op's credit line. Sawiak proposed, as a last resort, assigning the Co-op's accounts receivable and unattached inventory to the bank as security for a $20,000 line of credit. This would only be done if more loans could not be secured from the WBA – the Co-op's preferred lender – which already had a $30,000 stake in the Co-op, split between a $16,000 mortgage and $14,000 worth of demand loans.

In October of 1939, to help ease some of the repayment pressure (and to better secure its loans) the WBA converted these demand loans to a new mortgage. In November the Co-op took a $15,000 loan from the WBA and in February of 1940 another $5,000. The WBA converted these two loans into a second mortgage of $20,000 and loaned the Co-op another $5,000 in June of 1940. The WBA also helped the Co-op to secure further chattel and real property mortgages from the Local Mercantile Corporation in the spring of 1940, which allowed it to borrow up to $20,000 from this financial institution at 7 percent interest.

Clearly, the People's Co-op was in serious financial trouble throughout late 1939 and early 1940. Virtually nothing it "owned" was unencumbered by a mortgage or loan guarantee: indeed, a provincial auditor later argued that the People's Co-op was mortgaged well beyond the value of its assets in 1939–40.

As was so often the case, the Co-op turned to the people and to its workers for help in a crisis.

Mitch Sago planned a major membership and fundraising campaign for January and February of 1940, a campaign that started at home with a request for Co-op employees to launch the membership drive by taking part in a share-purchase arrangement. The employees would have a portion of their wages deducted and converted to People's Co-op shares for a period of six months – typically two shares per week, or a total of $4 per pay period. No one could have foreseen how the Co-op's enemies would use this plan to deepen its crisis.

THE SIMONITE INQUIRY

The Board took its share purchase proposal to the Co-op employees on January 12. After some debate, a standing vote was held and the workers approved the plan.

Some employees, however, did not take part in the plan. In the end, sixty-six of the Co-op's approximately one hundred employees participated in the share-purchase plan.

Edward Drage, the business agent for Local 119 of the Teamsters, heard of this plan when he stopped in at the Co-op to pick up union dues from the members on January 19. He became quite agitated when a couple of the workers told him that they could not afford both union dues and share purchases. After talking to some other men, including a recently laid-off driver, Drage concluded that this share-purchase scheme constituted a compulsory contribution to the employer, and as such, was a violation of the union contract.

Without any forewarning, Drage immediately took steps to have John Seter, the Co-op's representative on the Executive of Local 119, removed from that body and then to have the entire Co-op work force suspended from the union, a decision which

C.E. Simonite, businessman and alderman for Ward One, launched an inquiry allegedly to examine unfair labour practices at the Co-op, including the matter of wages. Ironically, Simonite's voting record on council was never pro-labour.

was enforced effective February 1, 1940. Both the Co-op's workers and management protested this decision. Typically, the matter would have been decided within the labour movement, and beginning on February 5, the former shop committee of the union local of Co-op employees turned to the Winnipeg Trades and Labour Council to help them arbitrate this dispute with their union. A special hearing before that body resulted in letters being written to both the local and international headquarters of the Teamsters on behalf of the Co-op workers. However, there was to be no in-house labour settlement of the matter. Firstly, Drage and other conservative members of the Teamsters Local were adamant that the suspension should stand. Secondly, the issue had come to the attention of Alderman Charles Simonite.

Simonite, no friend of organized labour, knew an issue when he saw it. He was very well aware that the People's Co-op was one of the larger suppliers of milk to Relief recipients, which by definition made it a supplier to the City of Winnipeg and, therefore, subject to its fair wages and practices regulations. If it was in trouble with its own union, then it might be possible to find the Co-op in violation of those regulations and strip it of all City business. At very least, it would give Simonite an unparalleled opportunity for some very public red-baiting. And the timing for such an anti-red campaign was perfect. Winnipeg's labour movement was embroiled in an internal struggle over the Winnipeg Trades and Labour Council's decision to condemn the government's use of the Defence of Canada Regulations to detain the editors of the Winnipeg-based *Mid-West Clarion* for running an editorial critical of the Canadian war effort. The Labour Council Executive saw this as a defence of freedom of the press and speech, but several unions left the Council in April of 1940, charging that it was too influenced by Communists. Thus, Simonite believed that he might even receive some conservative union support for his witch-hunt at the Co-op.

In April 1940 Simonite convinced City Council to create a special sub-committee to conduct a full-scale public probe into the Co-op's labour practices. Bileski saw this as a political crusade to deprive the Co-op of its Relief milk business, which in April of

The Inquiry—really an opportunity for red-baiting, with the Co-op as its main target—failed to show unfair labour practices. Even Edward Drage, the conservative union official who had set things in motion, had to grudgingly admit that the only union-ized dairy which had been willing to offer a wage increase to its employees during recent negotiations was the People's Co-op.

1940 accounted for 27 percent of its sales. That loss might have killed the Co-op. A former alderman, and a current member of the Winnipeg School Board, Bileski knew how much Simonite detested anyone or anything associated with the political left. He also knew first-hand and through Alderman Jake Penner (the Co-op's former bookkeeper and a close politi-cal ally) how often Simonite had voted against meas-ures which would have allowed the Co-op a share of City business.

The hearings, not surprisingly, were something of a three-ring circus. At an April 15 City Council meeting, Simonite threw down the gauntlet to organized labour. He expressed surprise that it was

he, who was certainly not connected to the labour movement, who had to bring the matter up in the first place. Playing on the recent fight within the Winnipeg Trades and Labour Council, Simonite argued that the Winnipeg TLC should have dealt with this question. He then said that there were

> **Eloise Popiel** attended the Simonite hearings about the Co-op's labour relations.
>
> "We used to sit up in the top row. They had a rail-ing around. I was there all the time—Nosey Rosey—I had to find out everything because I had also bought $25 worth of shares so I was protecting my interests. It was a big crowd. We gave the money in to save the Co-op. They told us that we'd get the money back when the Co-op got back on its feet, but Simonite took it that, instead of getting paid, we gave the money to the Co-op. It was a bad time for us. But we won. They questioned a lot of people that worked at the Co-op and everyone of them told that they loaned the money, they bought shares and they could cash the shares at any time. As a matter of fact, I just got money back from the shares, with interest, of course. So, that wasn't money that was given to them, it was loaned."

only two possible reasons why it had failed to do so: "Either they are too weak, or they are rotten with communism."[4] But as the "friend of the working man," Alderman Simonite was willing to step in where organized labour feared to tread.

The Winnipeg TLC was not going to take this lying down and, in a widely quoted retort, its Secretary, C.W. Foster noted, "if the worthy Alderman desires to go witch hunting, and singing his song of hate under the cloak or pretext of cham-pioning the cause of the poor working man, that is entirely his own affair, but we strongly protest his attempt to inveigle the Trades Council in such des-picable tactics." Foster then pointed out the poor labour record of the firm with which Simonite was involved and observed that the Trades Council "view with a great deal of suspicion the motive that prompted Alderman Simonite to press for an inquiry."[5]

Both the floor and the gallery of City Council's chamber were crowded when this special sub-com-mittee began meeting. The floor of the Council Chamber was a who's who of the Winnipeg left, labour, and co-operative communities. R.B. Russell of the One Big Union was there, as were R.G. Anderson and C.W. Foster of the Winnipeg TLC, along with (or rather, opposed to) Drage and Ed Houle of the Teamsters. Also present – at the request of the Provincial government – was John Ward, the Province of Manitoba's Registrar of

Open Membership

Alderman Simonite amateurishly attempted to use this enquiry for a "red baiting" campaign against the co-operative movement. He tried to use the fact that there are Communists in the co-operative movement to achieve his ends.

We have never denied the presence of Communists in the Co-op. We would be poor co-operators if we did.

One of the elementary and basic laws of the co-operative movement is Open Membership. Party affiliation, no more than religion, race or nationality can stand in the way of membership -- Communists being no exception.

Elected to Office

I occupy my present position in the co-operative movement, not because I am a Communist, but because the membership elected me. There is no objection in the co-operative movement to members because they happen to be Conservatives, Liberals, Socialists, Communists and others. I have never yet heard of a co-operative, with a Conservative as its manager, called a "Tory outfit." If there are such cases then it is out of partisan consideration and not out of considerations for the co-operative movement. The same is true in our case.

Our Co-operative is no more a "Communist outfit" than this committee, which has a Communist member on it.

Excerpts from the Co-op's submission to the Simonite Inquiry.

Co-operative Associations. Then there was the Secretary of the Manitoba Milk Producers' Co-operative Association and a representative of the Canadian Co-operative Wheat Producers. The Co-op's representatives were former Alderman Bileski, Sawiak and Sago. Finally, as part of the sub-committee itself, there was Alderman Penner and Winnipeg's socialist mayor, John Queen. And these were just the people who were admitted to the floor. The gallery was packed with representatives of the labour press, the daily press, and on more than one occasion, by dozens of quite noisy Co-op employees and shareholders. Judging by some very detailed RCMP reports on these proceedings – and on matters which were discussed in the gallery – at least one, if not more, plain-clothed police officer was helping to round out the crowd.

From the outset, it was apparent that Simonite and Drage were as committed to proving that the

Peoples' Co-op was dominated by Communists as they were in substantiating unfair labour practices. Among those Simonite called to testify were several people who had never worked at the Co-op and who had no real knowledge of its labour practices, but who were "experts" on Communism – such as the head of the Valour Road branch of the Canadian Legion. Many of the questions put to Simonite's most important witnesses – former employees of the Co-op – had little to do with the share purchase agreement, but focused on which Co-op officials were "admitted Communists," which causes Co-op workers donated money to, whether or not Communists were given preferential treatment in hiring and even whether or not someone had been approached to take out a subscription to a particular newspaper. Simonite's questions to Bileski were even more telling, for he wanted a complete list of the Co-op's Board of Directors indicating which ones were members of the Communist Party.

Mr. Allen Chunn, delegate appearing on behalf of the Co-op employees, put it this way to City Council:

"We are puzzled, to say the least, in Alderman Simonite's sudden interest in union wages and labor welfare, especially in view of his consistent opposition to labor on numerous occasions in Council.

"The fact," said Chunn, "that he has suggested an investigation into wage conditions in a union shop and has showed no concern about the really low wages in some non-union shops, exposes his whole proposal as a cheap political trick against co-operative enterprise."

An executive committee and shop stewards meeting of Local 35, U. G. W. A. declared by resolution that:

"Alderman Simonite, because of his own record as an employer, and because of his known hostility to labor, is by far the least qualified on Council to request any investigation into unfair wage conditions in industry, nor has he a place on such an investigating committee."

C. W. Foster, Secretary of the Winnipeg and District Trades and Labor Council, in a letter of protest to City Council, wrote:

"Therefore, under these circumstances, we view with a great deal of suspicion the motive that prompted Alderman Simonite to press for an enquiry regarding any firm on account of violations of trade union principles and fair wage rates."

As the hearings dragged on through late April, May and June, it became clear that the share-purchases had not been compulsory – if for no other reason than that thirty-four Co-op employees had not taken part in the plan and were still employed there. However, it was also clear that Bileski and some of the Co-op's other senior staff had been very forceful in pushing for acceptance of the share-purchase agreement and that peer pressure had induced some employees to take part when they probably could not afford to do so. At the very least, the vote on this matter should have been determined by secret ballot, rather than by a standing vote. And a few other matters were brought up pertinent to labour relations at the Co-op, such as having drivers do "beach runs" to Lake Winnipeg resorts on their own time, and having drivers pay to have their trucks washed. These were minor points, but the union was right to bring them up as infringements of the spirit, if not the letter, of the collective agreement. It was also of some note that once the union brought these practices to the Co-op's attention, they were stopped.

If one tried to be fair in judging the matters which were supposedly at the heart of the charges against the Co-op, it would have to be conceded that the People's Co-operative did not function as the typical union shop. But the reason for this was made obvious in the testimony of Co-op employees: as member-employees of the Co-op, the majority of them believed that support for their co-operative was the same thing as support for themselves. At worst, the Co-op and the majority of its workforce was guilty of being too zealous in trying to stay in operation – staying in business was, after all, the reason behind the share-purchase agreement. But this was far from evidence of unfair labour practices. Even Drage, under cross-examination, grudgingly admitted that in the last round of negotiations for a new contract, the only unionized dairy in Winnipeg that had proposed a wage increase was the People's Co-op – hardly the behaviour of an unfair employer. From a trade-union perspective Drage's actions were indefensible. He was not defending the interests of the Co-op workers, since he actually expelled the local from the union, leaving them without representation.

Unfortunately, those orchestrating this inquiry had little interest in getting at the truth about the Co-op's labour practices. Simonite was out to get the Co-op, more for the politics of its leaders and workers than for its labour practices. Another conservative member of the sub-committee stopped attending the hearings when the Co-op witnesses were being called. Many times it seemed as if only the Co-op's

representatives and Penner took the proceedings seriously. And as it turned out, the real decision on the Co-op's fate was being made elsewhere.

THE ROUND UP

Beginning in January 1940, when the Defence of Canada Regulations were amended to allow the government to arrest and detain individuals without laying charges or holding trials, a concerted effort was made to use these Regulations to go after the far left in Canada. The March arrest of *Mid-West Clarion* staff for its February 17 editorial criticizing the Canadian war effort, was the next step in this process. The most telling blow came on May 15, 1940, just as the Co-op inquiry was reaching its mid-point, when a judge of the Ontario Supreme Court ruled that the Communist Party of Canada was an illegal organization. On May 16, Manitoba Attorney-General W.J. Major told the press that he not only approved of the Ontario decision, but that his "department started action some months ago to have the Communist Party outlawed in Manitoba."[6] On the same day Major made his comments, a front page story in the Winnipeg Free Press raised the question of the fate of the five "known and admitted Communists" who had been elected to public office in Manitoba, a group which, it was pointed out, included both Penner and Bileski.[7]

The answer was not long in coming. On June 4, 1940, the federal government submitted a list of banned organizations, which included not only a few pro-fascist groups, but also the Communist Party and a series of publications and organizations which the government deemed controlled by it, such as the ULFTA. This was a severe blow for everyone involved with the Ukrainian left, as the Labour Temples and other properties and records of banned organizations were now subject to government seizure. An equally ominous event took place on June 12: Alderman Penner, the Co-op's greatest City Hall advocate was arrested and detained under the Defence of Canada Regulations.

A round up of high-profile Communists had begun. The provincial leader of the party (and a sitting MLA), James Litterick, was being sought by the police, and it was only a question of when the police would be coming for Bileski (and heaven only knew who else, among the Co-op's senior leadership).

Bileski had enough time to present the Co-op's final submission to the sub-committee on June 28, 1940, and to have forty thousand copies of his submission printed and distributed throughout Winnipeg to build support for the Co-op – but just barely. In one massive raid early in the morning of

MILKMAN ROUNDED UP: The government round up of Co-op leaders and employees in the summer gave rise to many stories: some frightening, some comic. The most memorable is **Tony Bilecki**'s account of the RCMP escorting him on his rounds.

It was a bright summer night, July 6, 1940. Dawn was beginning to break through as I delivered milk to my last few customers. I was about to go to the restaurant for a cup of coffee and to record the morning's deliveries in my book. Around 5 a.m., as I was driving along Selkirk Avenue in the north end of Winnipeg, two police cars stopped my wagon. The cop asked me if I was Anthony Bilecki. When I answered yes, they informed me that I was under arrest and had to go with them. I told them that I wouldn't go until I finished delivering the milk and took the wagon back to the People's Co-op. I jumped on the wagon and started driving.

Seeing my determination not to abandon the milk wagon and my responsibilities, two policemen boarded the wagon and travelled with me to the co-op on Dufferin Avenue and McGregor Street. Many people on their way to work witnessed this parade, one police car in front of my wagon, the other behind, and two burly RCMP men standing with me in the wagon while I held the reins of my horse.

As soon as we came to the co-op, I unloaded my wagon and gave all the money I had collected to the man in charge. I didn't have time to mark all the names of the customers in my book. They said they were under instructions from Ottawa to arrest me on the basis of the War Measures Act. There was suspicion I was being disloyal to Canada and thus could be dangerous to Canadian interests in wartime. At the RCMP barracks I came into a large room where I recognized several friends who used to work with me. The RCMP then began interrogating us.
(Excerpted from *Dangerous Patriots, Canada's Unknown Prisoners of War*, William and Kathleen Repka, New Star Books, Vancouver, 1982; pp. 50–1.)

COURTESY ALICE BILECKI

July 6, 1940, the RCMP and local police scooped up much of the leadership of the Ukrainian-Canadian left. Bileski was picked up, as was Mike Kostaniuk – creamery manager and now the President of the Co-op's Board of Directors. Also arrested was J. Dubno, manager of the Co-op's new grocery store and a member of the Board of Directors, M. Biniowsky, the Co-op's night man, J. Prossak, an employee in the storeroom and Tony Bilecki, one of the Co-op's deliverymen.

Although these six men were the only Co-op members caught in this raid, the toll was really much greater. Mitch Sago, for example, only avoided capture by going underground. Other Winnipeggers arrested and interned in detention camps, included at least six former members of the Co-op's Board of Directors; its first general manager, William Kolisnyk; many of the 1928 founders of the WFCA, as well as the six men already mentioned; and eventually Mitch Sago. Between 1940 and 1942 when most of these people were released, it would have been easier to find a quorum of People's Co-op directors at the Kananaskis, Petawawa, or Hull internment centres than in Winnipeg. All in all, it was a staggering loss of leadership for the People's Co-op.

The provincial government also joined forces with the RCMP and raided the offices of the WBA and the People's Co-op. All of their records were seized and examined to see if they could link these businesses to the Communist Party or to any of the other now illegal organizations. The minutes of a conference in the Attorney-General's office on June 21, more than two weeks before the raids, indicate the care with which the provincial government's part in these raids was planned. These minutes also indicate that the government was aided by some high-profile former members of the Co-op, the ULFTA and the WBA, who obviously had axes to grind. The information of Mr. Horbay (one of the real-estate agents who had been forced to pay back

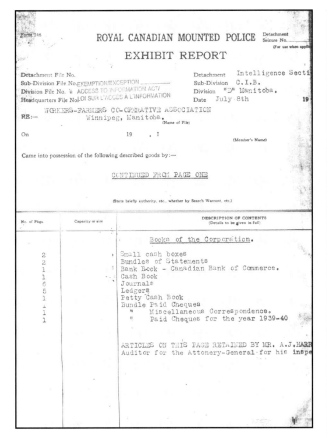

ROYAL CANADIAN MOUNTED POLICE

EXHIBIT REPORT

A document from the RCMP files on the Co-op. The Co-op's records, described here as "Books of the Corporation," were seized on July 8, 1940 by the Manitoba government – with help from the RCMP.

$3,200 to the Co-op in 1937) and of Messrs. Chomicki and Kobzey of the Lobay group was most useful to the government, as they knew exactly where the records were located.

Ironically, this raid somewhat helped the Co-op. While the seizure of its records made operations difficult, it forced the City of Winnipeg to defer final judgement on the Co-op until the province finished its investigation. Because the province was both slow and very methodical – ordering a full audit of all the Co-op's and WBA's records – the City's decision to deprive the Co-op of its Relief milk business was postponed until November of 1940 and not enforced until January 1, 1941. By then, enlistments and war-related employment had so drastically lowered the Winnipeg unemployment rate that the loss of this business was not as devastating as it would have been even a few months earlier.

This, however, was an awfully small silver lining to a very large cloud. On July 9, 1940, Walter Sawiak found himself catapulted into the position of interim general manager and President of the Board of Directors. And he was singularly hard-pressed to conduct business, first because the Co-op had no records, second because of the loss of key managers and employees (including Abe Greenberg, who had recently left the Co-op to take on the job of managing the ARG Creamery) and third because there was no one with signing authority left in Winnipeg. Sawiak was also worried about his sick and aging father, who had also been picked up in the raids.

SURVIVAL
—■—

Sawiak and the new Board, cobbled together from the junior officers of the previous Board, called an emergency membership meeting. They needed

■ WALTER SAWIAK ■

According to the March 21, 1929 Co-op minutes a "young Sawiak" was assisting part-time in the office while completing a bookkeeping course. Providing **Walter Sawiak** with a job while he learned the ins and outs of bookkeeping was a wise move on the Co-op's part. In 1940 when the Co-op's management was interned Sawiak found himself vaulted to the position of general manager.

This was a particularly difficult time in his life—his wife Helen had just returned from a tuberculosis sanatorium, they had a young son to raise, and Sawiak was trying to secure the release of his seriously ill father from the internment camps. In spite of all this, he steered the Co-op out of financial crisis to a more stable footing by the time Andrew Bileski was released in 1942.

Sawiak was an animated, handsome man, attentive to his family, often looking out for his two younger brothers. He kept active, enjoying bowling, curling and golf even beyond the diagnosis of multiple sclerosis in the 1950s. In 1957, he and his wife moved to Thunder Bay where he worked for a co-operative until the disease forced his retirement a few years later.

membership approval of the new Board and its officers, and they had to give a report on the recently concluded City of Winnipeg inquiry and to explain the events of the past few days. But this was rather complicated, because the usual meeting place, the Ukrainian Labour Temple, had been seized by the federal government and was boarded up.

Fortunately, the Hebrew Sick Benefit Hall had already been rented for July 10, when Bileski had planned to give a report on the City probe into the Co-op. At the emergency membership meeting, Sawiak gave a surprisingly upbeat report. He still thought the City would find the Co-op innocent of any unfair labour practices. He was more circumspect concerning the arrest of Bileski and the others, and the seizure of the Co-op's records, but thought that all would go well. And there was some reason for optimism, for at a meeting of Co-op employees two days earlier, the workers had unanimously voted to extend their share purchases for another six months, showing their faith in the Co-op to the tune of approximately $9,000 worth of additional shares.

But even when added to the new shares being purchased by farmers and cream shippers from the Glenella and Minnedosa regions, this was not enough to tide the Co-op over. There was concern that some depositors might pull their money out of their People's Co-op deposit accounts for fear that these funds might be seized by the government. And with the WBA currently under investigation by provincial authorities the Co-op could not turn to it for more loans.

The Co-op desperately needed more money to cover ongoing losses while Sawiak and the Board tried to figure out how to turn things around. One long-time supporter, John Korol, gave the Co-op a personal loan of $4,800 in August of 1940 in exchange for a chattel mortgage on the creamery's horses, harnesses and wagons. But even this was not enough, for the Co-op's milk department, the Minnedosa plant and the grocery store, were all losing money, while mortgages owed to the WBA were coming due.

Sawiak finally had to accept the bank's offer and pledge the Co-op's accounts receivable as security for an increased line of credit. No sooner had the Co-op taken this step towards financial stability, than word came from Vancouver that the Co-op's largest individual depositor wanted to remove her

entire $5,000. The Co-op's lawyer, who was vacationing on the coast, talked her out of making any hasty decisions, but in August, on the advice of an investment firm, she renewed her request for an immediate refund.

The Co-op simply did not have that much money, and probably could not raise it in a short time, so in a quite unusual move, the Board flew Sawiak to Vancouver to personally plead with the woman not to remove her money. It was well worth the $126.25 ticket, because he convinced her to limit her withdrawal to only $1,000.

But Sawiak must have felt rather like a firefighter, for no sooner had he returned from Vancouver than another hot spot flared, this time at the Minnedosa plant. As part of the purchase agreement, Mr. Anderson, the former owner, had been kept on as a butter maker and plant superintendent. By August of 1940, though, it was clear that the former owner was not only pro-Nazi, but was actively proselytizing everyone who came into the plant. Aside from the irony of a left-wing co-op employing a pro-Nazi, the Co-op did not need any charges brought against it for harbouring Nazis!

Anderson could not simply be fired, if only because the Co-op owed him money and it did not want to be called upon to make another sudden payment. Sawiak went to Minnedosa on August 14 to tell the former owner that he would have to "stop passing his pro-Nazi remarks" and cease giving his views on the war while at work.[8] A few days later Allan Chunn, the manager of the Minnedosa plant, called Sawiak in Winnipeg to tell him that Anderson was at it again. Sawiak now had little choice but to suspend Anderson.

Anderson immediately demanded the $1,600 he had invested in Co-op shares. What Anderson and his lawyer did not understand, however, was that, under provincial law and the Co-op's own constitution, Co-op shares, unlike on-demand loan accounts, did not have to be redeemed immediately. At a September 5 Board meeting, it was decided that all requests for share redemptions, including Anderson's, would be held in abeyance until December.

Fortunately for the Co-op, this was its last major crisis for quite some time. There were the occasional scares, such as the federal government's 1941 request for back taxes of $2,800 on Co-op profits between 1937 and 1939. The loss of Relief milk sales, commencing January 1, 1941, cost the Co-op almost $3,000. And the death of its accountant, John Wagner, in early 1941 was a serious loss for the Co-op.

Thankfully, Sawiak proved to be a very effective crisis manager. Not only did he step in and assume control at the lowest moment in the Co-op's history, but he also helped arrange long-term restructuring of the Co-op's debt and a whole series of economies which kept it in business. These were hard decisions to make, but with support from the Board and Co-op employees, Sawiak put all of his energy into keeping the Co-op viable. More routes were consolidated, paid holidays were cancelled, garage staff was cut back, extra equipment was sold, vacancies were left unfilled, fuel yard drivers were put on piece-work rates, and staff took on extra responsibilities to cover for employees who were laid off or who quit to join the armed forces or to take other jobs. Even the newly installed milk plant at Minnedosa, which had been a money-loser from the outset, was sold. Dividend payments were halted and it was decided to sell one or both of the Co-op's out-of-town plants in order to pay down the debt.

In February 1941, Dominion Poultry Sales bought the Glenella plant for $17,500. The deal called for the building, equipment and land to go to the buyer, while the Co-op kept the trucks and existing inventory. This was a fire-sale price, as the Co-op estimated it had invested approximately $27,000 in the plant. And even the new owner's agreement to sell the Co-op as much butter as it wanted for the next five years at market price, less a quarter of a cent per pound, could not disguise the fact that this deal was something of a giveaway − essential, though, if the Co-op was to climb out of its deep financial hole. Nor could it stop there. In December 1941 the Co-op sold the equipment and inventory from its Selkirk Avenue store for a slight loss. This small loss was well worth it to be out of a losing business.

The success of these measures was shown in an improved operating deficit. The financial year ending June 30, 1940 showed a deficit of $12,688 in the milk department, $1,100 for the store and $3,300 for Minnedosa. This was counter-balanced by a

$7,341 surplus in the butter department and some very small surpluses from Glenella and the fuel yard, but overall operating losses still exceeded $9,300. One year later the economy measures had reduced the net deficit to only $149.10.

Nineteen forty-one would be a turn-around year in more than just a business sense. After Germany invaded the Soviet Union in the summer of 1941, the Soviet Union and Communists everywhere suddenly became valued allies and the anti-Communist mood of 1939 and 1940 gave way to a far more tolerant attitude. Much of the animosity that had been directed towards the Co-op evaporated for the duration of the Second World War. Good times were about to return to the Co-op.

■ ■ ■

1   PCL, Box 4, Handwritten Minutes, 1939–40 "Minutes of the Board of Directors Meeting, September 21, 1939."

2   Ibid.

3   Provincial Archives of Manitoba, (hereafter PAM) GR 1528, Range 30, the JD Cameron Papers, Box 11, "Memo, J.D. Cameron to the Chairman, Re: Peoples's, November 1, 1939.

4   Cited in, City of Winnipeg Archives, City of Winnipeg File A-47, "CW Foster, Secretary of the Winnipeg and District Labour Council to the City Clerk, May 13, 1940."

5   Ibid.

6   "W.J. Major Approves New Ruling," *Winnipeg Free Press*, May 16, 1940, p. 1.

7   "Manitoba Prepares to Quell Communists," in Ibid.

8   PCL, Minute Book 2, "Minutes of the Board of Directors Meeting, August 29, 1940."

Winnipeg in the 1940s. Spared the massive devastation of the Second World War, Winnipeg reaped the benefits of the economic boom that the war brought.

CHAPTER SEVEN
THE CO-OP COMES OF AGE

THE WAR YEARS

As the Co-op settled into a more stable financial situation after 1941, it found itself a far leaner operation; indeed, almost too lean as a result of government-mandated rationing. For instance, the rationing of fuel, tires and other essential components of a delivery fleet caused some of the thirteen route reductions between 1939 and 1943. As the Co-op's business started growing again – 1943 sales surpassed its previous peak year of 1938–39 – it wanted to put more vehicles on the road. But, the Co-op, like everyone else, had to do more with less "for the duration."

Sugar and cream rationing reduced ice-cream production and forced the elimination of its ice-cream novelty line. Butter and butterfat rationing curtailed butter sales. Certain goods were taken off the market: coffee cream, with its 18 percent butterfat content, could no longer be manufactured or sold in Winnipeg; whipping-cream sales in anything

less than quarts were eliminated and then prohibited entirely; and even buttermilk could no longer be sold in pints.

The Co-op also lost many employees to the armed forces. Prior to 1941 the Co-op's enlistment rate had not been high, but in the fall and winter of 1941–42 there was a mass exodus of younger workers to recruiting stations. The letters of resignation these young men sent to the Co-op are charged with idealism and patriotism. They expressed no doubts about what they were doing: they were going off to fight the good fight against Nazism and fascism. Some, of course, worried that they would not be coming home, and they made arrangements to transfer their Co-op shares to loved ones, and in some cases, back to the Co-op itself. All of these letters virtually shone with an intensity of purpose and a desire to do the right thing for Canada, the people of occupied Europe and the world.

While the Co-op leaders wholeheartedly endorsed enlistment, these departures created severe labour shortages. For the last six months of

454 Minnigoffe St
Winnipeg, Man
Dec 20 #1940

To the management,
People Coop Ltd.

Dear Sirs:

I hereby give notice that
I intend to join the Canadian
Active Service Force on Jan 5th
and would ask you to grant me a leave
of absence, for as long as I will be
away.

Yours cooperatively

Bill Popowich

H-87765
Wm. Popowich
Corporal
85 Cdn. Bridge
Company
R.C.A.S.C.
C. A. O.

Hello Lottie and Friends:

I must seem like a stranger to you all, not writing for so long. As the saying goes it's a fight to the finish, first it was France, and it's there I saw the old fateful Vimy Ridge, then came Belgium, we were some of the first troops there and what a welcome, madness I called it, my sorrows are with all those people, for they sure have suffered, and now it is Holland, and still it is the same story - Nazi atrocities everywhere, everywhere there is sabotage also. Germany next. The days are short now, today being a lesser day I am straightening out my correspondence, and believe me I have a lot of it.

I am receiving the cigs regularly and they are welcome. It seems people never had cigs here during the Nazi occupation.

I like the bulletin that is being sent out. I should say we like it, as most of the boys read it after I am through.

Had a slight breathing spell just then one of those Jerrys came along. I made a hasty retreat to a slit trench the R.C.A.F. did the rest. Jerry no more. Well, Lottie so much for now, I hope to do better than I have done before.

Thanking you all again for the comforts received and wishing you all good luck and good health.

Wm. Popowich

Bill Popowich wrote from the Front to his Co-op co-workers via their newsletter.

Many Co-op employees enlisted in Canada's armed forces and saw action everywhere from the European theatre to Hong Kong.

Bill "Pop" Popowich (seen in uniform on page 93) was among the first wave of young men from the Co-op's ranks who enlisted in Canada's armed forces. Posted to England, Holland and Belgium during the War, he recalled the people there with fondness and developed a liking for British humour.

A native of Komarno, Manitoba, Bill had begun working in the plant at the Co-op in 1938, and resumed this work after the war. A calm and reasonable person, he was well liked by fellow employees who elected him president of the union for many years. He retired from the Co-op in 1981. After the sale of the Co-op to the employees in 1992, Bill served on its five-member Wind-up Committee until his death in 1997.

into the male bastion of milk delivery, much to the amazement of many of her customers. But female workers could not offset the effects of gasoline and tire rationing. As George Paulowich, the new sales manager observed in an issue of the Co-op News, the employees' newsletter, "We have thousands of cords of wood and tons and tons of coal, but only one man and one truck to deliver it with. Poor old Mike Kostaniuk, at the moment is the Manager, the Shipper, the Loader and if he was able to drive a truck, he would deliver it too."[1]

But there were substantial benefits as well from the wartime levels of government control and regulation. For example, the Milk Control Board (MCB) in March 1942 prohibited stores from returning unsold goods to creameries. In the past, stores had over-ordered, knowing they could return unsold product to the creamery for a full refund. The MCB also allowed only one delivery to be made to every store each day, and by only one creamery. This reduced truck use by the dairies, saving gasoline, tires and other truck parts. Strict regulation and tight controls on pricing eliminated cutthroat competition in the store trade, making it more profitable for the Co-op.

By far, the greatest advantage to the Co-op of wartime regulation came from the federal government's decision to establish milk subsidies. This was a two-part program, which granted separate subsidies to producers and consumers. For the producers, who got their subsidy in September of 1942, this was a 35 to 55 cent per hundredweight payment meant to

1943 the turnover rate was 41 percent, while 113 employees left in 1944–45 – an astonishing figure for an enterprise that had less than one hundred workers.

To ease this labour shortage, many more women were hired, particularly as plant workers. Before the war, the Co-op had employed women primarily as office workers. By 1944, a woman had finally broken

provide a living wage and to encourage more production of milk and butterfat for the war effort and home consumption. The consumer price subsidy, which was announced in December 1942, kept milk prices at ten to eleven cents per quart. This would prevent inflation and make a nutritious food source available to more people at a time when other foods were being rationed. It was estimated that by keeping milk prices low with subsidies, per capita consumption of milk in Canada increased by over 50 percent between 1942 and 1946. Like other dairies, the Co-op enjoyed increased sales thanks to the subsidies.

As an institution, the Co-op was intensely committed to an all-out war effort. When Andrew Bileski was released from the internment camp at Hull early in 1942, his first public statement, made at a special homecoming dinner, was a rousing endorsement for the upcoming plebiscite to release Prime Minister King from his no-conscription pledge. Bileski called for all-out mobilization to defeat Nazi Germany.

Nor was this empty rhetoric. The Co-op did all that it could to support the war effort. Every able-bodied employee was encouraged to enlist (in 1944 it was estimated that 46 percent of the Co-op's pre-war work force had enlisted) and a small enlistment bonus and farewell dinners became a regular feature of Co-op life. Even though it was still paying off its sizable debt load and reducing its operating deficits, the Co-op purchased tens of thousands of dollars worth of Victory Bonds between 1942 and 1946. The employees held separate bond drives, raising from $6,000 to $7,500 every year from 1942 onwards. The Co-op also sent parcels to soldiers

overseas, participated in blood drives and made financial contributions to many war-related causes. The Co-op and its leaders became the driving force behind support for the war effort in the Ukrainian-Canadian community – to the immense frustration of some of their enemies within that community. Former internee and reinstated

The Co-op employees on the home front provided moral support with parcels and news from home. Their newsletter, *Co-op News*, was one way of keeping in touch with their colleagues. Sophia Kicenko, "girl saleslady," (above) delivered milk to help ease the war-time labour shortage, and milkman Peter Kosman's column (left) kept a cheery note.

general manager of the People's Co-op, Andrew Bileski, introduced Chief Justice E.A. McPherson, the head of Manitoba's "Aid to Russia" fund, at a gala fundraiser held in 1943, and it was Bileski who handed the fund a cheque for $1,200 from the People's Co-op and its employees. The list of performers, contributors and organizers of this and similar events included many Co-op employees, shareholders, Directors and customers.

These activities were carried out because of a deep-seated belief that fascism and Nazism had to be defeated at all costs. At the same time, they greatly enhanced the reputation of the People's Co-op. Simonite's witch-hunt and the nationwide attack on radicals during 1940 was now largely forgotten. The Co-op was seen as a bastion of patriotism and activism, as well as a very good creamery.

THE CO-OP LOOKS TO THE FUTURE

The war years, at least from 1941 onwards, were good ones for the Co-op. Following Walter Sawiak's lead, the Co-op's financial situation improved considerably. Its mounting income in the 1940s was wisely used to give the institution a more solid financial footing. Despite shortages in staff and resources, the Co-op had continued to build its customer and shareholder base. In fact, while virtually every dairy in Winnipeg sold more milk during the war, the Co-op's volume of sales grew faster than any other dairy. Sales for Winnipeg's ten dairy plants were 23.79 percent higher for February 1943 than for February 1942, while the Co-op's gain was 37.52 percent. By 1945–46 the Co-op was selling approximately twice as much milk as it had in 1939 and it had almost ten thousand home-delivery customers as well as innumerable casual customers who bought Co-op products at an ever-increasing number of stores and restaurants. This was an impressive record for a dairy that had started out with only seven hundred customers fourteen years earlier.

The return of many former employees to Winnipeg to take up their old jobs, would further help the Co-op by reducing employee turnover. Demobilization would mean more consumers, all of

"V" for Victory: The cover of the *Co-op News*, June, 1944. The Co-op threw itself fully into the war effort, a reflection of the deeply held belief of its members, supporters and employees that fascism had to be stopped.

whom the Co-op hoped to serve. (And this didn't even take into account the coming baby boom, which would benefit every dairy.) The end of rationing meant that more trucks and better equipment could be purchased with the Co-op's growing depreciation fund, and all of the old products could be made and sold once again. There was even a new feeling that seemed to have enveloped Canada during the war, pushing the Canadian consciousness leftwards.

In this last regard there was little question that Canadians had come to see the world a bit differently during the war years. Government planning and involvement in the economy had been shown to work. In contrast to the chaos of the Depression years, when neither the Bennett nor King administrations had taken strong steps to direct the economy or improve living conditions, the government had successfully directed a multi-billion dollar war effort, run the economy, protected people from excessive profiteering and helped to provide virtually full-employment at decent wages. Few expected that this could be maintained completely once the war was over, but the growing popularity of the Co-operative Commonwealth Federation (CCF), the Labour Progressive Party (LPP), the labour movement and other progressive or left-wing groups was a reflection of the national mood. These were, after all, precisely the groups that advocated on-going government planning and involvement in the economy and which were most supportive of co-operative enterprise. If one added to this the left turn of the Liberal Party itself during the war years (cynics maintained that Prime Minister King was moving left in his labour and social policies solely to prevent an elec-

Then Oomah's father and mother came,
While Oomah hung his head in shame.
But they kissed his nose and hugged him tight
And dried his tears and soothed his fright.
Then Oomah's father sternly said,
"You really should be spanked, instead.
But never forget the lesson you've learned.
ALONE you were lost . . . and nearly burned . . .
But if you'd listened to our advice
You wouldn't be here. Next time think twice.
For TOGETHER we've trailed you all the day.
TOGETHER we drove the wolves away.
TOGETHER we'll take you home again,
In spite of the snow and the wind, and then . . .
Remember, Oomah, through thick and thin,
By pulling TOGETHER . . . we'll always win."

And safe at last . . . and comforted . . .
Oomah nodded his sleepy head.

And that was the tale the Trapper told,
To Jonathan . . . who was six years old.
And when he'd finished, he sat a while,
And then he said with a little smile . . .

"The folks who get along the best
Are the ones who Romp and Roar with the rest.
Dog or man . . . we're all the same . . .
It takes a TEAM to play the game."

OOMAH

by
Ray Darby
and
John Phillips

COMPLIMENTS OF
Co-op

CONTEMPORARY PUBLICATIONS

twenty-five cents

PCL

As part of its community outreach, the Co-op sponsored a children's radio program and provided storybooks like *Oomah*, a tale of co-operation.

toral loss to the CCF), it was clear that the People's Co-op would enjoy a much friendlier climate of opinion than ever before.

Still, if the Co-op had reason to be confident about the future, it would never forget the lessons it had learned during the bitter days of 1939–40. Nothing would be taken for granted. Although it was clear even before the war ended that the Dufferin Avenue plant was far too small for the Co-op's needs, there would be no expansion without careful planning and fundraising. If the Co-op was going to grow – and there was no question that it planned to – it was going to do so carefully, based upon increased support from its shareholders, from existing customers, from new customers in all parts of Winnipeg, from the North End community it had always served and from the larger Canadian co-operative movement.

The Co-op also knew that it had another kind of rebuilding to undertake first: an intellectual rebuilding that would focus upon re-establishing the co-operative spirit that had inspired its employees in the early days. The high labour turnover, and the fact that many of the old employees were not coming back, meant it would take serious effort to raise the level of employee commitment.

These were not simple tasks that the Co-op had set for itself. But if it was going to be a more cautious institution than in the past, it was nevertheless enthusiastic and confident about its future in the post-war world. Enthusiasm tempered by caution was the foundation upon which several decades of very successful operation would be based.

THE POST-WAR ERA

The Co-op emerged from the war committed to reaching out to more Winnipeggers than ever before. As early as 1942, Andrew Bileski had reinstituted regular radio advertising, but instead of using short advertisements or sponsoring programs of Ukrainian music, the Co-op now sponsored a children's show called "Cinnamon Bear," whose appeal went far beyond the North End immigrant community. Early in 1945 the Co-op launched its quite successful "Dollars for Scholars" show, and later it participated in a series of radio broadcasts about the

YOUR CO-OP IS ON THE AIR

Friday, July 26, at 1:30 p.m. Hear BILLY KOMAR and his Accordion, also a talk on the People's Co-op, over Station CKRC, Friday, 1:30.

The Co-op promoted cultural activities in many ways including radio programs which allowed it to reach a wider audience.

role of co-operatives in Canadian society. In a sense, the Co-op's original mandate to be a cultural and educational force within the Ukrainian working-class community was expanded to include the entire city.

But the Co-op's basic constituency would never be forgotten, and the sponsorship of music programs featuring North End performers such as Billy Komar, the son of a long time Co-op driver, remained constant. As its financial situation improved, the Co-op contributed to Ukrainian cultural events, sponsoring live performances of Slavic music at Ukrainian Halls, at music festivals across

Co-op established its own People's Co-op School, a three-month program of weekly lectures for its employees. Based on presentations by guest speakers from the Manitoba Federation of Agriculture and Co-operation (MFAC) and from the Co-op's own managers, it offered a course in the history, philosophy and contemporary problems of co-operatives in Canada and abroad. The Co-op was also heavily involved in the Prairie School for Social Advance, another educational initiative intended not only to raise

BUY CO-OPERATIVELY

PEOPLE'S CO-OPERATIVE Ltd.
PHONE 57 354

Programme

MUSICAL DIRECTOR — NICOLAS HOCULAK

MASTER OF CEREMONIES — Michael Sago   PIANO ACCOMPANIST — Mary Baron Bornoff

I

1. "THEME SONG" (Tuman chwyliamy liahaye) (From the Opera "Utoplena") — Lysenko
2. "OI TAM ZA DUNAYEM" — Ukrainian Folk Song
3. DANNY BOY — Weatherly
4. "WIJUT WITRY" (Ukrainian Song) — Arranged by N. Hoculak
   (Vocal Solo, Mary Bilecki and Orchestra)
5. A MESSAGE TO OUR PEOPLE — Ald. A. Bilecki
6. MY OLD KENTUCKY HOME — Stephen Foster
   (Chorus and String Orchestra)
7. RAYMOND OVERTURE — Thomas
   (String Orchestra)
8. "SHCHEDRYK" — Ukrainian Folk Song
9. "VECHERNYTSI" (Ukr. Selection in two parts) — Nischynski
   (Chorus and String Orchestra)

INTERMISSION

II

10. "ARTISTS' DREAM" — Waltz Adagio
    (Estelle Hussey and Manuel Finkleman)
11. GYPSY DANCE — Miss Mary Skrypnyk
12. VIOLIN SOLO (Selected) — Stanley Kolt
13. HUNGARIAN DANCE — Group
    (Cecilia Kusiak, Olena Hoculak, Annie Proskurniak, Olive Harrison)
14. "THE LONG AND SHORT OF IT" — Novelty Handbalancing
    (Ruth Buhnia and Paul Kuczma)
15. "HRECHANYKY" (Ukrainian Dance) — Group of Eight

INTERMISSION

III

16. "OI ZZA HORY" — Ukrainian Army Song
17. SONG OF THE VOLGA BOATMAN — Nikitina
    (Chorus and String Orchestra)
18. GIANNINA MIA (From "Firefly") — Rudolph Friml
    (Vocal Solo, Fred Paluk and Orchestra)
19. TWO GUITARS — Harry Horlick
    (String Orchestra)
20. OH, SUSANNA — Stephen Foster
    (Chorus and String Orchestra)
21. "OI NE SHUMY LUZE" (Ukr. Song) — Arranged by N. Hoc...
    (Vocal Solo, D. Nykyforak and Orchestra)
22. "WERCHOWYNTSI" — Arranged by N. Hoc...
    (Selection of Folk Songs and Dances of Western Ukraine)
    (Chorus and String Orchestra)

O'CANADA

LOOK FOR ON ALL YOUR   THIS LABEL CREAMERY PRODUCTS

AN ENTERPRISE OF THE PEOP...

FIRST ANNUAL CO-OP CONCERT

WITH THE

Canadian Ukrainian Youth Federation Choir and String Concert Orchestra

UNDER THE DIRECTION OF

NICOLAS HOCULAK

Thursday, March 2nd, 1939
WALKER THEATRE

Promotion and support of cultural and educational activities was part of the Co-op's commitment to the community life of Winnipeg.

Canada and in many other public forums.

As always, membership and share campaigns were ongoing, although well into 1946 there were too few people to send out as full-time canvassers or to run any large-scale campaigns. This was partially remedied early in 1946 when John Marshall became the first Educational Director in six years. He soon proved his worth to the Co-op by putting it on the front page of Winnipeg's papers while leading a dramatic campaign on the milk subsidy question.

Even before the Co-op hired Marshall, though, Bileski and the Board were working to rebuild the co-operative spirit at home. In December 1945, the

employee consciousness, but to create stronger ties between the People's Co-op and the co-operative and labour movements.

Building these ties was crucial to the Co-op's plan to reach a larger constituency. Just as it was reaching out to a broader audience with its radio broadcasts, it was also striving to become an integral part of the Manitoba co-operative movement. Early in 1946 the Co-op also became active in the Greater Winnipeg Co-operative Co-ordinating Committee and began taking part in national meetings of the Canadian co-operative movement. Through these

The People's Co-op School. The Co-op held classes for its employees about co-operatives' roles in society.

agencies it became involved in the nationwide fight by co-operatives to block the private sector's proposed changes to tax laws that would have made it almost impossible for co-ops to pay patronage dividends. Bileski also had the Co-op take out memberships in in the Elmhurst Golf Club, the North End branch of the YMCA and the Elks Club. These certainly did not fit the traditional image of the People's Co-op, but as Bileski argued, they were extremely useful for business and public-relations purposes.

While it is somewhat amusing to think of what Bileski, one of Winnipeg's best-known radicals, could have talked about at Elks Club meetings or out on the links with the decidedly more conservative gentlemen who frequented these institutions, this sort of public-relations work paled in comparison to the work that he and Marshall launched early in 1946. Marshall joined the Co-op at a particularly hectic time. A major recruiting campaign – whose goal was twelve hundred new home-delivery customers – was already underway, and

Marshall was to help run it. He was also responsible for the internal educational work in connection with the Co-op school and for creating the Co-op library which the Board of Directors and the Union had just agreed to fund on a fifty-fifty basis. But his most important job

◼ JOHN MARSHALL ◼

John Marshall, the Co-op's second Educational Director, saw hard times around him while growing up in the dust bowl that was Saskatchewan in the 1930s. After completing high school he got a taste of life as a construction worker on the Alaska Highway. Encouraged to attend university at Saskatoon, he became involved in campus politics while discovering an ability to write and a love of literature.

Marshall came to Winnipeg in the mid-1940s via the Co-operative Commonwealth Federation—he wrote briefly for the party newspaper, *The Commonwealth*. Moving farther left, Mitch Sago became his mentor. "I loved that man. I learned an awful lot from Mitch, his approach to life, writing." At the same time that he was filling the position of educational director at the Co-op, Marshall also worked with Sago and another young writer, Margaret Laurence, on the staff of *The Westerner*.

Marshall was at the meeting in Anne Ross's living room where the Housewives' Association was created, and worked closely with the Association on its campaigns for milk price controls and subsidies. He also helped found the Manitoba Peace Council.

After leaving the Co-op and Winnipeg in 1951, Marshall pursued a career in library science. In retirement since 1983, he helped establish the group Library and Information Workers for Peace and has written book reviews for various publications, including *Peace* magazine.

would be to lead the Co-op's campaign against the federal government's plan to end milk subsidies.

THE POLITICS OF MILK AND SUBSIDIES

————◼————

The removal of the government's war-time controls over the Canadian economy was a very contentious issue. No one wanted a repeat of the disastrous events following the First World War, when post-war planning had been largely non-existent.

But a strong business lobby wanted to remove both controls and the higher tax rates which supported them. The Liberal Party was committed to removing controls through a process called "controlled inflation." The recent experience of the United States, which had moved to decontrol its economy quite rapidly and had paid the price in runaway inflation, led many Canadians to believe that controls should be maintained longer, a view borne out by a 1946 Gallup poll.

When word leaked out of Ottawa in April 1946 that the milk subsidy was to be removed in a two-step process, the first hints of the protest to come were heard in Toronto. A Housewives Association, led by Toronto City Councilwoman May Birchard, held public meetings in conjunction with the local Trades and Labour Council and threatened to organize a women's protest march on Ottawa.

There was good reason for consumers to be worried about the removal of these subsidies, for milk had become an increasingly important component of many families' diet. By most accounts, overall milk consumption in Canada had risen by more than 50 percent while the subsidies were in place. Consumption figures compiled by the Milk Control Board of Manitoba for Winnipeg over a somewhat longer period, show that between September 1939 and March 1946 Winnipeg's milk consumption actually doubled.

Because milk had become so important a part of the diet of Winnipeggers, any price increase would have a dramatic impact on the family food budget. Worse, consumers were facing a double raise, for milk would go up by two cents per quart when the consumer subsidy was removed in June and by at least another one-and-a-half cents in October to make up for the loss of the producers' subsidy – and perhaps by even more if the price of feed and other components of the farmers' costs rose any higher. This worst-case scenario was a distinct possibility as other farm-based subsidies were removed throughout 1946. At the very least, consumers faced a 35 percent rise in the cost of milk over five months, not a pleasant prospect for families whose wages were certainly not rising at the same pace.

BASIC SOCIAL JUSTICE

The Peoples' Co-op resolved to lead the Winnipeg fight against the removal of milk subsidies. It saw the issue as a question of basic social justice since the poorest Canadians and those with the greatest number of small children would be forced to cut back on milk consumption if prices increased. The Co-op was the only Winnipeg creamery that took part in the campaign and it also became a vociferous supporter of all controls and subsidies that benefited working-class Canadians.

In April 1946, Bileski and Marshall contacted the housewives' and consumers' organizations which were already being formed in opposition to the inflationary impact of decontrol. And, on May 7 the Co-op hosted a mass meeting of these groups at Winnipeg's Playhouse Theatre, where resolutions calling for keeping milk subsidies were endorsed and sent to Parliament. Working closely with the leadership of the Housewives Association, the Co-op issued several press releases, lobbied for support of subsidies from the Milk Producer's Co-operative Association, the Milk Control Board and the labour movement, and printed and distributed thousands of copies of several pamphlets by Marshall and Bileski on the issue of price controls. Marshall attended every meeting of the Housewives Association, such as the May 20 meeting at Hugh John Macdonald School where he gave a particularly fiery speech, condemning the government's decontrol policy. He cited a recent newspaper article that suggested removing subsidies was a trial balloon to judge the public reaction to decontrolling prices. He argued that Ottawa must be sent a strong message that Canada's housewives, the people most directly responsible for managing the family economy, would not tolerate such decontrol until wages and family income rose to a point where they could afford price increases.

For the Co-op, maintaining subsidies and price controls on necessities was about basic social justice.

At this same meeting, two hundred members of the Housewives Association reconstituted themselves as a mass delegation of the Greater Winnipeg Housewives Consumers Association. They planned to visit the Chair of the Milk Control Board and the Provincial Minister of Agriculture to solicit their support for keeping milk subsidies, and to organize

---

We Don't Want You to Have to Pay That Extra 2 Cents Either!

•

The enclosed statement tells you why you now have to pay 12½ cents for your quart of milk instead of 10½. It simply amounts to this: that the government, instead of continuing to help consumers out, has decided not to help them out, as of June 1st.

You don't agree with this decision, and we don't either

But let's take a careful look at the whole question before we get too mad about it. We can't fight this issue intelligently unless we understand it. And one way to understand it is to ask:

Why the Consumer Subsidy in the First Place?

In December, 1942, when the government started to pay the subsidy, we were in the middle of a war which made us conscious of the health needs of the nation; a war in which the cost of living was going up. The government, therefore, had two main reasons for paying this subsidy:

(1) to help keep down the cost of living; milk is a big item in most family budgets, especially when there are small children; so the government decided to subsidize this essential food;

a city-wide signature campaign against removing subsidies.

The Co-op promised to help gather signatures and Marshall sent telegrams to organizations, such as the Royal Canadian Legion, asking for their support. He and others from the Co-op helped to organize a mass rally at Old Market Square against price decontrol – the first demonstration to be held there since the war had started in 1939.

The signature campaign of June 6 collected more than twenty thousand names in half a day, despite rain, and the "Stop Inflation" tags handed out with every signature were so popular that several campaigners soon ran out of them. By the time Co-op milkmen brought in protest cards from their customers and others were collected from stores across the city, the signature total rose to more than twenty-eight thousand. Clearly, many Winnipeggers were already feeling the two-cent increase in milk prices, which had come into effect on June 1.

Support for the campaign was widespread. Press coverage was positive and Mayor Garnet Coulter signed the first oversized protest post card that was mailed off to Ottawa. Thanks to lobbying by the Greater Winnipeg Housewives Consumers Association and the Co-op, several co-operative and labour groups endorsed the campaign. Winnipeg City Council, the Home and School Association of Manitoba, the Winnipeg School Board and the Provincial legislature had all passed resolutions protesting decontrol of the economy and the removal of the milk subsidy.

Despite the protest, the government refused to reinstitute the consumer milk subsidy. The Greater Winnipeg Housewives Consumer Association, the People's Co-op, and their growing body of allies, all vowed to keep struggling to have the subsidy restored and to prevent the removal of the produc-

Signature Tag Day Will Be Held Thursday

Signature day. when members of the Winnipeg housewives consumers association will seek signatures of citizens protesting federal price policy which, they fear, will lead to eventual inflation, will be held Thursday.

Representatives of the association will be on the streets from 10 a.m. until 4 p.m. and citizens will be asked to sign on large sized post cards. It is believed that such action will provide a sharp means of expression and will arouse public opinion on runaway inflationary prices and the subsequent rising cost of living.

The Co-op spared no effort in assisting the Housewives Consumers Association campaign to "Stop Inflation." It took a leading role, informing its customers, publishing thousands of pamphlets and holding mass meetings at Market Square and the Playhouse Theatre.

ers' subsidy on October 1. In August the CCF introduced a motion in Parliament, calling for the government to reconsider its decision to remove the producer subsidy. Amazingly, the government allowed a free vote, and even more surprising, enough Liberals supported the motion that it passed with 69 percent of the vote. However, this parliamentary victory was hollow, for Prime Minister Mackenzie King ignored the vote and removed the producer's subsidy.

As a result, milk prices rose 40 percent between June and October of 1946, as the Milk Control Board (back in charge of milk prices now that the federal government had vacated the field) passed along the full value of the producers' subsidy to the consumer plus a small additional increase to make up for the rising cost of animal feed. In addition, milk producers pushed for further price increases to cover the rising cost of their supplies. Twice they threatened to stage a milk strike and their strategy was successful. By January 1948 milk cost seventeen cents per quart.

In the twenty months since the first subsidy had been removed, the city's milk prices had increased by approximately 70 percent. As the Co-op and its allies had predicted, milk consumption dropped by 5 percent when the first subsidies were removed and by 9 percent early in 1948. Surprisingly, the Co-op's sales fell by only 2.5 percent and then quickly increased so that by 1949 they had risen beyond the record levels of early 1946. Its role as a pro-consumer organization during the fight for milk subsidies obviously stood it in good stead with many Winnipeg milk consumers. The Co-op remained active in this consumers' movement even after the initial battles had been lost. At every hearing of the MCB, in numerous publications distributed throughout Winnipeg and to trade union and farm organizations across Canada, in its resolutions at MFAC conventions and in several new organizations such as the Citizens' Panel, the Citizens' Conference on Milk, the Milk Lobby of 1947 and the Winnipeg Joint Council on Price Control, the Co-op continued fighting for price controls and subsidies. It argued that if Ottawa would not reinstitute subsidies then the provincial government of Douglas Campbell should provide aid. Through all of this, the Co-op was the only dairy in Winnipeg committed to providing consumers with ten-cent per quart milk – a commitment that was obviously appreciated by many.

A NEW PLAN FOR EXPANSION

When the subsidy battle was starting, the Co-op was also in the midst of a campaign to increase its customer and shareholder base, and both efforts continued simultaneously. The Co-op had to expand its aged and overcrowded plant in order to sustain the growth rate established during the war. But it was equally determined to avoid the financial troubles the last expansion had created. All future expansion would be carefully planned and would be paid for either by increases in shareholder capital or by selling bonds, not through loans.

Increasing shareholder capital was the least expensive method of financing and therefore preferable. But the Co-op would have to increase shareholder investments by several fold because a new plant or a major expansion and overhaul could cost hundreds of thousands of dollars.

Compared to the speed of expansion in 1939, post-war expansion took place at a glacial pace. First

Signature Day Brings Protesting Winnipeggers Out By Thousand

Thousands of Winnipeg citizens, agreeing with the Winnipeg Housewives Consumers' association, signed petitions on city streets Thursday — Signature Day — protesting against the trend toward inflation, and removal of the dominion government's subsidy to milk producers.

Business was mighty brisk at the corner of Portage avenue and Main street, where Mrs. M. A. Sloan, 1239 Wellington crescent, one of the convenors; Mrs. J. Zaikig, 243 Polson avenue, and Mrs. R. Nemy, 55 Cordova street, were in charge.

The booth in front of the Hudson's Bay company, also did a rushing business. Here Mrs. Kay Shefley, Mrs. K. J. Kerkham, 208 Lenore street and Mrs. E. J. Peto, 482 Wardlaw avenue, were officiating.

In charge at the table in front of the T. Eaton company, were Mrs. J. Walker, 422 Salter street, Mrs. F. W. Gray, suite 4, 255 Sherbrook street, Mrs. R. C. McCutchan, 503 Princeton apartments and Mrs. A. Palmer, 1211 Alexander avenue.

At one booth, business was so brisk that the little tags, bearing the words Stop Inflation, which were handed to every person who placed his [...]tion, ran o[...]

ever, brought more tags on the run about a month ago, when inflation threatened and milk prices went up. The membership now has grown to 425, with Mrs. Anne Rost[...] as president.

So enthusiastic were some citizens, that they signed every book they passed.

The organization was formed as president.

Caption: Winnipeg citizens, fearing inflation, heartily endorsed the Signature day staged Thursday by the Housewives Consumers' association. Above is seen a citizen signing the petition at a booth at the corner of Portage avenue and Main street. Mrs. J. Zailig, 243 Polson avenue, and [...], 55 Cordova street, are seen as they encouraged citizens

To Get Protest Signatures At Brandon

BRANDON, Man., June 8 (Special)—Brandon Consumers Housewives' association will endeavor to obtain 1,400 protest cards signatures against increased living costs affecting the family budget it was announced, following a meeting of the organization here Thursday evening, with representatives of a number of local womens' organization and other housewives present.

The cards, when completed, are to be forwarded to the Dominion government, protesting removal of price ceilings and asking restoration of price ceilings and subsidies on consumer goods "affecting the family burget."

Mrs. D. L. Johnson, temporary chairman of the initial meeting, was confirmed in office, as was Mrs. S. Sanders as secretary. A panel discussion was held, speakers being Mrs. D. H. Slemmon, Mrs. Geo. Lyons, Mrs. G. Snider and Mrs. Johnson.

The Tag Day was a huge success, gathering close to thirty thousand signatures in Winnipeg and Brandon. Unfortunately, the pleas from Manitobans and other Canadians fell on deaf ears in Ottawa.

came the efforts to increase the customer base by twelve hundred in early 1946 so that the volume of sales would warrant a new plant. Next, consultants were brought in to survey the creamery, suggest methods of improving short-term production and offer ideas for longer-term improvements. Over $20,000 worth of new equipment, which would increase present production capacities and be useful in any new plant, was installed. Finally, key staff members visited dairy plants in the U.S. and eastern Canada to study the best buildings and technology available.

No further steps were taken until the spring of 1947, when the Co-op launched another customer and share campaign. In April the Executive began a year-long search for a building site large enough to house a new milk plant, a large garage, and a stable and blacksmith shop. When the City of Winnipeg

Petition to Premier Stuart Garson and the Government of Manitoba

10c MILK

• TO THE •

CONSUMER

We, the undersigned, respectfully petition your Government for legislative action which will result in:

(1) The re-establishment of Ten Cent Milk by means of provincial and federal subsidies;

(2) Consumer Representation on the Milk Control Board;

(3) Study of co-operative and municipal systems of milk processing and distribution, under the provisions of the Milk Control Act; and

(4) A provincial grant for free milk to school children.

FREE MILK

TO SCHOOL

CHILDREN

NAME	ADDRESS

The Co-op was the only dairy in Winnipeg to remain committed to ten-cent milk and circulated petitions to that end. The 1948 "Million Signatures Campaign" – which was about price controls in general – presented seven hundred thousand names to Prime Minister Mackenzie King, including thirty thousand from Winnipeg, of which five thousand were collected through the Co-op.

agreed to sell the Co-op seven acres at the Old Exhibition Grounds (at the corner of Sinclair and Dufferin) for $16,500 in April 1948, the building campaign was ready to go into full swing. Preparations were made to hire fundraisers, but it was still uncertain how much money was needed because no decision had been made about the extent of expansion.

Everyone agreed that building a new plant, garage and stable complex on the Co-op's new property would be ideal. But cost estimates were over $580,000 and even if "frills" such as a milk bar were removed from this plan, the investment was still over half a million dollars. Such a plan was tempting, but the management did not think it financially feasible. Bileski pointed out to the Board in May 1948, that such a massive project would have to be financed by selling bonds, and that even at the base price of $500,000, interest and principle payments would cost $70,000 a year. This was impossible, given the Co-op's volume of sales and its fairly low profit margins.

At a series of Executive and Board meetings in May 1948 several alternatives were discussed. Because the Co-op's recently purchased site was only a few blocks away from its existing plant, the managers suggested building a garage and stable complex at the new site. The stable beside the plant

could be demolished, making room for an addition to the creamery. This construction, plus the modernization of existing facilities, could be carried out for $180,000, a sum that could be raised by selling shares.

Some Board members were still drawn to the idea of a new plant. Compromise suggestions included building a new creamery on the recently acquired property for $250,000 and converting the old plant to a garage, for a total investment of perhaps $300,000. Some more cautious Board members backed an $80,000 plan that called for no new garage, a small stable at the new site, some alterations to the old plant and the purchase of some new equipment. With so many alternatives, only two matters could be agreed upon: regardless of which plan was chosen, expansion would be financed through the sale of shares; and, the general membership would have to make the final decision.

At a membership meeting on May 18, 1948, all of the alternatives were discussed, each gaining quite a bit of support. And the shareholders added several other alternatives, including a very ambitious plan to build a brand new plant while simultaneously converting the old one to house yet another unspecified co-operative enterprise. Some members' faith in the future was clearly unlimited. What is most

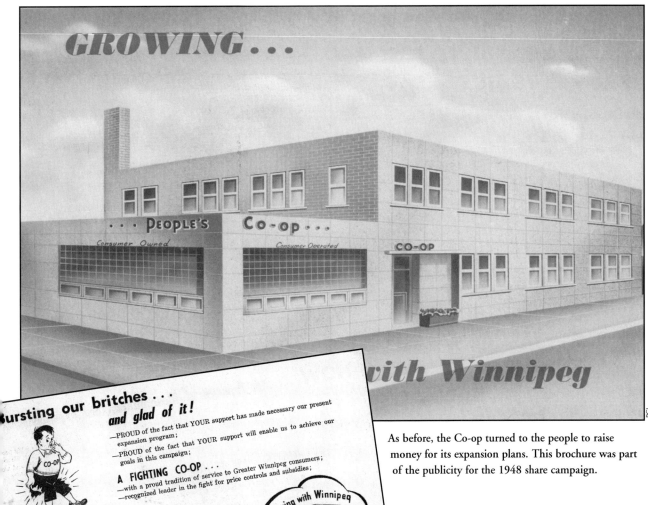

GROWING...

... PEOPLE'S Co-op...

Consumer Owned — Consumer Operated

CO-OP

...with Winnipeg

Bursting our britches...
and glad of it!

—PROUD of the fact that YOUR support has made necessary our present expansion program;

—PROUD of the fact that YOUR support will enable us to achieve our goals in this campaign;

A FIGHTING CO-OP...

—with a proud tradition of service to Greater Winnipeg consumers;

—recognized leader in the fight for price controls and subsidies;

A SOUND INVESTMENT...

—because of our record as a growing, expanding, live-wire business organization;

—because since 1928, we have paid an average share dividend of 3% per year on shareholders' investments;

—because we rest on the strongest of foundations—the people;

—because of our record in the consumer field, our leadership in the battle for higher living standards!

THE PEOPLE'S BUSINESS IS YOUR BUSINESS — BUY CO-OP SHARES!

Growing with Winnipeg
CO-OP
PEOPLE'S CO-OPERATIVE LIMITED
CONSUMER OWNED — CONSUMER OPERATED

As before, the Co-op turned to the people to raise money for its expansion plans. This brochure was part of the publicity for the 1948 share campaign.

interesting, though, is that the minutes of this meeting give no indication of a choice being made. The only clear decision was a resolution to launch a major campaign to increase membership and share sales as a way of financing expansion. Although never explicitly stated, it was clear that the nature of the expansion would depend upon how much money was raised through the sale of shares.

The Board quickly put together a highly flexible and open-ended building campaign intended to raise $100,000 through the sale of shares over three months. But this was just the start of a larger cam-

paign, as plans were made to alter the Co-op's constitution allowing its authorized share capital to rise from $100,000 to $350,000. (As the Co-op had slightly over $60,000 worth of shares outstanding in 1948, this meant that it hoped to raise a minimum of $100,000 and a maximum of almost $300,000 worth of new share capital.) A special campaign director was hired, Constantine (Kosty) Kostaniuk and special canvassers Roland Penner and Morry Zeilig. Five staff members, including John Marshall, were transferred to the special campaign staff and $10,000 was assigned for the fund-raising campaign – a king's ransom by Co-op standards.

The Board planned the campaign meticulously. Winnipeg was divided into fifteen canvassing zones, the names of all fuel yard and creamery customers were put on index cards, and a multi-pronged strategy was developed. There would be intensive canvassing of 10,000 to 15,000 households, primarily

GALA PICNIC EVENT TO MARK TWENTIETH CO-OP ANNIVERSARY

Twenty years ago the Co-op was born. This year, to commemorate that event ... was born a birthday. For weeks now your Board ... how best to celebrate this one. Then ... haven't had a birthday party for twenty ... a bang-u... ... friends. ... been pla... ... that's ... orget, a...

PICNIC EVENTS

Co-op "Hop"

"Dance to the stars beneath the stars" is the way a poet might put it. But it's not a bad description of the open-air dance being featured at the picnic. This, of course, is an evening event and will last from eight till late. One of Winnipeg's best orchestras will play the latest modern and the best in old-time music. Come young folk, come old folk, come, everybody come!

ADMISSION IS FREE!

(Continued on page 3)

PICNIC EVENTS
(CONTINUED)

The "Eat-Meet"

Do you like your shushliki well done? How many holuptsi can you eat in fifteen minutes? How much salt should a pickled herring have? How much sour cream do you like with your borsht? Do you like mustard or relish on your hotdogs? The answers to these and other similar questions will be asked and answered by lovers of food specialties at the picnic when they gather before the booths that various national organizations will be setting up.

Sport Shorts

For the muscle-bound, as well as for the ardent fan, for the kids as well as for adults, for mothers as well as fathers, there will be a packed sports program with plenty of action, and plenty of excitement. Besides such picnic favorites as races and tugs-of-war, there is going to be a baseball game between two fast teams equally matched. Sports specialties are also in the offing and you won't want to miss them. Grand prizes for all participants. Special prizes for winners!

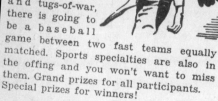

PICNIC EVENTS
(CONTINUED)

"Co-ops and Robbers"

During the course of the afternoon program there will be a short, but smart dramatic skit presented by a group of young people. Loads of laughs will be interspersed with punchy points aimed at . . . well come out and see for yourself.

Plans were made to celebrate the Co-op's 20th anniversary in grand style.

existing shareholders, customers, members of the various left-wing Ukrainian organizations and readers of the progressive press. Approximately one thousand individuals considered most likely to make larger investments were to receive more personalized attention during

the campaign. An additional 25,000–30,000 Winnipeg households would receive literature on the Co-op via mailings and advertisements in Winnipeg's co-operatively owned newspaper, the *Winnipeg Citizen*. Ads would be taken out in six of the larger "language" newspapers, as well as in *The Westerner*, *The Manitoba Commonwealth* and the *Manitoba Co-operator*. Finally, there would be news releases and a series of special publications – including a handsome four-page brochure, monthly bulletins to shareholders and a newsletter for customers – which would be delivered to approximately fifteen thousand households.

It seemed auspicious that eighty-six new shareholders purchased $3,000 worth of shares even before the campaign was launched at another special meeting of the membership on June 15. Here it was finally announced that for the present the plant would be extended rather than replaced.

Although the campaign started well, the sale of shares slowed quickly. By July 10 only five thousand shares had been sold. This was

Picnic Scenes

While the older folk danced to the music of Jack Shapira's orchestra, these young people enjoyed the novelty of an outdoor film showing at the People's Co-op 20th Anniversary Picnic on the evening of Saturday, Aug. 21. These youngsters, with their rapt, attentive faces, evidently found the films of great interest. The program included community-sing films and "Trappers of the Sea," a color film dealing with the Nova Scotia fishermen and their co-operative canneries. All films were produced by Canada's National Film Board.

The Twentieth Anniversary Picnic was like a North End Block Party, bringing thousands of people together. Festivities continued into the evening with dancing for the adults and films for the children, seen here.

quite worrisome, as orders for $44,000 worth of equipment for the addition had to be placed that month. Even worse, the Co-op's Minnedosa plant had just been inundated with flood waters when the Minnedosa dam burst, causing thousands of dollars of damage and temporarily closing the plant.

The situation worsened in August when Bileski learned that the structural steel that had been ordered for the plant addition would not be available until October or November – too late in the building season to do the Co-op much good. The basement design was changed so that reinforced concrete could be used but the building boom of the late 1940s was so intense that neither reinforcing steel nor concrete was available in time to start construction that fall.

Despite these setbacks, the huge public picnic on the Co-op's lot at the Old Exhibition Grounds – intended both as a Twentieth Anniversary celebration and the culmination of the building campaign – went on as planned. Mitch Sago was the master of ceremonies for this gala event that brought between four and six thousand people out for an afternoon and evening of picnicking, entertainment, speeches and sunshine. There was something for everyone: gifts for the children; ethnic food booths; a variety concert with singers, dancers and several orchestras; sporting events; Manny Finkleman and Walter

Kazor presented their comic boxing act; a satirical skit, "Co-ops and Robbers," had picknickers rolling in the aisles; films were shown in tents; and an open air dance, featuring Jack Shapira's big band, dominated the evening. And of course, Andrew Bileski told the assembled multitudes all about the People's Co-op, and urged everyone to buy shares in it.

It seemed to some that the whole North End had turned out to help the Co-op celebrate its birthday on that beautiful August day. No other dairy could have orchestrated such a community event, nor would they have wanted to. But the Co-op was a vital part of the community which took great pleasure in bringing the people of the North End together for such events.

Unfortunately, the picnic's success could not mask the fact that neither the financing nor the longed-for expansion was in place. Efforts were made to turn things around in September by making it a "concentration month" when five hundred shares were to be sold each day. Sales did improve, but the special canvassers could not come close to reaching the goal of $100,000. When the Annual Membership meeting was held at the end of September 1948 it was clear that some changes would have to be made in order to re-invigorate the Co-op and the building campaign.

■ ■ ■

1 PCL, *Co-op News,* Vol. IV, September, 1944, p. 2.

The "Hot" War – World War II – was followed quickly by the "Cold" War. Despite an increasingly hostile environment, many individuals and organizations voiced their concerns about peace, disarmament and other social issues. As in the past, the Co-op lent its support.

CHAPTER EIGHT
THE CO-OP AND THE COLD WAR

THE COLD WAR

A n internal memo discussing the share-selling and expansion campaign of 1948 pointed out that a possible drawback to selling Co-op shares to the general public was the "red-baiting campaign" going on at the time.[1] And this was no overstatement, for beginning in 1946 the positive view that Canadians had developed of the left and of Canada's war-time ally, the Soviet Union, underwent a massive change. The revelations of Igor Gouzenko, a cipher clerk at the Soviet Embassy in Ottawa, concerning a Soviet spy-ring in Canada and the United States were the first public shots in what would universally become known as the Cold War.

Everyone and every institution associated with the left became suspect. Although Canadian anti-communism would be a "kinder and gentler" version of the American witch-hunts – Canada never had a House of Commons sub-committee on "Un-Canadian Activities" – the Cold War hysteria of 1946 through to the 1960s took a serious toll on

Canadian civil liberties, on the careers of countless Canadians of radical political views and on the nation's labour and co-operative movements.

The People's Co-op, because of its association with the Ukrainian left and its Communist leadership, could not escape the persecution that was beginning to sweep the nation. Nor did it make any attempt to hide its beliefs and principles. This was a time when some institutions associated with the left tried to outdo even the business community and the government in their anti-Communist rhetoric in order to prove their "loyalty," and still others attempted to adopt a low profile. Rather than waiting for the storm to pass, the Co-op took the opposite approach.

Its work on the milk subsidy issue had pushed the People's Co-op to the forefront in Winnipeg just as the Cold War was beginning. The Co-op also spoke out against the suppression of civil liberties during the Royal Commission hearings and trials of the "spy-ring," against Quebec's use of the infamous Padlock laws, against the government-supported attack on the Canadian Seamen's Union, against the politically-motivated firings and layoffs of left-wingers at the CBC and National Film Board of Canada and against the internal labour war that was being waged upon radicals in many Canadian unions. Silence on these, and many other issues, was never an option for the Co-op's leaders and most active members. To them, fighting for world peace, for economic

But perhaps the most telling decision the Co-op made in the late 1940s was to replace Andrew Bileski as general manager with William (Bill) Kardash.

THE KARDASH ERA BEGINS

The Co-op could easily have turned to a lesser-known individual for leadership, but, as in so many other regards, this was not its way. When a new general manager was chosen in September of 1948, the Co-op turned to the man who, without question, was Manitoba's most prominent radical.

By 1948 Bill Kardash was well known not only to the North Enders whom he had been representing in the Provincial Legislature since 1941 but to Winnipeggers and Manitobans in general. As the only Communist in the Provincial House and as the provincial leader of the Labour Progressive Party, he was often the target of red-baiters both in the Legislature and in the press. But this wounded veteran of the Spanish Civil War was always ready to fight for what he believed in and had already become an icon of resistance for the North Enders who voted for him time after time. As it turned out, Kardash was not only an effective elected representative, but also a manager of considerable skill.

His background made him particularly well suited to his new position. Because he had grown up on a farm and worked as a farm organizer with both the ULFTA and the Farmers' Unity League in the 1930s, he was well aware of the problems and concerns of the Co-op's milk producers and cream shippers. Later, as an officer in the International Brigade in Spain, and then as a party leader during the 1940s, he had developed considerable leadership skills. His long-standing involvement with the ULFTA (recently reformed as the Association of United Ukrainian

---

October, 1949

CO-OP NEWS

Annual Meeting Reviews Record Year Endorses Gala Birthday Celebration

Another record year was reported to shareholders of the People's Co-operative in the 21st Annual Meeting, held Thursday, Sept. 29, in the Ukrainian Labor Temple. (See Special Supplement for complete text of Annual Report, delivered by W. A. Kardash, President and General Manager.)

Resolutions adopted by the meeting included one on **housing**, asking the federal government to initiate immediately a large-scale program of subsidized low-rental housing, and supporting the plan for 1,000 low-rental homes to be built by the City of Winnipeg, in co-operation with the provincial and federal governments; one on **freight rates**, calling upon the government to disallow the recent increase of 8% granted by the Board of Transport Commissioners, and to remove jurisdiction over rates from the Board, placing it in the hands of the government; one on **trade policy**, urging the Canadian government to "break away from the economic strait-jacket of dependence on the U.S. dollar and on decisions made in Washington," and to adopt an independent policy of two-way trade with Britain and all countries of Europe and Asia, based not on dollar agreements but on long-term credits and exchange of goods; and one on **civil liberties**, calling attention to the present mood of hysteria and red-baiting created by government and big business agencies, and to consequent violations of democratic rights; and urging, in conclusion, that proper democratic rights and safeguards be enacted into law in the form of a Bill of Rights guaranteeing fundamental freedoms to all Canadians.

Silence on issues of peace, economic justice, employment and civil liberties was never an option for the Co-op.

justice for working-class families, for full employment for Canadians and for civil liberties was far more important than being safe from the anti-Communist attacks, no matter how virulent. This, of course, took a remarkable amount of courage, for it is never easy to stand against state-sanctioned hysteria.

The Co-op's decision to push ahead with expansion just as the Cold War was hitting its stride was yet another manifestation of this courage. The building campaign would bring even more attention to the Co-op, for there was nothing low-key about it.

Canadians or AUUC) and the co-operative movement made him well known to everyone who worked at the Co-op. Kardash also had the uncommonly good sense to rely upon the knowledge and experience of the man he had replaced, Andrew Bileski, who remained with the Co-op as its creamery manager.

The first problem he faced was this: how to get the Co-op back on track with its building and fund-raising campaign? By the first week of October 1948 it was decided that, because of the lack of building materials, the plant extension would be deferred until the following summer. The fund-raising campaign, however, would be extended to the end of the year so that the goal of $100,000 could be met. (This was absolutely crucial, for at the same time these decisions were made, it was decided to draw up plans for a new stable and garage complex at the Old Exhibition Ground site.) Milkmen – the people who best knew the residents along their routes – were to be released from regular duties for up to two weeks to sell shares to their customers. "Co-op Nite" gatherings, with entertainment and refreshments, were to be held throughout Winnipeg, and the cost of the campaign was to be cut back, so paid advertisements were reduced while press releases were stepped up. John Marshall was specifically assigned to contact unions concerning share purchases, particularly those affiliated with the Congress of Industrial Organizations (CIO), which now represented the Co-op's workers. Finally, as another money-saving measure, the paid canvassing staff was cut back, and Bileski added the role of campaign director to his new job as creamery manager. All in all, an impressive set of decisions for Bill Kardash, a man who had been on the job for slightly over a week!

By December 1948, 1,200 new members had been recruited and 35,000 new shares sold – still 15,000 short of the original goal but twice the Co-op's pre-June share capital. This money allowed the Co-op to pay cash for the equipment it had on order, thus earning a 2 percent price discount on the order. Kardash took a series of fund-raising trips to other provinces to sell shares wherever a concentration of "progressive forces" could be found, such as Vancouver, Drumheller, the Lakehead and

■ W. A. (BILL) KARDASH ■

Bill Kardash was every bit the Marxist activist and intellectual, capable of providing astute critiques of world events or local politics on a moment's notice. Yet, he remained the farm boy who had developed his core beliefs not from books, but at the knee of his parents – hardworking Ukrainian Baptist immigrants who raised nine children on a Saskatchewan homestead. Indeed, it was his mother, not any theorist, that Kardash later credited with instilling in him the basic principles of co-operation. It is for the down-to-earth values of hard work, reliability and honesty as well as his approachability that he is best remembered by the people who associated with him at the Co-op and within the left-wing community.

Along with politics and the Co-op, Kardash's great passion was his family. His life-long partner Mary Kardash, daughter of Mike Kostaniuk, was one of the longest serving members of the Winnipeg School Board. Together these dedicated community activists raised two children and maintained close ties to their extended families.

Despite all of his other commitments Kardash always found time for the basic pleasures: a steam bath at Obee's (complete with oak brushes, kowbasa and vodka), chess games at the Hall and family time at Lake Winnipeg. For most of his thirty-four years with the Co-op, he worked six days a week and spent innumerable hours at Board meetings, contract negotiating sessions, and a host of other Co-op related activities. After retiring from the Co-op in 1983, he spent much of his time visiting shut-ins and helping seniors with their affairs and daily needs. He sang in a senior citizens choir at the Hall and campaigned for full benefits for veterans of the Mackenzie-Papineau Battalion with whom he had served in the Spanish Civil War.

Crow's Nest Pass. In March of 1949 another $100,000 share campaign was launched, this time to pay for the planned garage and stable.

Amidst this swirl of activity, regular business had to be attended to. The share-sale campaign was always linked with increasing basic patronage, and while other dairies continued to lose sales volume

The Co-op's Board of Directors, 1948. Back row, left to right: John Korol, David Weitzel, Frank Babienko, Andrew Bileski, F.C. (Chester) King, Myron Kostaniuk, Jacob Yanovsky. Front row, left to right: Zigmund Maytchak, R.W. (Reg) Slocombe, W.A. Kardash, Mischa Storgoff, and Walter Kaczor.

because of higher milk prices and the increasing sale of milk in stores, the Co-op's volume went up 4 percent in 1948–49. The fuel yard, meanwhile, posted an even more impressive gain of 17 percent, which meant that the Co-op's overall earnings were rising just when they were most needed.

But not everything was smooth sailing. As a result of the May 1948 flood, the Minnedosa plant had to be largely rebuilt and extended at a cost of $9,000 beyond the $2,362 that the Manitoba Power Commission paid as compensation for the damage done when its dam burst and flooded the town. In addition, this plant's cream receipts and butter production was falling. But worst of all, its recently reinstalled milk plant (which serviced the town of Minnedosa and the surrounding vacation spots with pasteurized milk) was now facing serious competi-

tion. In the summer of 1949 the Brandon Pure Milk Company hired a former Co-op driver and established a route in Minnedosa – a move which, in so small a market, threatened to make the Co-op's Minnedosa milk plant a money-losing proposition. John Kosmolak, the Co-op's manager at Minnedosa since 1942, was instructed to fight back. Eventually the Co-op was selling milk in the non-controlled Minnedosa market for fourteen cents per quart, at a time when it cost nineteen cents per quart in Winnipeg. The Co-op's Directors indicated they would even be willing to take the fight to the Brandon dairy's home turf and have Kosmolak establish a delivery route in Brandon.

Clearly, the People's Co-op was in a very positive frame of mind that summer and fall of 1949. Construction on the new stable had commenced in

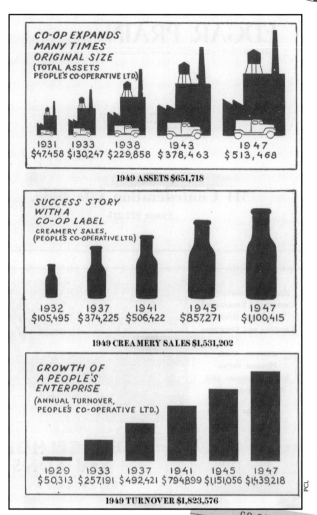

1949 ASSETS $651,718

1949 CREAMERY SALES $1,531,202

1949 TURNOVER $1,823,576

The search for more funds was continued and another share drive was begun in 1949 to support plans for the Co-op's expansion.

March and was completed before the summer was out. The garage had been started a bit later, but by September it was almost ready for use. And work on the plant addition had finally been started and was proceeding well, although not as quickly as everyone would have liked. Better still, the Co-op was setting new all-time sales records, its staff had grown to 130 (rising

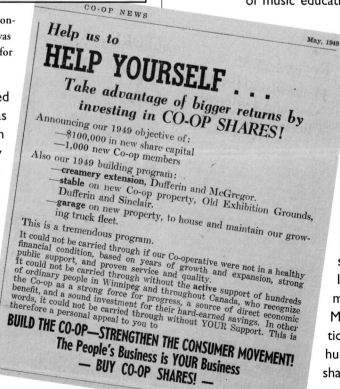

to 150 during busy seasons) in the various branches, its membership was up over three thousand, and more than twelve thousand households were being served by fifty delivery personnel. These were glory days indeed.

COMMUNITY SERVICE

As in the past, the Co-op was intent upon becoming even more a part of the community, not just a successful business. To that end, in the winter of 1949–50 the Co-op built a public skating rink next to its new stable and garage. And while the Co-op had been far too busy with construction work in the summer of 1949 to host another picnic, in December it held a huge concert and dance at the Civic Auditorium in honour of its Twenty-First Anniversary which drew over three thousand people. Plans were made to sponsor more youth activities for the summer of 1950, particularly sports teams and events. There was even talk of creating a summer camp for children, setting up a drop-in nursery centre for the community and establishing scholarships for young people, especially in the field of music education. Clearly, the Co-op believed in the cultivation of the younger generation, a theme that Bill Kardash continually stressed during his time as General Manager.

In the spring of 1950 the Co-op found itself taking part in an entirely new type of community service. The flood of 1950, which inundated much of southern Manitoba and many sections of Winnipeg, also hurt the Co-op. Sales fell sharply, seven routes had

The new stable on the Co-op's property at the old Exhibition Grounds was completed by the summer of 1949.

The new garage was also begun and completed during this same time. *The Co-op News* (Vol.1–7, October, 1949) said, "Not only are these fine new buildings our banner achievements of 1949; they also represent the biggest step ever undertaken by the People's Co-op in its 21 years of business expansion and consumer organization."

to be temporarily discontinued, many of its milk and cream shippers were cut off from the creamery for several weeks and all work on plant alterations had to be suspended. But the Co-op's creamery and fuel yard were safe from direct flooding. Since it was spared the worst of the catastrophe, the Co-op was able to offer aid to less fortunate Winnipeggers.

Co-op vehicles and personnel helped in the mass evacuation of St. Vital and Norwood, ferried hundreds of people to the Point Douglas evacuation centre and helped to save the Rover Street power station. Naturally, the Co-op donated milk, cream and other dairy products to the canteens that served the dike workers and to several of the evacuation centres. It also contributed $500 to the Manitoba Relief

Fund and provided relief for some of its customers who suffered flooding. The Co-op also took part in the public campaign to have the provincial government give flood victims full compensation.

Even as the Co-op was helping in the flood recovery effort, a new set of challenges was emerging at its creamery. Every advance in the building project, which by the summer of 1950 was almost completed, seemed to raise new problems. The entire old portion of the plant had to be redesigned and altered to accommodate new equipment, even as daily production of milk and other products went on. Employees had to contend with construction crews in their workplace, learn how to handle new equipment and reorganize their work patterns on

---

Announcing . . .

Preparations for a

Gala Co–op 21st Birthday Party

To celebrate the 21st Anniversary of the People's Co-operative!

PLANS INCLUDE:

VARIETY CONCERT: Classical, popular and folk selections. Featuring the best talent in town!

CO-OP HOP: Dancing for all, young and old, to music in many moods—sweet and hot, fast and slow, modern and traditional.

MANY OTHER SPECIAL AND NOVELTY FEATURES

Time, date and place to be announced.

There's **room for all** at the Co-op Birthday Party—Bring family, friends, and neighbours. It's the party of the year!

For more details

WATCH FOR FURTHER ANNOUNCEMENTS

PCL

Even though a repeat of the 1948 Picnic was not in the cards for the summer of 1949 due to the construction, the Co-op still intended to celebrate its achievements with the community it served. (*Co-op News*, Vol 1-7. October, 1949)

The Twenty-First Anniversary Concert and Dance at the Civic Auditorium drew 3000 people as guests of the Co-op.

an almost daily basis – all while setting new production records to match the increasing demand for Co-op products. Then, because the expanded plant was still not large enough, the entire ice-cream plant was shifted to new quarters. The old garage was converted to an ice-cream

---

■ SOPHIE BILECKI ■

Sophie Bilecki came to Winnipeg from Montreal in 1949 with her husband Roman and their young son. She worked in the plant during the 1950s; her husband worked at and managed the Co-op garage for 25 years.

"I worked in the cheese room, I packed cottage cheese. I wasn't supposed to put the pressed cheese into the cold storage because it was too heavy, but I was told to. I did a few times and I got ruptured. I didn't like it, but I had to work. Rubber boots, cold water, and then hot water to rinse the cheese, water standing on the concrete floor. That's why I suffer on my feet now. It was very hot in the cheese room.

"Next I worked in the butter room. I had to stand and wrap it in paper. Still on concrete floor, still in rubber boots all day long, but no water and better temperature.

"After the butter room, I went to the ice cream room. It was much colder than the cheese room. I pulled the ice cream from the mold. That was very heavy; I had a blister on every finger."

AUUC/WBA

making room and joined to the main plant with a new storage and refrigeration facility. This project, and the ongoing alterations and repairs in the old part of the plant, added almost a full year to the construction work, and tens of thousands of dollars to the cost. When everything was completed in 1951, well over $300,000 had been spent on construction, repairs, alterations and new equipment.

Between 1949 and 1951 many nerves were frayed by working in this never-ending construction zone. And, although

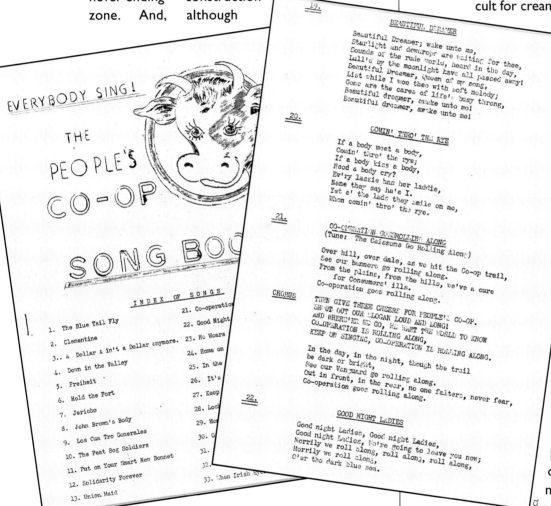

The Co-op song book, with one of the songs "adapted" lyrics.

efforts continued to increase share capital, the Co-op raised little more than half of the cost of rebuilding and remodelling. Still, all this would not have been quite so bad if 1951 had not turned out to be such a difficult year for the Co-op in other ways.

AN INDUSTRY IN TRANSITION

By 1950 it was clear that the milk trade was entering a period of transition. Like many other industries, it was caught up in the inflationary spiral of the late 1940s and early 1950s. Labour costs had risen dramatically and supply prices increased almost daily, as both milk producers and dairy workers tried to keep up with inflation. It was very difficult for creameries to keep pace with rising costs without continual increases in milk prices. Milk sales were already being subsidized by the higher prices for cream, and several dairies complained that they were losing money on each quart of milk sold. But increasing the price of milk was no solution, as each increase lowered overall sales.

Just as worrisome to home-delivery dairies was a small, but noticeable, trend between 1946 and 1950 towards buying milk at the store. Although the store/home-delivery price differential was still only one cent per quart more people had bought cars and refrigerators with the money they earned in the boom years. This made it easier for people to travel to stores and then pick-up, transport, and store their own milk and other dairy products.

As long as the price difference between home delivery and store prices was only one cent, this trend was a minor irritation for home-delivery dairies. But the Winnipeg chain stores such as Safeway, along with the new Shop-Easy and Jewel

The 1950 flood hit Manitoba and Winnipeg hard. The Co-op's manager, Bill Kardash, who was also the MLA for North Winnipeg, criticized Premier Campbell's "wait-and-see" attitude in the legislature. The Co-op called for full compensation for flood victims.

and Jewel Junior stores, were pressuring the Milk Control Board to increase this differential to two cents or to end consumer price regulation entirely.

The MCB resisted this pressure from 1946 to 1950, but early in 1951 the Agriculture Committee of the Provincial Legislature recommended that the MCB set minimum prices that had to be paid to milk producers and a maximum price at which milk could be sold to consumers. In effect, mandatory price differentials between store and home-delivery prices were to be done away with. A firm like Safeway, which had just built a new dairy to supply its thirty-four Winnipeg stores, would have a huge advantage under such a system. Because it had no home-delivery costs, industry analysts thought that Safeway

Your Co-op Helps Fight the Flood

When the final story of the flood is written, the real heroes of the crisis will be the people themselves—the plain, ordinary people who do the work. By their labor, by their capacity for organization and leadership, they saved many portions of Greater Winnipeg from the relentless flood waters.

Men, Equipment Released

As an organization of the people, the People's Co-operative is proud to have been a part of this widespread community effort. From the outset, the Co-op made available as much manpower and equipment as it could spare, consistent with the maintenance of essential services to our customers. All our drivers were asked to use their trucks to help evacuate people from threatened areas. This was done in St. Boniface-Norwood, East Kildonan, Pt. Douglas, St. Vital, and other flooded districts. Many hundreds of people were safely evacuated with the help of Co-op vehicles and personnel. Special mention should be made of the Co-op's participation in the mass evacuation of St. Vital, when Co-op trucks operated a shuttle service between the fire hall and the railroad station, at a time when every available vehicle was needed.

Products Contributed

From the fuel yard, five trucks were on loan to the Point Douglas Relief Centre in the Ukrainian Labor Temple on Euclid. Three men were released on full pay to help operate these vehicles, for periods of from one to two weeks. Contributions of Co-op milk, ice and other products were Point Douglas

The addition to the creamery and the installation of new equipment like the pasteurizers seen here, presented problems and higher than anticipated costs. Plant supervisor, **Peter Stastook** remembered:

"When we changed equipment, that was done at night. We kept on going. I was there when they still had the cream-top bottles, and then they went to a round bottle and then to a square bottle because they fit better into the milk case. Then we changed from glass to carton and then to jugs. And then after that we went to pouches. We would just have to scrap all that equipment. Pouches didn't last too long. Milk didn't keep. They said that coolers with fluorescent light shining on them would de-oxidize the milk. Then it was back to cartons."

could sell milk for as much as three cents per quart below the wagon price. An even more frightening prospect for home-delivery dairies was that Safeway might use milk as a loss-leader to get people into its stores, just as Piggly Wiggly had done in the 1930s. Although the Agriculture Committee had recommended that no one be allowed to sell milk at below cost, it was debatable that anyone could determine Safeway's actual production cost .

Despite the drawbacks of this plan, the possibility of cheaper milk in Winnipeg was so appealing that the government quickly endorsed these recommendations. The results were dramatic. Milk sales at Safeway's Lucerne Dairy in September were almost 100 percent higher than for the previous September, according to an MCB survey. Overall, Safeway milk sales rose by almost three hundred percent between 1946 and 1951, while most other dairies saw a substantial drop in their store sales, particularly in 1951.

The impact of this pricing change was potentially disastrous for the Co-op, which still did over 50

VOL. 58 — NO. 149   28 PAGES   PRICE FIVE CENTS; WITH COMICS 10c   WINNIPEG, THURSDAY, MARCH

MANITOBA TAXES TO ST

Milk Price To Rise One Cen

Distributors Ask
Further Increase

Residents of Greater Winnipeg will start paying a cent a quart more for milk within the next two weeks, and the entire increase will go to the producers.

In addition, a further three-quarters-of-a-cent increase was asked Thursday by the Association of Milk Distributors.

Margarine
Price Rises
Two Cents

A two-cent rise in the retail price of margarine in all food stores Thursday brought the cost of most standard grades to 47 cents per pound.

In some stores it reached 48 cents.

Cause of the increase, manufacturers said, was a rise in the cost of cotton seed oil in the United States imported for manufacture of margarine in Canada.

This boosted the wholesale cost two cents per pound almost two weeks ago, they said, but the effect

EASTER LILIES

McPhail Clarifies Policy
On Distribution Of Milk

Although the milk control board has been assigned the task of ensuring an adequate supply of milk for the Greater Winnipeg area, the board accepts no responsibility for where milk is sold" once it has reached the distributors, according to Roy McPhail, chairman.

The question was raised in the light of daily milk shipments to non-controlled areas outside the jurisdiction of the milk control board at the same time that powdered or re-constituted milk was being sold in the metropolitan area to supplement low supplies.

Board Fixes Prices

The milk board has the power to fix consumer prices for Greater Winnipeg (including Charleswood, Transcona and Selkirk. It also establishes the price paid to producers who supply firms distributing milk in this area.

But these same distributors, whose intake is checked by the board, also sell milk (purchased at board-set prices) to outlying areas where the board has no power to set selling prices, and where consumers pay competition prices.

"The board does not attempt to direct companies as to where their milk should be sold," Mr. McPhail stated. "Nor are we empowered under the milk control act to prevent distributors from selling where they wish. That would be regimentation.

"We see that quota milk for all fluid sales is paid for at the set tion late Thursday

price, but beyond that we don't interfere."

Mr. McPhail said he had no figures to show how much of the milk received by distributors in the Greater Winnipeg area was sold outside the board control area. He agreed that the milk sale figures listed in the board's annual report included, therefore, all milk sold.

See MILK Page 11

Suspect's Life
In Jeopardy;
Hearing Oper

Daniel Biegun, 47-year-old worker Saturday morning still ered between life and death Winnipeg General hospital, reported.

Meanwhile, preliminary quest into the fatal shooting of Mrs. Adeli shooting of Mrs. Adeli Klassen, 253 Chambers st last Tuesday was schedule open at 12.15 p.m. Saturda central police station.

Mrs. Klassen, who was employed as a chambermaid in a W room last Wednesday morn a bullet through the head. Biegun, who is suffering bullet wound which is bel self-inflicted, has been in c condition since the shooting underwent a delicate brain opera-

Milk Up
One Cent
Sunday

A one-cent increase in the price of milk goes into effect Sunday, the control board announces Saturday.

This will make the price of raw and standard milk, delivered to homes, 19 cents a quart, with Jersey milk set at 21 cents. The store price differential still remains at cent.

The increased cost will all go to the producer. He will be paid $4.25 both his hundred pounds for ondary milk (the compulsory 10 per cent and sec- 10-cent bonus quota) plus quality milk to top quality bringing it to $4.35.

Previously the producer was paid for quality milk for his quota milk and $2.90 for 10 per 10 per cent of quota, making blended price of $3.99.

Would Need More

However, if dairy employees wage demands now being negotiated are met, distributors would require an additional three-quarters a quart to cover wage costs.

The new schedule still allows the storekeeper a one-cent spread between his buying and selling prices. This also applies to other bulk prices such as to other bulk prices chasers and schools, hospitals, restaur Home-delivered prices for other forms of milk are: buttermilk, 20 cents a quart; cereal cream, 20 cents a pint; coffee cream, 34 cents a half pint; whipping cream, 20 cents drink, 20 cents a quart. chocolate-flavored dairy

Decisions by the Milk Control Board had a dramatic impact on small dairies like the Co-op.

percent of its volume in the home-delivery trade. Consumers were not going to pay a two-cent premium on home delivery, especially when the basic price of milk was once again forced upwards by the MCB's decision to raise the price paid to milk producers. Even worse, impending settlements with the unions representing dairy workers in Winnipeg would probably necessitate another increase of three-quarters of a cent per quart. Finally, pressure to lower delivery costs was forcing all the home-delivery companies to consider cutting deliveries from six to five days per week, a move that many analysts predicted would hasten the shift to store sales.

THE COLD WAR HEATS UP

Change in the milk industry was just one of the Co-op's problems in 1951. The Cold War took a toll upon the People's Co-op several times between 1946 and the early 1960s. Despite all of its hard work building ties to the larger co-operative and labour movements, the Co-op was estranged from both during this period. By the early 1950s it had

been expelled from the Manitoba Federation of Agriculture and Co-operation by those who wanted to rid that organization of any "red" taint.

Meanwhile, in 1947, the Co-op's workers, who had joined Local 271 of the CIO's Food, Tobacco and Agricultural Workers' Union found themselves cut off from their union because of the anti-Communist purges of the labour movement during the Cold War. When they tried to rejoin the CIO and the Canadian Labour Congress in 1954 they were turned down flat because of the Co-op's political connections. Then there were countless Canadian and local Chamber of Commerce publications, plus a

---

■ BETH KRALL ■

Beth Adams began working in the office in the late 1930s. Soon after, she married Ernie Krall, who was already working alongside his father, John, eventually succeeding him as plant supervisor.

Her family had a long history of involvement in the Ukrainian left. As she recalled, "the unemployed used to jump off the trains and come to our house on Selkirk Avenue."

She recalled that for left-wingers, the Co-op was a haven in a harsh world. "At the Co-op we were all friends, so you wouldn't be 'exposed' because of what you believed in." At the same time she felt the Co-op was not immune to common attitudes towards women workers. "Women working at the Co-op were always considered as just the workers. Men were hired even though sometimes we doubted their ability. Women never actually advanced."

COURTESY BETH KRALL

steady stream of newspaper and magazine articles concerning the "Red Peril" which, on more than one occassion, mentioned the People's Co-op and Bill Kardash by name.

But even in this Cold War atmosphere, 1951 stands out as a particularly difficult year for the Co-op. Anti-Communist sentiment had reached new heights with the outbreak of the Korean War in

---

THE CO-OP'S UNIONS AND THE COLD WAR

Even after being forced out of Teamsters Local 119 in 1940 the Co-op's workers had not abandoned their belief in unions. Accordingly they formed their own union in the early 1940s, calling it simply "The Creamery Workers' Union, Local 1." Although this union had no backing from any national or international office, it succeeded in negotiating contracts with the Co-op's Board of Directors which guaranteed them essentially the same wages and benefits as other workers in the industry.

Still, both the Co-op and its workers wanted to rejoin the mainstream labour movement, although not if that meant rejoining Teamsters Local 119. But when the CIO entered the field of creamery organizing with its Food, Tobacco, Agricultural and Allied Workers Union of America, the Co-op's workers joined Local 271 in 1947. And they did well with this union; indeed, the 1949 contract between the Co-op and its workers saw dramatic improvements in both pay and benefits. Unfortunately, this was also the same time when the CIO was fighting its most bitter internal battles against the Communists, former Communists, and assorted leftists who had been among the CIO's most effective organizers and leaders. Not surprisingly, the Co-op's local was a natural target for such attacks, and once again the Co-op's workers found themselves cut off from any union centre, although they continued to bargain collectively with the Co-op as Local 271 for several years.

Early in 1954, after four years on their own, another chance to rejoin the larger union movement seemed to present itself to the Co-op's workers when another union began to challenge the Teamsters for the allegiance of Winnipeg's creamery workers. The leaders of the Co-op's Local 271 applied to the Retail, Wholesale and Department Store Union (CIO-CCL), asking for affiliation with that union. However, Walter Kinset, the union's Toronto-based national organizer, refused to even contemplate this application, telling the Co-op's workers that "they had to clean their house of communists from top to bottom before they could join the CIO local."[2] There was little chance of the workers turning on the Co-op: instead they turned away from the broader trade union movement and eventually re-established the Creamery Workers Union, Local 1, which represented them until 1992.

CIO-CCL Dairy Union Woos Rival's Members

A CIO-CCL dairy workers' union has begun a drive to woo more workers away from its rival, the AFL-TLC Teamsters' union, it was learned Tuesday.

Local 755, Retail Wholesale Dairy Workers union (CIO-CCL) has sent pamphlets out to employees of Silverwood Dairies Ltd., inviting them to join the union. At present the employees' bargaining agent is the rival Local 119, International Brotherhood of Teamsters, Chauffeurs, Warehousemen and Helpers of America (AFL-TLC).

The drive at Silverwood's came following Monday's report that the Teamsters' Local 119 had been defeated by Local 755 in a vote Friday on which local would be bargaining agent for employees in three other Greater Winnipeg dairies.

2 DEVELOPMENTS

Two other developments came to the fore Tuesday:

● An official of the Retail, Wholesale and Department Store union, Local 755's parent body, reported that a request from employees at People's Co-operative Ltd., 610 Dufferin avenue, to join the CIO local had been turned down on the grounds that the co-op was "Communist-dominated."

● The resignation of Albert Cowley as president of the Teamsters' Local 119 was accepted at a meeting of the local Monday night. It was reported that Mr. Cowley had resigned three weeks ago to accept a full-time job with the Teamsters' Credit society and that therefore his resignation had no connection with the results of Friday's representation vote at the three dairies.

The local elected Ken Howard to Mr. Cowley's unexpired term. Ed Houle, business agent of Local 119, said Tuesday there was nothing else to report on the meeting. (The press is not allowed to attend.)

He said he had no comment to make on Friday's representation vote or any other matter pertaining to the switch of the men to the CIO union.

The leaflet sent out by the CIO local to Silverwood's employees compared wage rates and other benefits in various Silverwood plants across Canada, which have contracts with the CIO union, with rates and benefits in the Winnipeg plant, whose workers are represented by the AFL Teamsters' union.

Walter Kinset, of Toronto, national organizer of the Retail, Wholesale and Department Store union (CIO-CCL) said Tuesday his union is interested in representing the employees of all dairy plants except the People's Co-Operative, because "it is Communist-dominated."

He said a delegation representing the People's Co-op employees had been told "they have to clean their house of Communists from top to bottom before they could join the CIO local."

"We understand that the People's Co-op's top officers are Communists and employees too," said Mr. Kinset.

W. A. Kardash, Communist member of Manitoba legislature for North Winnipeg, is president of the People's Co-op.

PCL

The campaign against the "Red Peril" was also directed at the Co-op's employees. They were barred from membership in the Retail Wholesale Dairy Workers Union of the CIO-CCL because "the People's Co-op's top officers are Communists and employees too [sic]." (*Winnipeg Free Press*, April 13, 1954)

1950. A series of articles in *The Financial Post* sought to expose Communist involvement in various institutions and to highlight the threat Canadian Communists posed to the nation. In a front page article of February 24, 1951, Ronald Williams turned his attention to how the Labour Progressive Party (LPP) financed such "nefarious" Communist activities as the "ban the bomb" movement, the "Peace Petition" campaign, support for the diplomatic recognition of the People's Republic of China and its warnings against too much Canadian economic, political and military involvement with the U.S. (According to this series, peace, diplomacy, an independent foreign policy and Canadian economic nationalism were all subversive in the Canada of 1950–51.) Right below the banner headline, "There's Big Money in Communist

Despite the attacks against it, the Co-op retained the support of its workers, who formed their own union. Seen here, a meeting of employees and management. Third row, left to right: Nick Mateychuk, Walter Roscoe, unknown, Ed Slugoski, Joe Small, Paul Meda, Ernie Krall, unknown, A. Gerelus. Second row: unknown, Louis Pollock, Leonard Bodnar, Bill Patryluk, Clyde Adams, unknown, Myron Kostaniuk, unknown, Eddie Adams. Seated: George Paulowich, John Harrison, Andrew Bileski, Hamil Chopp, unknown. **Bob Pawlyk**, an employee at a later time, recalled: "Those were probably the first times that I ever did pay union dues. Thinking about it now, I think a union at the Co-op was almost a contradiction in terms in today's standards because the Co-op was a co-operative; they were for the people, they wanted their workers to be happy, so having a union in a co-op almost wasn't necessary."

Business Network," was a picture of the People's Co-op plant on Dufferin Avenue![3]

In and of itself the article was not that damaging. There was some inflammatory rhetoric about Kardash, but Williams had gotten his hands on a two-year old People's Co-op Annual Report, so many of his facts on the Co-op's operations were accurate, and almost flattering in a strictly business sense. There was no proof for his charge that the Co-op and other "Communist-dominated" businesses were improperly siphoning off money to support the LPP, but the accusation was nonetheless

troubling, especially when the Co-op was trying to raise money for its ongoing building program.

What was most damaging about this artfully constructed pastiche of fact, supposition and insinuation was its spin-off effect. On March 7, 1951 the *Winnipeg Free Press* picked up on Williams' article and ran an op-ed piece catchily entitled "Comrade Tycoon" which, tongue-in-cheek, suggested that the Provincial Legislature and the *Free Press* owed Kardash an apology for not recognizing him as one of "the leading tycoons of the Communist commercial empire in Canada."[4]

The Financial Post

Vol. XLV   Member of Audit Bureau of Circulations   Publication Office: Toronto, February 24, 1951   Fifteen Cents an Issue, Six Dollars a Year   No. 8

There's Big Money in Communist Business Network

Stores, Insurance, Professions, Co-ops Mean Big Profits for Campaign Chest

By RONALD WILLIAMS

People's Co-operative at Winnipeg

This is one of the buildings owned by the Peoples' Co-operative, a $2 million Winnipeg milk products and fuel-yard business controlled by Canada's Communists. It is the biggest of half a dozen co-ops from which the Reds derive revenue to maintain their $1 million political and propaganda machine. The milk distributing end of this big business has 50 routes, 10,000 customers in Greater Winnipeg and employs 150 persons. Turnover in 1949 was $1.8 million. Total annual business done by Communist-run co-ops is over $4 millions.

From Businesses Like This—

(above) This front-page article in the *Financial Post*, February 14, 1951, was typical of the Cold War posturing of the 1950s. It targeted several left-wing organizations including the Co-op. While it did accurately quote figures from the Co-op's own Annual Report of 1949 the rest of the article was almost purely speculative.

(right) **Joe Zuken**, prominent labour lawyer, and long-time Winnipeg school trustee and alderman, acted as the Co-op's legal council for over thirty years.

The Co-op took these insinuations seriously enough to have their lawyer, Joe Zuken, look into filing a libel and defamation suit against Williams and the *Post*. Zuken in turn consulted with one of Winnipeg's larger law firms. The consensus was that while there were grounds for a suit, the cost and publicity would do the Co-op more harm than good. Reluctantly, the Co-op decided not to take legal action.

It is difficult to say what role these articles played in the Co-op's drop in business in 1951. The *Ukrainian Toiler*, a Ukrainian-language paper associated with some long-time rivals of the Co-op, certainly tried to whip up more anti-Co-op sentiment

by publishing an ersatz version of Williams' piece. And the right-wing national publication, *The Ensign*, tried to revive the matter in July and August by asking Manitoba's director of co-operative services if the law governing the connections between co-operatives and political parties should be changed in

one-horse little town.

COMRADE TYCOON

Mr. William Kardash, Communist M.L.A. for North Winnipeg, occasionally receives less than his deserts at the hands of the Manitoba Legislature. There is a disposition to dismiss him as a mere party tub-thumper, rather than to recognize him for what he is as the representative of big business. It will perhaps be gratifying to Mr. Kardash to learn that his role as one of the leading tycoons of the Communist commercial empire in Canada has at last received prominent mention in The Financial Post.

Some time ago, in an article dealing with the great Communist free enterprise, profit-taking system in the United States, the Free Press expressed some doubt that the Canadian Communists possessed adequate talent for exploiting the workers of this country in similar fashion. It seems that this was unjust. The Post's article, by Mr. Ronald Williams indicates that the Canadian organization, extending to all sorts of businesses and professions with particular-emphasis on co-operatives and insurance, is pretty much a carbon copy of that in the United States. It may perhaps be a bit reticent, like the big combines, about disclosing profits but they seem ample to finance a national headquarters, eight provincial offices, some 200 organizers and assorted help, apart from subsidizing various papers, paying the expenses of delegates to demonstrations and congresses, sending the chosen to Europe, covering the costs of propaganda and paying for expensive election campaigns.

Mr. Kardash rates publicity in the Toronto journal of Finance for his job in running the People's Co-operative in Winnipeg. When not talking to himself in the Legislature, he bosses a modern, two-plant dairy and fuel yard, controls the destinies of 50 milk routes, employs 150 workers, caters to 10,000 customers. The 1949 turnover is given by the Post as $1,800,000. It is explained that Mr. Kardash gave up the party leadership to join the ranks of the business elect, which doubtless qualifies him, if Mr. Buck ever forms a Ministry for a seat in the Senate where the prevailing color scheme is already red.

The *Free Press* followed the *Financial Post*'s lead with its own attack. The Co-op's radical reputation was well deserved. But in the post-war years, when many of its workers were non-political, it stressed toleration as well as class struggle.

John Wityshyn, the last manager in Minnedosa, recalled one Co-op Christmas Party where **Bill Kardash** told the crowd "'We don't care if you're black, you're white or whatever, as long as you do your job, it's fine with us', and I really appreciated that. We knew that they belonged to this organization and we didn't, we were just the opposite because we were Catholics. But they would come and ask us about the church, they'd ask us how we carried on. So they didn't interfere with your religion or with anything. As long as you did your job, they seemed to be happy. So we had to be proud of it."

al years and had built up considerable support among area cream and milk shippers. However, the Minnedosa plant had never become as integral to its community as had the Winnipeg branches of the Co-op. And while it was an assured source of butter, the tens of thousands of dollars that had been poured into this almost fifty-year-old plant really had not paid off. The costly impact of the Minnedosa flood of 1948 and the new competition for milk sales from the Brandon Pure Milk Company only made matters worse.

These factors, plus Kosmolak's resignation, probably explain why in December of 1950 the Co-op entertained an offer to purchase the plant. This potential solution eventually led to a new round of problems. When the Manitoba Dairy and Poultry Co-operative offered $50,000, Kardash and Bileski concluded that the Co-op had invested $85,000 in the plant. Adding another $15,000 for the goodwill and patronage that the new purchasers would acquire with the plant, they asked for $100,000.

Both Manitoba Dairy and Poultry and the owner of the local newspaper, *The Minnedosa Tribune*, were

light of the People's Co-op case. However, given the recent change in price structure and the move to five-day delivery – which were hurting all home-delivery firms in 1951 – it is almost impossible to judge whether or not all this fuss was playing a role in lowering Co-op sales. But it certainly indicates the type of opposition with which the Co-op had to contend during this period.

RED-BAITING IN MINNEDOSA

In Minnedosa, an operation which had always been somewhat troublesome for the Co-op, there was no question that the adverse publicity took a toll. Under local Manager John Kosmolak, the Minnedosa operation had showed a small operating surplus for sever-

outraged by the Co-op's bargaining position. In comments published in the *Tribune*, authorities from the provincial and local branches of the Manitoba Dairy and Poultry Co-op were bitter. They questioned whether the plant was worth even $50,000, denied that the People's Co-op had any goodwill in the community and even called into question its status as a real co-operative. By January 1951 there was considerable talk of establishing a new milk plant to compete with the Co-op in Minnedosa. The *Tribune* reported that some townspeople were advocated boycotting the Co-op to force it into "a reasonable bargaining position."

It was in this increasingly hostile atmosphere that the red-baiting campaign of 1951 would be played out. As no immediate replacement was found for Kosmolak, Andrew Bileski and the Co-op's accountant, John Fedirchyk, were sent out, on alternating weeks, to run the

Minnedosa plant until April, when a full-time manager was hired.

By the time that John Miller, recruited from the Worker's Co-op store at Kirkland Lake, Ontario, took over as the Co-op's manager in Minnedosa, the

■ JOHN KOSMOLAK ■

John Kosmolak's family was very active in the Ukrainian Labour Temple in the Point Douglas area of Winnipeg. After graduating from St. John's Tech in the late 1930s, John began working at the Co-op – as can washer, driver, ice cream- and butter-maker. In 1942, he was moved to Minnedosa as the Branch manager, and remained there for almost ten years. During that time, he saw the plant assets increase threefold, and steered the operation through the rebuilding that followed massive flooding when the Minnedosa dam broke in 1948.

He recalled, "Co-operatives at that time were something frowned upon in this district, and the first few years found the little plant struggling to make ends meet." John approached this challenge with a very personal style, both in management and community involvement. Through his contact with people and imaginative advertising campaigns, he attempted not only to make the Co-op viable in Minnedosa, but also to build the local economy and boost civic pride.

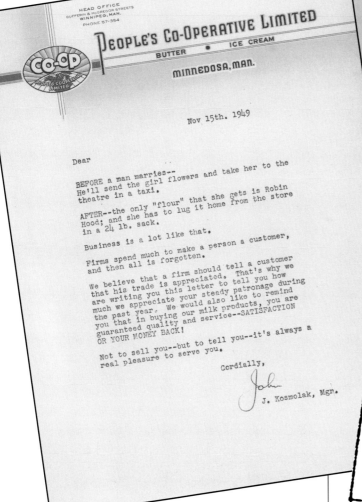

situation had deteriorated considerably. Sales had fallen so drastically that plant income was $17,000 below the previous year, while expenses had risen $6,000. Staff from Winnipeg were sent to canvass lost customers and cream shippers and to reassess production methods. Both they and Miller had a very tough row to hoe, for the anti-Co-op campaign in Minnedosa was now in high gear. On March 15 the local paper reprinted the *Winnipeg Free Press* op-ed piece, which gave those who already disliked the Co-op more grist for their mill. On April 5, just after the Co-op cut milk prices in an effort to win back customers, the *Minnedosa Tribune* greeted this news with a slashing piece focused upon the Co-op's political connections. The opening line of this report was rather telling: "The price of milk in this town has been cut to fourteen cents a quart by the Minnedosa branch of the Communist-headed People's Co-operative of Winnipeg..."[5] Just in case anyone had missed the point, it went on to give a brief overview of the Williams piece from the *Financial Post* and then quoted a lengthy section of it.

This article had the desired effect, for the April 26, 1951, edition of the paper carried an impassioned – but unsigned – letter to the editor. Although the editor's note stated that it was not the paper's policy to publish unsigned letters, "in view of the subject discussed, it has been decided to allow the letter below to be reproduced for the benefit of our readers." In the finest Cold War tradition the anonymous author linked the purchase of milk in Minnedosa with the buying of arms and munitions used to destroy "our boys" who were fighting Communism in Korea.[6]

Editor's note—It has not been the custom during the past to publish unsigned letters to the editor. However, in view of the importance of the subject discussed, it has been decided to allow the letter below to be reproduced for the benefit of our readers. We will give equal prominence to any letters received advocating another point of view than that discussed in the letter.

Minnedosa, April 23, 1951.

Mr. Editor.

Dear Sir:

No doubt it would be quite a surprise to a number of our citizens to learn, in a recent issue of your paper, through your article "Milk Prices Slashed Here", that our local dairy is a Communist-headed concern, even though rumors to that effect have been circulating for some time.

We are all thoroughly convinced that Communism is a menace to the Democratic world; its way of life and all it stands for. Our religious leaders all condemn it— "They can't all be wrong".

The democratic countries are building up armies and equipment to meet its menace; our boys are going out to fight it.

Are we, as loyal Canadians, going to give our money to or in any way knowingly, patronize a firm that is Communist owned?

What is a few cents more per quart for milk? The important question is, where do the profits from these concerns go? Yes, there isn't any doubt about it, it goes to buy arms and munitions to destroy those (our boys) that oppose Communism.

How about it? Are we going to be short sighted enough to fall into this trap (now we know) or are we going to take a stand for the right and show them we will have no part in supporting Communism, as that is what we are doing if we continue to buy our milk from the People's Co-operative dairy in Minnedosa. We are simply giving our money to buy bullets to destroy our own sons. Not so good, is it?

Thanking you, Mr. Editor, for your enlightening article and hoping it will awaken us, as you no doubt intended it would.

APR. 26, 1951   Subscriber.

No matter how ludicrous these charges were, the Co-op found nothing funny in either this letter to the editor or the April 5 report that inspired it. Still smarting from its inability to take action against the *Financial Post*, the Co-op's Board instructed Zuken to launch a libel action against the Minnedosa paper, which eventually resulted in an out-of-court settlement. The Co-op got a retraction, the right to publish a rebuttal to both the April 5 article and the April 26 letter to the editor, a $100 cash settlement (the Co-op had wanted $500 for lost business, and while the paper's lawyer agreed that the Co-op was entitled to this, he demonstrated that this would bankrupt the paper), $100 of free advertising and a promise that the paper would refrain from libelling the Co-op.

The damage, however, had already been done. Co-op milk sales in Minnedosa fell by 40 percent, its best cream hauler in the district switched to a dairy in Erickson. The anti-Co-op agitation also spread to nearby towns and villages, with the result that the Co-op was shut out of Strathclair and then, by action of the local council, was refused a license to sell milk at Shoal Lake for the summer season of 1951.

The Co-op refused to throw in the towel, mindful of its responsibility both to shareholders and cream shippers, milk producers and patrons of the Minnedosa region who had supported it since 1939. If the Co-op left Minnedosa, there might be no place for those producers to ship their milk and cream, as the Brandon dairy got all of its milk from the Brandon milkshed. Moreover, the Co-op's leadership was convinced that it had to keep fighting red-baiting and the inroads of capitalist firms – no matter how difficult the struggle.

Miller and the Co-op's Board of Directors decided that the way to rebuild lost business in Minnedosa was to recruit lost customers and cream shippers and then drive the Brandon Pure Milk Company out of the Minnedosa market entirely. In June 1951 Miller launched a campaign among local milk shippers to petition the town council to protect their interests. The petition sought to prevent any dairy that did not purchase its raw milk locally from selling its products in Minnedosa. The

What your Creamery means
TO MINNEDOSA

For the year ending June 30th, 1951, the Minnedosa Creamery spent locally:

$29,700.00—WAGES (Highest local payroll, with 12 of its 15 resident employees working for the milk department)

$38,500.00—TO MILK SHIPPERS (Largest portion of which is spent locally)

$8,500.00—GAS, OIL and TRUCK REPAIRS (all spent locally)

$6,700.00—TO RAILROADS (local station)

$815.00—TAXES TO THE TOWN

$1,200.00—PLANT MAINTENANCE (spent locally)

$85,415.00—TOTAL

The Minnedosa Creamery Makes for a BIGGER TOWN

Support Your Local Creamery!
Support Your Local Milk Shippers!
Support Your Home Town!
Support Minnedosa's Largest Industry!

The Co-op responded to the Milk Control Board's decision to keep it out of Brandon with this statement in the Minnedosa paper. It also went on public record about its role in the local economy.

Council and Mayor, however, were not inclined to help either the local milk shippers or the Co-op and sat on the petition for over a month. After meeting with the Mayor in August, Miller met with a representative of the milk shippers and the Town Council. This gathering did not go well. Not only did the Council refuse to take direct action to protect the local market for the Co-op and its shippers, but it also refused to ask the Milk Control Board of Manitoba to establish milk control in Minnedosa. Local newspaper coverage made it sound as if Miller had threatened the Council with a shutdown of the Co-op's milk plant (but not the butter-making or ice-cream portions of the plant) and the loss of twelve jobs if it did not support milk control.

In mid-August Miller tried to correct this impression with a letter to the editor. He noted that the Co-op was doing everything possible to keep the milk plant going, while the Town Council, by refusing to protect the plant, its shippers and employees from the competition of a Brandon firm (which had no presence in, and no commitment to, the town of Minnedosa) was putting those jobs at risk. As well, Miller, the Board of Directors and the local shippers who had signed the original petition, applied direct-

ly to the MCB for the establishment of milk control in Minnedosa. By September of 1951 the MCB had agreed to hold a public meeting early in October.

By the time this meeting was convened on October 2 everyone was well primed. A petition circulated by the Brandon firm, and signed by 249 people, was presented. It asked that there be no change made that might deprive the people of Minnedosa of the services of the Brandon Pure Milk Company. This dairy's manager and lawyer were there to present its case against MCB control. The Co-op was represented by Miller and Bileski, and many of the Co-op's milk shippers were in attendance. Despite a steady rain, this mid-afternoon hearing at the local Legion Hall drew about three hundred people.

Roy McPhail, the Chair of the MCB, made it clear to the crowd that the Board was not interested in politics, and that all political commentary was to be left out of the meeting. Still, for all of his attempts to control the meeting, the hostility that had been developing towards the Co-op over the past year spilled out. The Co-op was raked over the coals by many of those in attendance and it was a minor miracle that things did not get more out of hand. McPhail later wrote to Bileski that, "I know I reflect the feeling of the Board when I state my regrets at the attitude adopted by many of those present at the meeting. Your own courteous bearing in spite of aggravating circumstances was noted by all members."[7]

Unfortunately for the Co-op no points were being awarded for gentlemanly conduct, and the same letter of October 12 informed the Co-op that its application for MCB control of the Minnedosa

John Miller had long been involved in the labour and co-ooperative movements when he applied for the manager's position at Minnedosa. Later, Miller headed the Co-op's sales department in Winnipeg during the worst years of the Cold War period and is credited with creative campaigns that helped maintain and even increase the Co-op's sales.

COURTESY C. KOSTANIUK

market had been refused. The Co-op decided that if a Brandon company was going to be able to sell into its market, it would take the fight to Brandon. However, because this market was already under MCB control the Co-op had to apply for permission to sell milk in Brandon. On December 28 this application was turned down on the grounds that Brandon's two existing milk companies were more than enough to serve that market. Strangely, the MCB had concluded that a city several times the size of Minnedosa could support only two milk distributors, but that Minnedosa should be wide open to all comers.

THE WORST OF TIMES

■

Aside from the completion of its building program, 1951 would have to rate with the era of the milk price war and the disastrous year of 1939–40 as a low point in the history of the People's Co-op. Within a month of the MCB's decision to allow a two-cent differential between store and home-delivery prices in Winnipeg (and its imposition of five-day milk delivery) the Co-op lost 454 home-delivery customers – a total that would continue to rise despite every effort to stop the flow. By September, eight retail milk routes had to be taken off, and their volume was only partially made up for by introducing two new store routes. Meanwhile, in Minnedosa, losses were mounting steadily. Its 1949–50 surplus of $968 became a deficit of $3,822 for 1950–51, and over $5,000 for the fiscal year 1951–52.

And there were even more ominous signs on the horizon. In September, Safeway's Lucerne Dairy introduced a non-refundable paper and wax milk carton. Although the technology and materials were more expensive than the reusable glass containers, Winnipeg consumers seemed to like the lighter weight and convenience of non-returnable containers. Safeway's milk sales rose, forcing other Winnipeg dairies to consider ordering the new "Pure-Pak" bottling machines. By December of 1951 it was apparent that a new milk price war was brewing, as a number of milk companies were cutting milk and butter prices to their store customers to compete more effectively with Safeway. The Co-op would either have to follow suit – and lose money on each quart of milk it sold – or stick to its current price and lose even more sales.

Add all of this to the red-baiting, and the demoralizing effect it had on employees and management alike – and the best that anyone at the Co-op could say about 1951, was that on December 31 it would be over.

■ ■ ■

1   PCL, Box 2, 1948 Co-op Campaign, "Publicity Memo," n.d.

2   *Winnipeg Free Press*, April 13, 1954.

3   Ronald Williams, "There's Big Money in Communist Business Network: Stores, Insurance, Professions, Co-ops Mean Big Profits for Campaign Chest," *The Financial Post*, February 14, 1951, p. 1.

4   Unsigned, "Comrade Tycoon," *Winnipeg Free Press*, March 7, 1951, p. 19.

5   "Milk Prices Slashed Here," *The Minnedosa Tribune*, April 5, 1951, p. 1.

6   Ibid., April 26, 1951.

7   PCL, Box 3, Milk Control Board, "Letter, Roy McPhail to Andrew Bileski, October 12, 1951."

WTPA, II-33

For the twenty years between 1950 and 1970, Winnipeg followed the trend of other cities – more suburban sprawl, more reliance on cars, more shopping malls and retail chains. The growing prevalence of cars allowed people to "shop around," but at the same time, made it harder for the Co-op to keep their small-store and home-delivery customers.

CHAPTER NINE
COMPETITION, INNOVATION AND DIVERSITY IN A CHANGING WORLD

A CHANGING CITY

The ability of the People's Co-operative to survive many crises between 1928 and 1951 would be put to an even more severe test over the next two decades. This test would not come from any particular crisis but from that most basic challenge of all – the ability to cope with change.

In many regards, the world in which the Co-op had operated for its first twenty years had remained fairly constant. Until shortly after the Second World War, Winnipeg was very stable in terms of size and ethnic composition. Its population had grown by less than 5 percent, and although the surrounding suburbs were beginning to grow more rapidly than the city, Greater Winnipeg still had a very low growth rate until 1946. Until 1951 the North End was still where most eastern and central Europeans lived, while the southern and western precincts were home to the majority of the city's Anglo-Saxons.

The way in which people lived had not really changed all that much either. They still had most of their milk, bread and other necessities delivered to their homes, often by horse and wagon. The Co-op itself still had twenty-six horse-drawn rigs when World War Two ended. Most Winnipeg dairies and other businesses still made heavy use of horses and wagons, and prominent firms such as Eaton's prided themselves on their delivery rigs and beautiful teams of horses well into the 1950s.

Most people still heated their homes with coal and many still used wood stoves for cooking in the 1940s. Cars, although certainly more common, were still not ubiquitous in 1946, and many working-class families still relied on public transportation and walking. In most parts of the city there was still a grocery store on almost every corner. Even the seventy-four Safeway, Shop-Easy and Jewel stores had not surpassed the approximately 830 small independent stores where most Winnipeggers still did their grocery shopping in 1951.

When it came to milk, the only real innovation of the past twenty years had been homogenization, a

process which stopped the separa-
tion of the cream from the rest of
the milk. In 1951 there was still no
2 percent or 1 percent milk, while
skim milk was still used primarily in
making cottage cheese and powdered milk, or for feeding animals,
but certainly not as a regular drink.
Nor were there any such things as
two- or three-quart containers, or
pouches, or jugs – or any other
sort of packaging other than the
glass quart, pint and half-pint containers that had been used for the
last half century.

Just as the industries in which
the People's Co-op were involved
seemed to be relatively unchanging
during the 1930s and 40s, so too
were certain aspects of the economy itself. Inflation was certainly not
a problem until 1946. A comparison
of prices from 1928, when the Co-
op first went into business, with

Saul Simkin joined the Co-op in the early
1950s and served as its accountant and
office manager for fifteen years. A member
of the Jewish left-wing community, Simkin
had been a labour organizer and activist
since the 1930s.

those eighteen years later, gives evidence of price
stagnation or even deflation, not inflation. Much the
same could be said for wages, although they did rise
somewhat during the war. Even after experiencing
the wage and price inflation of 1946–51, anyone or
any institution that had come of age during the
"dirty thirties" and war years would have found it
difficult to believe that a day would come when milk
would cost a dollar a quart or a worker would make
over $10,000 a year.

In the years following the war, but especially after
1951, all of this changed dramatically. Wartime savings and pent-up consumer demand had created a
huge market for consumer goods such as cars and
refrigerators, but it did not stop there. Electric
ranges were bought to replace old, unsafe wood
stoves in most homes. And new homes themselves
came into great demand. A post-war building boom
started slowly in 1946, gathered speed throughout
the late 1940s, took off in the 1950s and continued,
largely unabated, well into the 1970s.

Almost all of this new construction took place in
the suburbs, which would have been impractical if

car ownership had not become
almost universal. What the distinguished historian A.R.M. Lower
once referred to as "the great
God-Car" had now taken over
the streets of Winnipeg, allowing
more and more people to live further and further away from where
they worked, and from where
they had grown up.

An exodus from older parts of
the city to new suburbs was clearly underway. From 1951 to 1971
the City of Winnipeg's population
grew by only 10,500, or 4.5 percent. The suburbs, however, almost
doubled from 115,452 to 219,900.
This not only altered population
distributions, it also changed the
ethnic composition of certain
parts of Winnipeg. The North End,
for example, lost almost 10 percent of its Ukrainian population
between 1951 and 1961, a decline
that became even more noticeable in the 1960s and
1970s. Almost 50 percent of the Jewish population
left the area during the same period.

The degree of ethnic group cohesion among
eastern and central Europeans was clearly declining.
Aside from the small group of displaced persons
who came to Canada from Europe in the post-war
period, Winnipeg's eastern European community
was overwhelmingly Canadian-born after the
Second World War. These people spoke English as
their first language, travelled in more cosmopolitan
social circles than their parents and increasingly
married members of other ethnic groups. By the
late 1950s and 1960s, short of knowing someone's
last name, there was almost no way of telling what
ethnic group a person had come from, for all tell-
tale accents had been lost except among the aging
population of original immigrants.

This did not mean that these groups lost all sense
of their ethnic identity, but rather that it was not as
strong as it had once been. And the sense of social,
political and economic alienation which had caused
Winnipeg's ethnic community to maintain close ties

Adapting to the changes at hand, the fuel yard began supplying oil along with wood and coal for home heating in 1952. The Co-op's patronage dividends, which reached 8 percent in good years helped keep a steady number of customers.

escaping the demise of coal and wood. The Co-op needed to meet this change in technology (in the 1950s approximately 85 percent of all new homes were being built with oil furnaces) while continuing to serve its traditional customers, who proved to be somewhat resistant to change. In the North End some homes had coal furnaces and wood stoves well into the 1970s. In 1952 a truck and tanks were purchased to get into the heating oil business in a small way. This venture proved so successful in its first year of operation – and profitable, given the mark-up on fuel oil – that the Co-op added another fuel oil truck in 1953, and a third in 1955. Between the sale of its traditional wares (wood, coal, coke, hardware and paint), fuel oil and increasing amounts of gasoline, the fuel yard made spectacular gains during the 1950s. Regular patronage dividends, which started at 3 percent and eventually climbed to 8 percent, no doubt helped to keep old customers and attract new ones.

Fuel yard Manager Mike Kostaniuk, General Manager Bill Kardash, and the Co-op's Board of Directors were always looking for ways to make the fuel yard a year-round venture, so in the early 1950s it supplied a broad range of electrical appliances, which patrons could get at the Co-op's wholesale cost plus a small mark-up for handling. This never developed into a major revenue source, but another plan for making the fuel yard busier year-round did.

Since 1929–30 there had been talk that the fuel yard should go into the building supply trade, and a few steps had been made in that direction by selling paint, hardware and some other lines of goods. But going into this business on a large-scale and establishing a full-sized lumber yard had been prevented by lack of money, lack of space at the fuel yard and a preoccupation with the creamery branch. In 1954, it was decided to move the fuel yard to the Co-op's site at the Old Exhibition Grounds because only a

was also dissolving. After the war and the full revelation of the horrors of the Holocaust, anti-Semitism decreased and became far less socially acceptable. For Ukrainians, social and political inclusion was perhaps best symbolized by the repeated election of Steve Juba – the populist Ukrainian-Canadian Mayor of Winnipeg – from 1956 on. By the close of the 1960s, the ethnic composition of both the provincial government headed by Ed Schreyer and of City Council, demonstrated that the various eastern European groups now held considerable political power in Winnipeg and Manitoba. Moreover, these ethnic groups were breaking out of the old occupational and educational ghettoes that prejudice had forced upon them, even further weakening group cohesion.

ADAPTATION TO CHANGE AT THE FUEL YARD

What all of this meant to the People's Co-op was that it would have to operate in an environment where the only constant was change. All of its activities would have to be revolutionized. Its original business, the fuel yard would have to adapt to the coming of gas and electric heating. There was no

small fraction of the property was being utilized. The Co-op could then sell the old fuel yard at Pritchard and Battery, amalgamate operations at one location and build the long-desired lumber yard. This addition would make the fuel yard a year round operation and provide an important new service to the people of the North End.

However, it was seven years before the lumber yard was built, and another four years for the fuel yard to move to the Old Exhibition Grounds and amalgamate its operations with the lumber yard. The delay was not caused by financial problems; rather, it was almost the reverse: business was going so well at the fuel yard that there was not enough time or staff to undertake the project. With fuel oil and gasoline sales rising so rapidly, and coal sales rather surprisingly holding their own, the fuel yard had major sales increases throughout the 1950s. Success stood in the way of making even more changes for the fuel yard.

ADAPTATION TO CHANGE AT THE CREAMERY

Emerging from the calamitous year of 1951 in shaky fiscal condition, the Co-op had to make some tough decisions in order to turn things around in the creamery. The first problem that had to be addressed was competition from the big chain stores which were taking an ever larger share of the milk business away from home-delivery dairies and seemed to be the wave of the future for all grocery merchandising.

The chain stores took full advantage of the changing nature of the city. An informal 1951–52 Milk Control Board study showed that the three major chains of the time – Safeway, Shop-Easy and

Jewel – understood the real-estate maxim of "location, location, location" very well. They were all on major thoroughfares, close to areas where relatively affluent populations were growing. As the author

The large grocery chains that were becoming more common in Winnipeg were concentrated on the thoroughfares that ran through more affluent neighbourhoods toward the suburbs. In 1953, the Co-op served 441 stores, almost all of which were "Mom and Pops" located mainly in the North End and other less affluent areas of the city.

of the report noted, "the chain stores hunt in packs."[1] And so they did: Academy Road, Broadway, Portage Avenue, St. Mathews, Westminster, Corydon, Osborne, Kelvin, Henderson Highway, St. Mary's Road and the northern portion of Main Street (outside of the Winnipeg city limits) had the vast majority of Winnipeg's chain stores, all of which, with the exception of Broadway, were thoroughfares that served the burgeoning suburbs. The only densely populated region of the city and the only major streets the chains had not yet colonized were in the North End. There, for all of its population density, only four chain stores had been established, two on Mountain and two on Main Street. The author of the report felt that this was because the chains still could not compete with the "Selkirk Ave. 'Markets.'"[2] He may have been correct in this, but then again, it might have been that the chains were more interested in serving affluent parts of the city rather than the poorer North End.

This lack of representation in Winnipeg's North End gave the Co-op an obvious opening. Over the years it had been gradually increasing its percentage of store milk sales, and in the process, had strengthened its relationships with the small, independent storekeepers. Now that the price differential between home delivery and store sales had risen to two cents per quart, the Co-op knew that it would have to rely upon these stores to sell even more of its milk.

By February of 1952 the Co-op's Board of Directors was planning to establish a "united front with the small storekeepers"[3] and within a few weeks the Co-op dropped its wholesale milk price so that it could compete with the big chains. The Co-op knew that this would cut into its own home-delivery sales, but, faced with a choice of increasing store sales to raise its sales volume, or focussing upon a clearly diminishing market, the Co-op pursued store sales.

This was not an easy decision, for it meant reorganizing the Co-op's entire delivery system. Increasingly uneconomical routes had to be consolidated or discontinued – particularly the small volume horse-drawn wagon routes. This shift would be partially offset by creating more store truck routes, but losing eleven retail routes between 1951 and 1952 was not balanced by adding two new store truck routes. However, because of the booming economy and the tendency of the Co-op's younger drivers to move on to jobs with better pay or better hours, there was no need for layoffs. The greatest problem was convincing some of the older milkmen to give up their horses and start driving trucks – a change that proved impossible for two older deliverymen. Instead of letting them go or forcing them into early retirement, the Co-op kept on two horse-drawn wagons until 1958, even though neither route had enough volume to make it profitable.

The Co-op's reorientation towards store sales would not, however, be enough to save the dairy if it did not keep up with other changes. In 1951 Safeway's Lucerne Dairy had started to put milk in a new type of container, essentially a paper "bottle" that was coated in wax and held together by wire

■ JOHN SAS ■

John Sas began at the Co-op in the early 1960s as one of the young people hired for the summer. Starting as a deliveryman on the notorious Beach runs, he held the position of sales manager when he left the Co-op 29 years later.

Sas was a milkman when Anne Ross, the director of the Mount Carmel Clinic, worked with the Co-op on campaigns to keep milk prices down and to get milk into schools. Eventually the Co-op was running a large-scale school milk program that was the bane of every driver's life. Sas recalls, "You had to go to each room, stand there with all your cases of milk, then the kids would come and give their six or eleven cents and you went from door to door. I used to hate going on those routes that had all those big schools. You'd come out weighed down and then you came back and you had to count all that change. And heaven forbid that the Co-op should have a coin counter."

Not all customers were as wholesome. The Co-op also used to sell to approximately fifteen private gambling clubs on Main Street. Deliveries to these clubs, which were open around the clock, would start at 3:00 am. Sas said, "You came, the little slit opened up, the guy would look, 'Oh, it's the milkman,' close it, let you in. You'd go in there in the smoke-filled rooms; there were a lot of guys with nice suits, playing cards all night."

COURTESY MELODY AND JOHN SAS

and adhesives. This non-returnable bottle was terribly expensive compared to the old glass bottles which, despite breakage and cleaning costs, were very economical. Still, consumers – especially those who had switched from home-delivery service to store purchasing – liked the lighter weight, the convenience of just throwing them away when empty, and the novelty of not having to pay a deposit.

Because of the 2.2 cent per quart cost of such packaging, late in 1951 all of Winnipeg's creameries (save for Lucerne) had entered into a "gentleman's agreement" to not use these bottles or the costly, and patented, Pure-Pak machines needed for the process – at least not without informing the other dairies well in advance. Realistically though, because paper cartons had proved such a success – between 1950 and early 1952 Safeway's share of Winnipeg milk sales jumped from 1.9 to 5.9 percent – it was a question of when, not if, some dairy would break the pact.

Crescent moved first, and ordered Pure-Pak equipment and cartons without telling any of its competitors. But, in the incestuous world of the Winnipeg milk business, where almost everyone running a milk plant had at one time or other been an executive with another firm, the word spread like wildfire. Long before Crescent received its machinery from Detroit, Modern and some of its subsidiaries had ordered their own equipment. The Co-op, which was not part of this "fraternity", did not find out about Crescent's plan until just three weeks before that dairy started selling milk in paper containers.

When the Co-op's competitors started putting these paper cartons on the market in August 1952, the impact was immediate. By the end of the month the Co-op had lost five stores, while in five others the sales dropped sharply. The Co-op's management tried to put a brave face on matters, noting at a Board meeting that these losses were partly counterbalanced by increased glass bottled milk sales at other stores. This gain was "partly due to difficulties the competitors have experienced with the paper bottle and mainly due to the large amount of goodwill the Co-op enjoys among the storekeepers and consumers."[4]

Goodwill notwithstanding, only one month later Co-op sales had declined to the point where it had no choice but to order Pure-Pak equipment. Indeed, the losses were so severe that the Co-op had Modern Dairies custom package its milk until the new equipment arrived three-and-a-half months later.

All of this was clearly a gamble. The cost of having milk custom packaged and of the Pure-Pak machine (obtained on a lease-to-purchase arrangement) and the various supplies needed for the cartons was very high. In a typical month the lease fees plus packaging materials added $7,000 to the Co-op's operating costs, while the machinery and cartons had to vie for precious plant space with the glass bottling operations, as glass bottles were still in demand on home-delivery routes and by many store customers who thought the paper cartons gave the milk a "funny" taste.

The gamble paid off though. By February of 1953, only one month after the Co-op's own Pure-Pak machine was up and running, it had made up for the 7 percent dip in sales it had experienced when its competitors introduced paper cartons. In fact, sales were up by over 12 percent, and by March the Co-op had surpassed its all-time volume sales record. In a matter of months, all the volume losses occasioned by price inflation, by the establishment of the 2 cent per quart price differential, and by its competitors early start in the new packaging system were overcome. The sale of high-profit items like cream and butter also increased.

The greatest victory for the Co-op in all of this was a moral one. David had taken on Goliath, and if the giant wasn't exactly vanquished, David was still standing. And in a sense, at least one Goliath had been slain, for early in 1953, Silverwoods (the owner of City Dairy) announced that it would no longer package milk in paper cartons because of the cost. Perhaps this should have worried the Co-op – if the deep corporate pockets of this national dairy giant could not afford the new packaging, how in heaven's name could the much smaller People's Co-operative afford it? – but it was taken as a good sign. As the Coop managers saw it, the milk industry in Winnipeg was now broken up into three camps: Crescent Creamery, which sold only paper cartons; Silverwoods, which sold only glass bottles; and Co-op and Modern (and its subsidiaries), which sold both. The Co-op's managers were convinced that they and Modern had made the proper decision – a mixture of the tried and true with the new and (at least, temporarily) popular.

Besides making the appropriate business decisions, the Co-op was also determined to both keep its supporters abreast of recent developments and involved with the Co-op in a social, as well as business sense. To this end, it launched a new campaign to inform its customers, shareholders and other consumers about the changes in the milk industry, and to explain the Co-op's recent decisions. Over three months it hosted a series of family-oriented

percent in 1952–53, the two People's Co-op plants saw increases in cream shipments of 25 percent and 40 percent respectively over the same period. Minnedosa would continue to be a money-losing operation for most of the 1950s, but so long as it kept the main plant well-supplied with butter, most other shortcomings could be overlooked.

As a result of these changes, by the mid 1950s the Co-op had not only recovered from the problems of 1951, but was in better financial shape than at any time in its history. In 1954, for the first time ever, the Co-op's 10 percent statutory reserve

The Minnedosa creamery started up milk production again in the late 1940s, but, like many other small rural dairies, could not make it pay. Still, the creamery did very well throughout the 1950s with butter production.

The Minnedosa plant was in very rough shape when **John Wityshyn** became manager. "They had a house next to the plant which was around four feet from the plant and it was falling apart. The floor, you could have put an egg in one corner, it would have rolled right up to the plant. We were improving the plant all the time and we improved the house. We lived in the house, it was heated from the creamery, it was steam heat, and water was from the creamery. The house and utilities were free, but you were on call twenty-four hours a day."

"Co-op Nites" all over Greater Winnipeg, where informational lectures by the Co-op's managers were interspersed with films (from the Winnipeg Public Library), short concert programs and food. For the children, a series of Saturday afternoon entertainments was held, with a heavy emphasis on movies and ice cream. Later in the year the Co-op inaugurated a special series of get-togethers with the Board of Directors, management and the storekeepers – they were open-houses, really, where food and spirits flowed quite liberally.

Attempts were also made to improve the Co-op's situation in Minnedosa. Cream shipments, the plant's bread and butter, had to be increased somehow after the events of 1951, so the Co-op turned back to an old practice. The special cream bonus (one cent per pound of butterfat) that had worked so well in the 1930s when the Co-op first entered the butter-making trade, was reintroduced in 1952, primarily for the benefit of Minnedosa-area cream shippers. While this did not solve all of the Co-op's problems in that town, it certainly had the desired effect on cream shipments and butter production. Whereas cream production in Manitoba rose by 10

deduction would not have to be used to pay down deficits from previous years. In almost every respect, the Co-op had turned the corner: Minnedosa was sending more butter to Winnipeg; the fuel yard's adaptation to oil sales had been hugely successful, allowing it to make major contributions to the Co-op's surplus; and the complete reorientation of the creamery's business, while at times difficult, had worked. True, it was strange for some of the old-timers to see that almost 70 percent of the Co-op's milk – much of it sold in strange new containers – was being sold through a network of five hundred stores, and that some of it was even that "blue"-hued skim milk, that everyone had once known was fit only for animals. Stranger still, all of this milk was being hauled to stores by men who didn't even know how to handle horses! But no matter how strange they seemed, the changes had worked. And for the rest of the decade business would continue to improve for the Co-op.

PROSPERITY SHARED

With the Co-op in a surplus position and with the future looking reasonably bright, managers, board members and shareholders once again started thinking about expansion and diversification, particularly into the building supply trade. Some voices, however, urged that instead of expanding, the Co-op

Dr. Milton Tenenbein grew up in North End Winnipeg. He has been the head of emergency services at the Winnipeg Children's Hospital for over 20 years. While attending university and medical school, he worked for several summers as a milkman on the Beach runs beginning in the later 1960s.

"My mom and dad had a store on Sargent and Young which was called Family Grocery and Confectionery and my dad exclusively sold Co-op products. So, when the time came for me to make some money so I could support my education, I guess he called in a couple chips with the dairy and respectfully requested that they might find a job for me, which they did. It was a great job for a university and medical student. It was well-paying. Of course, I worked hard, but I made my tuition and some money to support my education.

"On the Beach run I had an old beat-up truck. You didn't have to worry about speeding because one couldn't. If you had someone who was going five or ten miles slower than you in front, passing was like a five-minute operation. The step vans that they had in the city, the motor was right beside you, and we used to drive around with the sliding doors open. You had to or else you'd cook in there.

"At the loading dock, I was called 'Doc' and I have fond memories of those other drivers. I always got along very well with them."

COURTESY DR. M. TENENBEIN

should use the good times to consolidate its recent gains, put more money into the reserve fund, pay higher dividends to the shareholders and start taking better care of its own work force.

There had always been many on the Board who advocated improvements in working conditions and

fringe benefits for the Co-op's workers. Some, like Chester King, were quite prominent in the union movement, and all were very progressive on most social issues. The Co-op's workers certainly agreed that improvements were needed, for while the Co-op had tried to keep up with Winnipeg's big dairies in terms of wages, fringe benefits and working conditions, still, its work force had fallen behind some of Co-op's counterparts during the early 1950s. And the greatest need – the union and the Board agreed – was for a pension plan. Not only was it the right thing to do, but keeping high-quality personnel in the booming 1950s and 1960s required some provision for retirement.

When the Co-op introduced its pension plan in 1957, it immediately made company contributions far greater than the amounts specified in the union contract. The Board adopted a policy of making additional payments, many times those specified in the agreement, for every year that it was in a surplus position. This made up for the lean years when it had wanted to introduce a pension plan but had been unable to do so, and it was also a hedge for the workers against potential bad years. Because the pension plan negotiated by the union was a profit-sharing plan, the Board did not want its workers to be penalized just because the Co-op might not have enough of a surplus to make sizable contributions in future years. Thus, the Co-op heavily "front-loaded" its contributions to the plan, and continued to over-contribute to the pension fund on a regular basis. In fact, it became a habit – and rather a pleasant one so far as the employees were concerned – for the Board not only to put additional money into the pension fund, but to make special contributions to increase pension payments to workers who had retired at low rates because of their relatively short period of contributions.

It became a source of pride to the Co-op that its pension plan was soon recognized by the insurance industry and other dairies as one of the finest and best financed plans of its kind in Winnipeg. When added to improved medical benefits and substantial wage increases, the work force's prosperity was moving in lock-step with the Co-op's prosperity – a situation the founders would have found extremely gratifying.

Opening of the Red River Co-op's first shopping centre in Winnipeg, 1958. While People's Co-op patronized Red River for its gas, their patronage for dairy products was not reciprocated. The shopping centre turned to a private company instead, and only began to stock People's Co-op products five years later.

THE CHAIN STORES AND THE MILK MONOPOLY

————————— ■ —————————

While the middle and later years of the 1950s were good ones for the Co-op, there were some ominous developments in the milk industry. Competition became more severe as the decade progressed, largely because of concentration in the grocery trade and dairy industry.

The growth of the chain stores continued unabated during this period. Safeway built more and larger stores and had its own dairy, so there was no chance the Co-op could sell any milk there. Shop-Easy expanded and it also swallowed up the Jewel and Jewel Junior chain in its bid to win a larger share of the Winnipeg grocery market. It did not build its own dairy plant, but it signed an exclusive supply contract with Modern Dairies, so once again the Co-op was shut out. Before the close of the decade,

the eastern Canada-based Loblaws chain entered the fray, soon to be joined by A&P and Dominion stores – none of which would deal with the People's Co-op. One large consumers' co-operative, Red River Co-op, established two huge shopping centres of its own in the late 1950s and early 1960s, but both of these stores initially refused to handle People's Co-op milk. (This was truly irksome to the Co-op, not only because this co-operative was buying its milk from a private company, but also because the Co-op patronized another branch of the Red River Co-op for all its gasoline!) In short, just as the Co-op became more dependent than ever upon the small independent grocers for sales, these independents were being squeezed out of business by the big chains. As they had done in the 1930s, when Piggly Wiggly and Safeway had first threatened their existence, small retailers again banded together to take advantage of group-purchase savings. Innumerable small stores suddenly become part of the Tom-Boy, Solo, IGA and Red and White groups –

most of which were organized and run by grocery wholesalers. And it was difficult for the Co-op to get the milk business of these small chains, because its larger competitors were able to offer group rebates that were almost impossible for the Co-op to match.

■ JOHN WITYSHYN ■

When **John Wityshyn** came to work at the Co-op in the early 1950s, he had no intention of staying on for any length of time. A farm boy from Komarno, he had come to the city looking for work. His parents had shipped cream to the Co-op, so he decided to drop in as he drove by one night. "I stopped in, they hired me and I started working that same evening."

Wityshyn worked his way through every job in the plant. Six years after he started at the dairy, he was asked to become the manager of the creamery in Minnedosa. " And I was quite shocked because I didn't even know where Minnedosa was!"

Wityshyn's territory extended as far as Brandon, St. Lazare, McCreary and Amaranth. Over the next thirty-one years, he slowly built up the Co-op's sales: "When I first got there, about 60 cases of milk were being sold. Later, we used to sell 1500 cases a week."

Wityshyn served the community, making sure the Co-op patronized local businesses: "With truck repairs, [the garage] said they had one or two employees on account of us." He also sat on the town council for fourteen years.

Wityshyn looked after Co-op customers – "It was 7 days a week. We never went away on a long weekend because we felt that the customers needed you for the long-weekends. This is one of the reasons we had good relationships with the customers." He also fostered good service and loyalty among the employees. "We had good drivers. We had one guy with 40 years, one with 42 with us. I had 37, Stan Funk, the bookkeeper had 34. They were devoted employees to the co-operative. We trusted one another."

COURTESY JOHN WITYSHYN

The larger creameries had the economies of scale on their side, particularly Modern Dairies. It had always been the most aggressive of the Co-op's rivals, taking over an ever-increasing share of dairy production with its buy-out program of Winnipeg

dairies and smaller milk and butter plants throughout Manitoba. In the mid-1950s this buy-out program went into overdrive. In 1955 Modern acquired the Brandon Pure Milk Company (the Co-op's old rival in Minnedosa), which was forced to sell after a Milk Control Board investigation proved that it had been underpaying its milk shippers for years. Far more dramatic though, was Modern's takeover on January 1, 1956, of the plants and equipment of its oldest and largest rival, Crescent Creamery, including its huge Winnipeg operation and plants in Portage la Prairie and Swan River. Modern now owned its original plants, plus Standard Dairies, Medoland (the old St. Boniface Creamery) and Crescent; bottled milk for Winkler Creamery, Cambridge and Royal Dairies in Winnipeg; and owned major plants in Brandon, Portage, Rivers, Gimli and Flin Flon.

And Modern was only one of the Co-op's rivals in the Winnipeg milk market. There was also City Dairy and, of course, Safeway's Lucerne Dairy, which in many ways set both price and packaging trends in Winnipeg. How was a small, two-plant operation like the Co-op to compete against firms such as these?

THE CO-OP'S RESPONSE TO MONOPOLY

Bill Kardash actually saw something positive in standing up against this growing monopolization of the milk industry. When he reported on Modern's recent acquisitions to Co-op shareholders in March 1956, he told them that this might work to the Co-op's advantage, as many customers were anti-monopoly and would turn to the People's Co-op as an alternative. He felt that the Co-op's market share, which he estimated at between 11 percent and 12 percent, would grow if the Co-op spread the word that it was the only real alternative in Winnipeg for those opposed to the monopolization of the milk industry.

Judging by the Co-op's sales trends over the late 1950s and early 1960s Kardash's optimism was at least partially warranted. By keeping pace with each new change in the industry – selling 2 percent milk,

138

packaging even more of its products in paper cartons, adding half-gallon containers and items such as orange juice and juice-like drinks such as Beep to its product list, and converting to the more efficient new bulk tanker method of shipping milk from the farms – the Co-op did remain competitive. Moreover, it was always looking for new areas into which it might expand, and by 1958–59 had finally secured permission from the MCB to sell milk from its Minnedosa plant first in Neepawa and then in Brandon. It also broke into the summer market at Falcon and West Hawk lakes, then expanded this seasonal business into routes serving the year-round communities of Lac du Bonnet, Great Falls, St. George, Powerview, Grand Beach, Seven Sisters, Whitemouth and Rennie. The Co-op even briefly served Steinbach, although that route soon proved impractical and had to be taken off after only a few months.

The Co-op also became more adept at certain marketing strategies. In an effort to boost ice-cream sales in 1957–58, it entered a give-away marketing promotion – giving bricks of ice cream to new customers as an introductory offer. This strategy induced 204 stores to handle Co-op ice cream and more than doubled the sales of ice-cream products in only two months. The Co-op also became more willing to grant loans, mortgages and the use of freezers and refrigeration units to the stores and restaurants which handled its goods, in order to help them stay in business – and keep selling Co-op products.

But the Co-op's wisest move of all during this period was probably the appointment of John Wityshyn as its new Minnedosa plant manager in 1959. This hard-working farm boy was a jack-of-all-trades and master of many. He personally carried out many of the much needed repairs at this aging plant; served as the primary butter maker; handled sales, advertising and public relations; and on more than one occasion, climbed into a truck and handled deliveries. He truly fit into this rural community and was able to make the Co-op plant financially viable while integrating it into the surrounding community during the 1960s and 1970s. Wityshyn made the Co-op's Minnedosa branch into a mini-marketing empire, as his drivers added to their wares not just

■ BOB PAWLYK ■

Bob Pawlyk worked at the Co-op in the late 1960s, one of the many young people who got summer and part-time jobs there.

"I was a member of Ukrainian folk dance at the Ukrainian Labour Temple. I was 17 and the Co-op was looking for summer drivers and I got a call from John Sas asking me if I was interested in driving a milk truck on one of the beach routes. I thought that was just the greatest thing."

Bob recalled the management's commitment to co-operation was more than rhetorical. It provided service to many rural communities long after it was profitable. "During the winter, I also drove the Whiteshell feeder route, Co-op would sell milk to anybody who wanted to buy. There were a couple of broken-down stores that used to be general stores maybe back in the 1930s and 1940s and the only route in was a gravel or mud road in behind a bunch of farms, but they still had farmers who lived up there, and we still serviced them. Nobody else would, but Co-op would serve them, so I guess from that point of view, it really was a people's dairy."

new milk, dairy and ice-cream products, but a growing array of frozen food products, which varied according to the best deal he could arrange from suppliers.

PLANS FOR THE FUTURE
■

As the 1960s dawned, the Co-op was clearly in excellent shape. There was even an improvement in the climate of political opinion. Although the Cold War continued, the most virulent red-baiting was over. For the first time in years the Co-op felt able to make overtures to the larger co-operative movement, and they were well received. In 1960 its application for membership in Federated Co-operatives Limited (FCL) was accepted, as was its 1961 application to the Co-op Union of Manitoba.

Membership in the FCL would prove to be particularly important. It not only helped the Co-op get back into the larger co-operative movement, but also gave it access to a broad range of goods to sell, as the FCL was a prairie-province-wide wholesaler of goods to consumer co-operatives. Through the FCL the Co-op finally realized its thirty-year-old dream of creating a building supply business. When it set up its lumber yard on the Old Exhibition Grounds in 1961, it was the FCL which helped to plan the layout and buildings, offered low-cost financing for the upfront costs and became the Co-op's supplier of choice for lumber, hardware and most other building supplies.

Even as the lumber yard was being planned, several members of the Co-op's Board of Directors were convinced that the time had finally come to build a new creamery plant on the Old Exhibition Grounds site. The projected $1 million cost, while daunting, did not seem out of reach considering the Co-op's annual turnover of almost $3 million. The recently adopted policy of putting all share dividends into a five year revolving account – a standard practice in many co-operatives – plus the mounting statutory reserve fund, indicated that if the Co-op creamery continued to increase its market share, plant expansion would be essential and affordable.

It was also clear that the fuel yard would finally have to be moved to the Old Exhibition Grounds so that it could be amalgamated with the lumber yard. This raised the question of what to do with the fuel yard property. Should the Co-op sell the land or should it use it as a developer might – perhaps by building apartment blocks or a series of single-family dwellings? The relocated fuel yard itself would not take up much room at its new home. The abandonment of coal and wood was now being matched by a decline in fuel oil sales as Winnipeggers increasingly converted their furnaces to natural gas. Everything but the fuel yard's gasoline sales would

WINNIPEG BRANCH

FEDERATED CO-OPERATIVES

LIMITED

Official Opening

TUESDAY, MARCH 22nd, 1960

at 8:30 p.m.

1615 KING EDWARD STREET, ST. JAMES

Aerial Photo of New Office Building and Warehouse
at 1615 King Edward Street, St. James, Manitoba

The Federated Co-operatives Limited, which itself expanded in 1960, played an important role in helping the Co-op open its lumber yeard in 1961. The Co-op's membership in the FCL indicated a lessening of the isolation imposed by the Cold War.

be phased out of existence over the next decade.

The entire operation – the lumber yard, the Co-op's garage and truck repair facilities and a new creamery – still would not make full use of the land, so all sorts of plans were put forward. Why not, for example, build a sports and entertainment complex – including a curling rink, bowling alley, banquet hall and a restaurant and milk bar for the general public. Such a complex would make good use of the land, generate revenues and bring even more people into contact with the Co-op.

Another business opportunity that was explored in 1960 concerned the Soviet Union. It was now interested in exporting certain goods to the West, particularly the Moskvich line of automobiles as well as tractors and other farm implements. Bill Kardash and the Board explored the possibility of becoming the sales agents for a whole series of Soviet-made goods out of the lumber yard and fuel yard offices, and in 1961 even bought two Moskvich cars as demonstrators. They must not have been very popular, as the Co-op's records make no mention of any further purchases of them.

When the new lumber yard opened in September of 1961 the future could not have looked much better. The Co-op's old enterprises were doing well, ambitious plans were being laid for the future, and it had just branched out into what everyone thought would be a sure thing – a North End lumber yard. Since Winnipeg's housing market was growing, the demand for lumber and other building supplies would be considerable. As there was no other co-op lumber yard in the area, it was assumed that all co-operatively-minded people would patronize the Co-op. The fuel yard's trucks and yard equipment, always

The lumber yard was housed in the converted stables and surrounding area. Such an undertaking had been part of the vision of the Co-op ever since the 1920s.

idle over the summer months, could now be put to use during the busy construction season, while the fuel yard employees would now have year-round employment, shifting over to the lumber yard when the fuel business slowed for the season. Last, but not least, the lumber yard would bring an ever-increasing number of customers into contact with the Co-op, which would heighten its public presence and increase business in its other lines.

Unfortunately, the success story did not materialize, although the grand opening in September was certainly a successful social affair. An introductory sale, a ribbon-cutting ceremony at which Alderman Jake Penner, Councillor for Ward Three and the Co-op's former accountant, did the honours, and entertainment, prizes, food and speeches kept a sizable crowd happy. But opening a building supply yard so late in the construction season presented some economic problems, as costly inventories had to be car-

Alderman (and former Co-op employee) **Jacob Penner**, representing Winnipeg City Council, cut the ribbon in September, 1961 to officially open this new Co-op venture.

ried over the quiet winter months. Despite some expert advice from FCL, no one at the Co-op had any real expertise in the building supply trade or in dealing with contractors. Both the lumber yard's staff and management had to travel a very steep learning curve, and some would fall off along the way. For several years the lumber yard recorded considerable deficits and would not produce anything even approaching a surplus until 1966–67, when its sales were boosted by the Co-op's decision to develop a

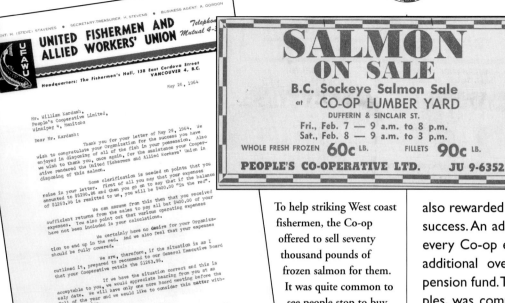

branches of the Co-op were in good enough shape that strong surpluses were generated in 1962, 1963 and 1964. These surpluses were celebrated with higher share dividends, patronage dividends, cream bonuses and contributions to the statutory reserves. The workers were also rewarded for their contribution to the Co-op's success. An additional week's salary was granted to every Co-op employee in each of these years and additional over-contributions were made to the pension fund. The Co-op, living up to its own principles, was committed to sharing its prosperity with those whose support and hard work made it possible.

To help striking West coast fishermen, the Co-op offered to sell seventy thousand pounds of frozen salmon for them. It was quite common to see people stop to buy lumber or get gas at the pumps, then snag a couple of sockeye from the refrigerated unit set up on the Co-op grounds.

A NEW FORM OF COMPETITION: MINI-MARTS AND JUGGED MILK

Taking its cue from some U.S. and Toronto retailers, a new chain – the Mini-Mart – came to Winnipeg late in 1964. The idea was to establish a series of convenience stores (located in former corner stores) which would be open seven days a week for extended hours and have as its trademark product three-quart jugs of milk. These would be sold as cheaply as possible in order to get people into the stores, while profits would come from groceries, snack foods, cigarettes and other such goods. As was later discovered, a deal had been struck almost a year earlier to have Modern Dairies serve as the new chain's sole provider of milk.

When the first nine Mini-Marts opened in December of 1964 (with forty more scheduled to open in the near future), Winnipeggers flocked to buy the cut-rate milk. Three-quart jugs cost only fifty-nine cents while individual quarts in other stores cost twenty-three cents apiece. Naturally, every store in Winnipeg lost milk sales and wanted jugged milk so that they could compete with Mini-Mart. Modern, as Winnipeg's only dairy possessing the appropriate bottling, filling and washing equip-

housing sub-division on the grounds of the former fuel yard.

Still, if the lumber yard was a disappointment in the early 1960s, there were considerable successes for the Co-op's other branches during this period. Minnedosa and Winnipeg both held their own in terms of volume sales, and the Winnipeg branch added several new out-of-town routes and additional home-delivery routes in Winnipeg during the early 1960s. Better yet, late in 1963, after putting some pressure on Red River Co-op through their joint supplier, FCL, the Co-op finally got some shelf space in its two supermarkets. And in what many people must have thought was the strangest development ever, the Co-op briefly entered into the salmon selling business. To help striking West Coast fishermen, the Co-op agreed to market over seventy thousand pounds of frozen salmon in Winnipeg. Throughout 1963–64 there was no question that the Co-op was the only dairy that could offer its customers a full range of dairy goods and salmon to boot. Nor was there any other lumber yard where workers could ask customers – with an almost straight face – if they wanted some sockeye along with those two-by-fours.

Even with deficits from the lumber yard running in the neighbourhood of $20,000 per year, the other

A Winnipeg white out. Sales manager **John Sas** recalled that it was a badge of honour for the Co-op to get the milk out no matter what the weather. The proudest of the Co-op blizzard fighters was **Fred Billows** (below), who delivered milk for the Co-op for 26 years. During one blizzard, Billows was the only milkman in the city to complete his rounds, spending 17 hours battling the elements.

WTPA

COURTESY C. KOSTANIUK

Ribbons awarded the Co-op for its high quality butter. **John Sas**, sales manager: "The guy that could really make butter was a guy by the name of **Johnny Wnuk**. We always were winning awards at the CNE. We had tons of ribbons, cups. Andrew [Bileski] would pick up on that and put it in the literature, 'Award-winning butter'. We played that up. It wasn't just that the Co-op did it, the workers did it. It instilled pride in all the workers, also helped us in our advertising, and in marketing, where people thought that if you had award-winning butter, everything else was award-winning."

ment, was able to provide its store customers with the same sort of three-quart jug, while Canada Safeway scrambled to get a three-quart plasticized carton on the market, even though it lost money on the new packaging.

Milk had become a loss-leader in the fight for grocery sales, and the Co-op had to join in the fight since its volume sales had fallen precipitously as soon as the new jugs hit the market. However, just as when the Pure-Pak containers had come out, it would take three to six months for the $40,000 of equipment to be delivered. Like Royal Dairies and the small Selkirk-based dairy, Lakeland, the Co-op had no choice but to have Modern custom bottle three-quart jugs for them. For six months the Co-op had to sell this milk to its store customers for the same price it was paying Modern. Matters did not improve much when the huge new machines were finally installed. Not only did they crowd the plant, but the jugs, while a solution to the

problem of volume sales, cut into revenues. The Co-op found that it was losing 3.3 cents of revenue on one third of its total milk sales by the spring of 1965.

At roughly the same time, the Co-op was informed that all of its Pure-Pak machines had to be converted to the production of plasticized cartons early in 1966. As the patent and leaseholder, Pure-Pak could enforce this decision, even though it increased the Co-op's costs substantially at a time when the creamery could least afford it.

The Co-op was also having a staffing problem. With all of the recent changes in the industry, the increased weight of containers, pressure to hold onto customers and a booming economy, the Co-op could not keep deliverymen. Seven retail routes were taken off and two wholesale routes added, but the Co-op still could not maintain a full roster of drivers. Between April and August, nine drivers quit, one was let go, five gave their notice and two were on sick leave – a critical situation for a company whose deliverymen were a key to getting and keeping customers.

So difficult was 1965, that for the first time in nineteen years, the creamery showed a deficit. In 1966 the creamery deficit rose to $27,000, before being erased the following year. The Co-op's volume sales eventually returned to their 1964 level, but even with improvements between 1967 and 1969

In contrast to the rapid turnover among its drivers, the Co-op's office enjoyed some stability among its staff. Joining Eloise Popiel, Gerry Eremco and Beth Krall in their long tenure were women like Tanya Storgoff, Vera Weremiuk and, seen here, (second row, right) **Ann Kostaniuk** who all worked in the office for many years.

the creamery was less profitable than in the early part of the decade. Far more worrisome, its sales were not growing as quickly as the population of Greater Winnipeg. Still, the situation had stabilized and it must have been a bit rewarding for the Co-op to see Modern lose its exclusive contract with Mini-Mart in 1967. That chain's corporate parent, Westfair Foods (part of George Weston's bakery and grocery empire) had taken a leaf out of Safeway's book by purchasing its own dairy – the old St. Joseph's plant – and bottling jug milk.

Homes on the site of the fuel yard. The land vacated by the fuel yard gave the Co-op the opportunity to build seventeen homes and provide low-cost housing to potential purchasers.

CO-OP HOUSING

There was one bright spot for the Co-op as the 1960s ended. When the fuel yard finally moved in the winter of 1965–66, plans were in place to turn the old yard into a mini-housing subdivision. All the other potential uses of this land had been thoroughly discussed and rejected for one reason or other. One real-estate developer suggested selling the land as a parcel for approximately $35,000. While a sizable gain over the original purchase price, it was decided this was far less than the Co-op would get if it developed the land itself. The idea of building apartment blocks was also appealing, but the construction costs would have forced the Co-op to go into considerable debt – not something it was willing to contemplate in 1966. The Co-op had little trouble attracting seventeen purchasers who could either make their own building arrangements or use the Co-op as the general contractor. Those who did not have the Co-op build the house had to agree to buy their building supplies from the Co-op's lumber yard.

This strategy worked exceedingly well. For the first time in its history, the lumber yard showed a surplus – before bad debt accounts were factored in – largely because of the construction of these houses. The sale of these lots yielded $65,760 – almost double the value of the land as a parcel. Meanwhile the lumber-yard staff gained experience in the contracting business while supervising the construction of eleven homes. Perhaps most importantly, the Co-op had helped provide good and affordable housing in the North End (the homes and land had an average value of $16,500). Moreover, it helped seven families finance their homes by providing long-term mortgages. It had once more combined sound business practices with playing a positive role in the community.

So successful was this endeavour – plus the construction of one other home on Redwood – and so valuable was it to the lumber yard, that in 1968 some of the profit from the land sales was used to purchase building lots on Leila Avenue. Four more homes were built and sold there by the Co-op in 1969, another good year for the lumber yard. Anyone watching the flow of traffic in and out of the lumber yard and its neighbouring Co-op gas pumps and garage, would have had good reason to think that they might be looking at the Co-op's most important ventures for the future.

■ ■ ■

1 PAM, RG 1528, Box 4, File 28, "An Analysis of Store Distribution in the Greater Winnipeg Area," p. 1.

2 Ibid.

3 PCL, Minute Book 2, "Minutes of the Executive Meeting, February 24, 1952."

4 Ibid., "Minutes of the Board of Directors Meeting, August 28, 1952."

In the 1974 Annual Report, Bill Kardash said, "We are living in a period of rapid changes ... We in the People's Co-operative will have to contend with the same issues that face the rest of the working people throughout the country – inflation, unemployment, higher taxes, housing shortage, higher cost of living ... but we know our strength and success lie with the people."

CHAPTER TEN
THE ROLLER COASTER RIDE

A REMARKABLE RECORD

W hen Bill Kardash addressed the crowd of over one thousand assembled at the Winnipeg Auditorium in November of 1970 for a dinner and dance in honour of the Co-op's Forty-Second Anniversary and Manitoba's Centennial, he recounted a proud history of the Co-op's contribution to Manitoba. Its fuel yard, lumber yard, garage and creameries had provided employment to thousands of Manitobans over the years. It had pumped millions upon millions of dollars into both the rural and urban economy through its milk and cream purchases, its wages and its purchases of wood, equipment, trucks and other necessities — even as it paid out over $600,000 in dividends to its shareholders, patrons and cream shippers. The Co-op had also built more than twenty reasonably priced homes in Winnipeg and financed many more over the previous four years. Meanwhile, its 160 current employees were serving twenty thousand home-delivery customers and five

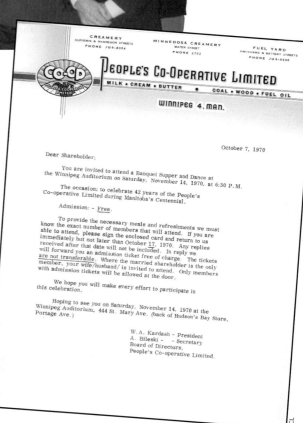

In 1970, Manitobans observed the centennial of their province. The Co-op, acknowledging that event and its own 42nd Anniversary, once again staged a large community celebration.

■ MURPHY DOLA ■

Murphy Dola worked at the Co-op from 1962 until 1993, during which time he was very active in the union, serving as its president for many years. He recalls that there were some years at the Co-op where veteran deliverymen like himself made more than management.

"I was involved with the union for about 25 years. I would have to say that the Co-op did a tremendously good job; they always managed to give us what every other dairy in Winnipeg had gotten for wages. We had better benefits and it was amazing what we got for pensions.

"The union had a mutual-aid sick fund started in the 1960s. The company had to pay into it $1.00 a month per employee. If you were off sick, you had 6 weeks that you could collect. Eloise Popiel and I looked after the sick fund and we were very strict – there were people who missed every Monday. We built that little fund up to $100,000. For a small union to have their own little thing going, it came back to we always had the worker in mind."

NEW CHALLENGES

But Bill Kardash was also a realist. He recognized that for all the obstacles the Co-op had already overcome, the future would be even more difficult. Through numerous resolutions at its shareholders' meetings the Co-op had been an early and vociferous critic of the growing domination of the Canadian economy by the United States. And the Co-op had firsthand experience of this through its long competition with Safeway and its Lucerne Dairy. However, as Kardash knew only too well, earlier in 1970 this competition with a well-heeled US corporation had intensified when Modern Dairies,

PCL

Encouraged by the lumber yard's sales of close to $1 million in 1972 and a net profit that even outdid the creamery branch that year, the Co-op expanded the lumber yard's operation. Seen here is **Tim Kostaniuk**, third generation Co-op employee, who later managed the garage as a full service facility open to the public.

"We got accounts with Brinks and City Bread, Display Fixtures, Canadian News, servicing their fleets of trucks. Individuals could bring their vehicles in as well. I was there for 11 or 12 years. We had a fellow on parts, a shop foreman who would greet customers and line up the work for the mechanics. At one point, we had 5 mechanics working during the day, one in the evening, a night man to keep the place secure. We had a gas bar and a parts counter where do-it-yourselfers could come in and buy parts and accessories for their cars."

hundred small stores with dairy products that continued to win honours at competitions across Canada, while thousands more were being served at its gas pumps and lumber yard. And this was far from the end of the Co-op's accomplishments. It had played a role in numerous public campaigns on behalf of consumers and it had taken public stances on all sorts of issues, ranging from milk subsidies, to world peace, to its recent support for the erection of a statue of Louis Riel to commemorate Manitoba's Centennial. Moreover, it had been a very good citizen of the North End, supporting that community with charitable contributions, jobs and services. It was an enviable record and Kardash was justifiably proud.

with nineteen dairy plants in rural and urban Manitoba, had been bought by Chicago-based conglomerate, Beatrice Foods. Modern would be even tougher to fight now that its corporate pockets contained billions rather than merely millions of dollars.

The growth of supermarkets and convenience store chains had also continued unabated, squeezing even more small stores out of business – stores that were an important part of the Co-op's distribution system. Several new chains such as Pic-a-Pop, Mac's Convenience Stores and the Southland Corporation's 7-Eleven stores were cutting deeper into the independents' dwindling neighbourhood business.

Even in its newest endeavour, the lumber yard and its allied house building program, the Co-op was facing problems. Although the housing subdivision and the project on Leila Avenue had been successes, there were trends that made further such investments questionable. In 1970 six more building lots had been purchased – five in what would become The Maples and one in St. James – but high mortgage rates (now running from 10.5 to 11 percent) and volatile lumber prices made building a risky business.

Internal renewal was another challenge for the Co-op. The general work force had undergone startling transitions from the days of World War Two. There were few long-service employees left by the 1970s, as the first generation were almost all retired, while the majority of employees hired during the 1950s and 1960s had tended to move on to other jobs fairly quickly. The same, however, could not be said for the managers, the Board of Directors or the shareholders of the Co-op. On the one hand, this provided stability to the Co-op and ensured a continuation of its traditions of political, social and economic activism. On the other hand, it meant that the Co-op was facing the future with a leadership that was, on average, more than sixty years old, and an aging shareholder base.

Kardash had called for an infusion of young blood into the management and Board many times during the 1960s. Younger men such as Nick Ursuliak, Mike Yakimchuck and John Sas were hired and groomed for future leadership roles, in the early 1960s.

However, it was getting harder to find talented and committed young people within the left-wing Ukrainian Canadian community than it had been during the 1930s and 1940s.

Part of this was due to the Cold War, which had scared many of the younger generation away from the left, while the events of 1956 in Hungary and 1967 in Czechoslovakia caused many to leave the various left-wing organizations from which the Co-

■ **PETER STASTOOK** ■

Peter Stastook worked in the plant at the Co-op, beginning as a butter printer and finishing as the plant supervisor. During his 42 years there, he won many awards for his butter and ice cream. He was proud of the way the staff pitched into to ensure the high quality of product and the cleanliness of the plant.

"We were all like one. In the last year that I was there, when I was supervising, we cleaned up our plant. And we were the tops in Canada. The government inspectors go by rating, by points. We were top-rated in Manitoba and then throughout Canada. In their spare time the employees were willing to clean up and paint the whole plant. It was the 'Tidiest Small Plant in Canada.'"

COURTESY PETER STASTOOK

op had traditionally drawn its leaders. But, there was another trend that also limited the old Ukrainian left's ability to attract younger members.

The growth of radicalism so often associated with the 1960s, which might have been expected to revitalize the Ukrainian left, actually had the reverse effect. During the 1930s, 1940s and 1950s the choices for those who thought capitalism inhumane came down to the social democracy of the CCF or the Marxism of the Communist Party. But the rise and fragmentation of the New Left after 1956 opened many alternatives to those on the political left. With these options, the baby-boom generation of radicals was far less likely to align itself with the old left, of which the Co-op was still a very proud part.

There was a certain irony to this, for rereading

the resolutions of the Co-op's general membership meetings of the 1940s, 1950s and 1960s, and comparing them to the concerns of the New Left in the 1960s and early 1970s, it would be easy to conclude that the new generation of radicals borrowed their program from the People's Co-op. Canadian economic nationalism, a distaste for American foreign policy – particularly in regards to Vietnam, trade with China, the Soviet Union and Cuba – concern about multinationals, demands for an end to nuclear proliferation, support for an independent Canadian foreign policy, support for Canada's aboriginal peoples and calls for a much more active welfare state, all became common to most parts of the New Left and were even incorporated into the policies of Liberal administrations during the late 1960s and early 1970s.

However, having the New Left and even Prime Minister Pierre Trudeau catch up to the Co-op in many of its concerns did not help the Co-op rebuild its leadership. The increasingly frequent illnesses, retirements and deaths of long-time managers such as John Miller, John Fedirchyk, Saul Simkin, Ernie Krall and Andrew Bileski was a cause of great concern to Kardash and the Board even though the Co-op had been able to attract some talented people. Kosty Kostaniuk, for example, the director of the 1948 fundraising and building campaign, was recruited to the Co-op after a twenty-one-year absence, as was Harry Stefaniuk from the WBA, while several employees of long-standing such as Peter Stastook were promoted into management ranks during the late 1960s and 1970s. But, while these individuals were valuable, none of them was young, so the leadership crisis was postponed, not done away with.

Motorists going to and from work via Arlington or McPhillips could easily swing by the Co-op grounds to "fill 'er up" and save on each tank of gas. The Co-op's price was often the lowest in the city, which the Board felt was the best way for "savings to be passed on to the consumers." (PCL, Annual Reports, May 2, 1977)

KEEPING PACE WITH CHANGE

The Co-op's leadership might have been aging, but its commitment to keeping the Co-op successful was as strong as ever. In the creamery each new technological change was studied and, if deemed worthwhile, adopted. For instance, while the Co-op had not rushed into the production of yet another new form of packaging, the plastic pouch, when Silverwoods introduced it to the Winnipeg market, once its value was firmly established the Co-op bought the equipment to keep up with the competition. And, despite some ongoing problems with the lumber yard, the Board of Directors decided in 1973 to expand these facilities, followed by a further $100,000 expansion in 1978. The Co-op's gas pump service was expanded in the early 1970s as part of a broader plan to allow the garage to service the Co-op's fleet, other truck fleets and the general public. This plan was fully realized in the early 1980s, by which time the Co-op offered automotive services of every description, including the sale of diesel and propane.

New opportunities were always being studied. Proposals to distribute Cheemo brand perogies and Kefir – a Ukrainian health food – were discussed several times during the 1970s and several parcels of land were examined as sites for a new Co-op housing subdivision, including a thirty-seven-acre parcel north of Grassie Boulevard. But this interest in the new was balanced by careful attention to the Co-op's largest business, the dairy. Although its Winnipeg store sales diminished throughout the

1960s and 1970s because of the closing of small stores, this was balanced by a resurgence in home delivery and the further development of out-of-town routes. In 1973 the Co-op had forty-six home-delivery routes in Winnipeg, six store truck routes and six country routes which served small stores and consumers' co-ops in Beausejour, Morris, Stonewall, Riverton, Vita, Pine Falls, Pinawa and the districts surrounding these towns. It also had three ice-cream trucks on the road, three special-delivery trucks and four separate summer beach routes. From Minnedosa the Co-op distributed products to fifteen towns in the surrounding region. Clearly the Co-op had established some fairly valuable niche markets in rural Manitoba.

This all indicated a management team still very much at the top of its form, and the Co-op's financial picture reflected this. Surpluses in the 1970s kept on hitting new records: the Co-op's "best year ever" of 1970 – with a surplus before taxes of $286,285 – was surpassed in each of the next five years. Rather wisely, given the inflation rate, not only were the appropriate depreciation reserves made, and patronage and shareholder dividends increased, but the Co-op's statutory reserves were also upped so that costly new equipment could be purchased without borrowing money at rapidly rising bank rates. In fact, the interest earned on monies set aside for statutory reserves, depreciation and a Milk Control Board bond (which guaranteed payment of one month's worth of milk shipments in case of bankruptcy and to cover member deposits) would become an important source of funds during lean times.

THE GOOD TIMES END

Ironically, it was a federal milk subsidy program that brought the Co-op's wave of prosperity to an end – at least indirectly. Late in 1973, the federal government had decided to grant a five cent per quart subsidy on milk as part of its effort to stem inflation. The Co-op, which had been calling for a restoration of milk subsidies since 1946, was enthusiastic and

distributed twelve thousand fliers announcing the subsidy, noting that the government had finally caught up to the Co-op. And even though this subsidy was split up by the Milk Control Board of Manitoba in a fashion disadvantageous to milk processors, it did encourage consumers to buy more milk, which fell in price by three cents per quart.

There was a fatal flaw to this program though: there could be no milk price increases for the life of the subsidy. All increases in labour and delivery costs would have to be

> TO ALL CO-OP CUSTOMERS
> MILK SUBSIDY AT LAST!
>
> As a milk consumer you are entitled to know the position of People's Co-operative Ltd. on the Federal Consumer Subsidy on milk.
>
> On Sept. 4, 1973 the announcement was made in the House of Commons of a 5¢ a quart consumer subsidy. It was to roll back the price and hold the price for 1 year. It was clearly declared as a consumer subsidy.
>
> A week later, after waiting for action from government bodies, People's Co-operative Ltd. issued a PRESS RELEASE.
>
> In it we: * repeated our stand favoring a milk subsidy over the past many years;
> * welcomed the federal policy of a consumer subsidy on milk;
> * offered our co-operation for its implementation;
> * indicated it meant an annual saving of $5-$6 million to the consumers of Manitoba and an addition of $5-$6 million to Manitoba's economy from the Federal treasury;
> * asked why the delay – who was stalling. Each day that passed meant a loss of $15,000 to consumers.
>
> The PRESS RELEASE met with a conspiracy of silence – total black out – on the part of the news media. Apparently a price reduction on milk was not newsworthy.
>
> Last week, Sept. 26, in our submission to the Milk Control Board at a public hearing we proposed a roll back of 4¢ to the consumer with 1¢ going to meet the commitment made by the Milk Control Board Aug. 8/73, allowing a further increase in the price of milk to the producers and a portion to the processors to cover, in part, the increased cost of raw milk.
>
> We urged that any increase in the costs of production and/or processing be met by a further increase in subsidy from the Federal treasury -- in addition to the 5¢ a quart. Such cost increases should be reviewed periodically by all the parties concerned.
>
> Proposals submitted by others at the public hearing ranged from the entire subsidy being given to the producers, no reduction in price to the consumer, to a partial subsidy to producers and processors.
>
> Ours was the only proposal that called for a consumer reduction of the price of milk.
>
> The decision announced last Saturday Sept. 29 comes close to the proposals of People's Co-operative. The price is reduced by 3¢ a quart. Of the other 2¢ subsidy, 1¼¢ goes to the producers and ¾¢ a quart will go to the processors.
>
> As a consumer we hope you will agree with the position we have taken.
>
> Your support is appreciated and we thank you for your continued patronage.
>
> PEOPLE'S CO-OPERATIVE LIMITED
>
> P.S. If you want a copy of our PRESS RELEASE or submission to the public hearing, please leave your name and address with your milkman or write us.

Flyer on 1973 subsidy. When the subsidy ended in 1974 and inflation pushed milk prices to astronomical heights, the Co-op's submission to the Milk Control Board argued "that a portion of monies spent unnecessarily or wasted on military projects could adequately cover the costs of the milk subsidy." As an alternative, it proposed, yet again, "to make the milk industry a wholly public utility." (PCL, Co-op Submission to the MCB, May, 1975)

absorbed by the dairies and increases in the milk producers' costs would have to be borne by the farmers. In a period of profound inflation such as the early 1970s, it was inevitable that these costs would rise dramatically, setting the stage for a disaster in the milk industry.

When the federal government announced that it was not going to extend the subsidy past September 30, 1974, it was obvious that milk prices would sky-rocket to cover both the value of the subsidy and the increased costs of milk production. At hearings conducted by the MCB in August of 1974, the milk producers requested an increase of ten cents per quart, while most Winnipeg dairies asked for an additional 3.13 cents per quart. Adding in the loss of the five-cent subsidy, Winnipeg's consumers faced a potential price jump of eighteen cents per quart, a 50 percent increase over the prevailing store price of thir-ty-seven cents.

The Co-op did not take part in the joint presentation of the other dairies. It argued that the federal and provin-cial governments should implement a national pro-gram of milk subsidies which would assure producers and processors a fair return while keeping milk at affordable levels. In addition, it called for a free milk program in elementary schools and heavily subsidized milk for school children in senior grades. Unfortunately, neither the Co-op's presentation, nor that of Anne Ross of the Mount Carmel Clinic or any of the other consumers groups who called for keeping the subsidy program, had any impact.

Given the circumstances, the MCB had no choice but to increase milk prices. On October 1 the price rose by seven cents per quart while another four-cent increase was phased in over the next few

Orest Kowalewich (centre) played a leading role in the cultural life of Winnipeg's Russian and Ukrainian commu-nities before coming to the Co-op in 1964. Over the next seventeen years, Kowalewich worked as a milkman, engi-neer then plant manager. His innovative procedures suc-cessfully steered the plant through major technological changes.

months. However, production costs were rising so rapidly that another three-cent increase had to be implemented in September of 1975 – which still did not come close to matching costs. But there was only so much that consumers could handle in a short period of time. A fourteen cent per quart increase, or 38 percent, in just under a year was high even by the standards of the 1970s, and as might have been expected, milk consumption dropped.

The Co-op's sales fell throughout late 1974 and 1975 – a problem that was compounded by a rash of small store closures. As a result, the Co-op had to take seven routes off in the sum-mer of 1975. As Kardash had pointed out to the MCB in May 1975, the Co-op would not be able to carry on much longer without sub-stantial price increases. Unlike its competitors, he said, "We have no concen-tration of wealth to back us up, nor can we fall back on a national or multi-national structure in case of need."[1] Reluctant to call for higher consumer prices, Kardash argued, to no avail, for gov-ernment subsidies.

By 1976 the creamery was showing a sizable deficit and most of the Co-op's operating surplus came from its investments in bonds and mortgages, and from – of all places – the lumber yard. Nor did matters improve much in1977, particularly as the Co-op had to start reconfiguring its plant and equipment to prepare itself for Canada's switch to the metric sys-tem in the spring of 1978. This changeover cost the Co-op almost a quarter of a million dollars and increased its labour costs on each unit of milk by approximately 12 percent.

With high rates of inflation, a diminishing base of corner stores to sell its products (approximately 50 percent of these stores went out of business between the 1960s and 1978) and a frightening fall in home-delivery customers (in 1978 Kardash estimated the Co-op's home-delivery service reached only slightly over twelve thousand households, a decrease of eight thousand since 1970) the Co-op, or at least its biggest branch, was in serious trouble as the decade drew to a close. Reorganizing its operations could only help so much. Switching all butter production to Minnedosa, making the Winnipeg plant more efficient and upping the load on each delivery vehicle were of assistance, but such measures could not reverse the downward trend.

The Co-op's policy of carefully husbanding its resources during the good years allowed it to avoid incurring any major debts when the times got lean. Even after all of the bad years of the late 1970s, it could report to the shareholders in 1980 that the People's Co-op was in good financial shape. The value of its assets continued to rise and the share capital and deposit accounts were well protected by physical assets and investments – certainly not a claim that could have been made at any time in the 1930s, 1940s or even the 1950s.

It was, however, an inescapable fact that the Co-op's core business, the creamery, was in decline. Despite relentless campaigning to recruit home-delivery customers and determined efforts to retain store and restaurant customers with rebates, a strong commitment to service (including providing dairy cases, freezers and milk dispensers at cost) and excellent products, the customer base was diminishing. On many products, such as ice cream, the Co-op could not compete against much larger plants, which had economies of scale and the newest equipment on their side. More to the point, the Co-op could not compete with the loss-leader marketing strategies of the new "superstores."

The vast new Safeways, Economarts, Food Barns and SuperValus and even some gigantic IGAs, which came into existence during the late 1970s and 1980s, were engaged in a brutal price war in which the main weapon was the loss-leader. When ice cream and other non-controlled dairy products became part of the loss-leader arsenal, the Co-op could not keep its market share. Its plant, while often expanded, reorganized and updated, was small by the standards of its competitors – including not only Beatrice, Lucerne, and Silverwoods, but also the greatly expanded and renamed Manitoba Dairy and Poultry Co-operative, Manco. Despite being able to use surpluses from its other operations to subsidize the creamery, any more dramatic changes in the market would probably sound the death knell of the Co-op's dairy operation.

But change, if nothing else, is inevitable. Manitoba's Conservative government, very much committed to the free market, set the stage to completely change the structure of control over milk prices when it passed the Milk Prices Review Act in July of 1980. Under authority of this Act, the new Manitoba Milk Prices Review Commission (MPRC) ruled that as of January 1, 1981 price control at the consumer level would be done away with and that for a one-year trial period, "retail prices are to be established by the market place."[2]

A NEW MILK PRICE WAR

This was the worst news the Co-op could have received. The economy was entering a profound recession, which would see unemployment rates skyrocket and consumer buying power plummet. Most people would have to get the best deals possible on every product, including essential foodstuffs such as milk. This meant that the already cutthroat competition between Winnipeg's grocery chains would further intensify. Now, however, the big stores could add milk to their list of loss-leaders to get consumers into their stores – and this would prove to be a very attractive draw, as milk was one of the most standard items on the family shopping list.

Canned or dry goods could often be bought in bulk when the goods were on sale. Indeed, with the increased use of freezers in middle-class and even working-class homes, meat, bread and some vegetables could also be stored in this way. But milk and a handful of other perishable products had to be bought and consumed quickly. It made sense for the larger stores to lose money on milk in order to attract as many customers as possible.

This strategy threatened to destroy any company whose sole or primary business was the dairy trade

◾ KOSTY KOSTANIUK ◾

When **Constantine (Kosty) Kostaniuk** came to Winnipeg from Sudbury in 1934, fresh out of high school, one of the first things he did was to take courses in accounting and business practice. Thirty-five years later, he applied those skills when he became the Co-op bookkeeper, and eventually its general manager in 1983. In the intervening years, he served overseas in World War II, married, raised three children, attended the Khaki College for returning veterans in London and the University of Manitoba and worked as a journalist.

The son of Myron Kostaniuk, he grew up in the ULFTA, serving as a teacher of Ukrainian language and music and director of choirs and orchestras in several provinces during the 1930s. He went on to work for the Workers Benevolent Association, and then worked as a journalist at the *Ukrainian Word*, both of which were housed in the Ukrainian Labour Temple. He and his wife, Ann, who, for twenty-five years, worked at the Co-op a few blocks away, could often be seen on McGregor Street, walking together to and from their respective places of work.

After retirement from the Co-op in 1985, Kostaniuk remained on the Board of Directors and then became the driving force within the Wind-up Committee formed after the sale of the Co-op to its employees. He participated in Veterans Against Nuclear Arms (VANA), and supported many other activities aimed at peace and social justice. He continued to write, research and speak, and despite the loss of an eye, continued playing in the Winnipeg Mandolin Orchestra and the Mandolin Quintet, and singing in the senior citizens' choir at the Ukrainian Labour Temple.

"The whole idea of the Co-op was to make people realize the significance of co-operation. If you want to co-operate, then you'll begin to listen to somebody else because you can't co-operate without listening. When you listen, you begin to get the opinions of others and you begin to have consensus on how to work together. This whole feeling was part of the ideology that the system needs to be changed and the co-ops can play a role in helping people to get that sense of importance that they can make change, and change for the good."

COURTESY C. KOSTANIUK

– unless it had huge volume sales, an exclusive contract with a major chain, or the money to survive prolonged losses. As the Co-op had none of these, it was unlikely to survive a lengthy milk price war.

As usual though, no matter how uneven the fight might be, the Co-op was not prepared to roll over and accept defeat. Since protests to the MPRC about the "unfair trade practices" were ignored the Co-op had to fight for market share in any way it could. In this case it increased rebates to its wholesale customers and tried to increase the home-delivery trade.

Volume-based rebates to the Co-op's wholesale customers, which had ranged up to 8 percent in the late 1970s, rose sharply. By 1983 store rebates ranged from 5 to 20 percent – with additional per litre discounts for consumer co-ops. Despite rebates, though, milk still cost more in the small stores, so they continued losing sales. With store sales falling, and becoming a money-losing proposition, the Co-op tried hard to recruit new home-delivery customers.

Focusing on new housing subdivisions where there were plenty of small children – and a market for the costlier but convenient home-delivery service – the Co-op had some success. Considerable effort was made to service the "shut-in" market of older customers, including those in senior citizen's homes, who needed home-delivery service. And, taking a leaf from the book of Minnedosa's manager John Wityshyn, the Co-op also began selling a broader array of frozen foods – anything to increase its overall sales volume.

But, no matter how hard sales manager John Sas scrambled and wheeled and dealed with wholesale clients or how diligently creamery manager Kosty Kostaniuk worked to reduce production and delivery costs, the creamery was in critical condition. Lost volume, high rebates (which in 1981 cost the creamery almost half-a-million dollars) and prices that could not meet costs, combined to cause an operating loss of $162,265 in 1981. And even though the Co-op's "other income" – primarily from investments – allowed it to show a small net surplus on its overall operations, matters were degenerating quickly.

DESPERATE TIMES

—————— ■ ——————

Drastic action was now necessary. The Co-op announced that for the first time in thirty years no patronage dividends would be paid. In June of 1982 a plan was developed to put the creamery on a four-day workweek. This would cut labour costs by 20 percent and provide some savings in operating costs. Nor was this to be carried out at the employees' expense, as the Co-op applied to the Unemployment Insurance Commission (UIC) for a special work-sharing arrangement whereby its workers would qualify for a one day per week UIC benefit to help counterbalance lost wages.

This arrangement was put in place and was then extended from its original "temporary" status to a much longer-term arrangement. UIC's contribution to the plan was extended well into 1983 and, even after this assistance ran out, the four-day workweek in the plant, the office and delivery departments became standard. This was partially compensated for by higher percentage wage increases for those working at the creamery than in the Co-op's other departments over the next few years, but no matter how humanely enacted, the four-day week was a sign of the Co-op's growing desperation, as were its other moves. Delivery routes were consolidated, positions were left unfilled and early retirements were encouraged. When Kosty Kostaniuk took over as general manager at the beginning of 1983 his former job as creamery manager was eliminated.

There were no easy solutions to the Co-op's dilemma. The downturn in the economy and the price wars were even driving large stores out of business. Dominion Stores left the Winnipeg market, the smaller Loblaws stores were replaced by the SuperValus, but most shocking and disheartening to those in the co-operative movement was the October 1982 announcement that the Red River Co-op's shopping centres were closing. The economic downturn also hurt the Co-op's building supply and garage businesses. In 1982 these two branches suffered mounting losses, while the operating losses of all branches now amounted to $216,012. Income from various investments barely covered these losses. Amazingly, on sales of over

$13 million a year, the Co-op had an after-tax income of only $20,000. As a result, not only were no patronage dividends declared and no funds put into statutory reserves, but the Board had to dip into reserves to make a small shareholder dividend available.

The last thing that the Co-op needed at this point were any sudden losses, such as a customer bankruptcy. This, however, was one of the hazards of being in almost any business during the early 1980s, and the Co-op was not immune to the losses it had to accept as an unsecured creditor. It tried to stay on top of its various accounts, but because all its operations granted credit to customers, it was inevitable that some had to be written off as bad debts. Throughout the 1970s and 1980s the Co-op's records are littered with the dry legal notices which represent the failure of a growing number of small businesses (and their owners' dreams) and of the Co-op's attempts to recover some of its investment. However, as accustomed as the Co-op was to business failures, nothing could prepare it for a truly staggering loss in 1983.

THE NORSEMAN AFFAIR

—————— ■ ——————

With the decrease in Winnipeg home-building during the early 1980s, the managers of the Co-op's lumber yard looked long and hard for new places to sell lumber and hardware. And they soon found an area where the demand for building supplies was growing — the north. With the federal government finally providing some much-needed money for native bands to improve reserve housing, there was a strong northern demand for building supplies. It seemed wise to get in on this trade, particularly since payment would be backed by "irrevocable band council resolutions," a more secure form of financing than that offered by most contractors.

As it turned out though, the lumber yard manager dealt not with the band councils, but with an intermediary, Norseman Enterprises. Although no one at the Co-op knew it, this company was over-extended and had been facing financial problems for a number of years when it signed its first contract

School children (above and right) check the Co-op's display at the Manitoba Dairy Centennial, 1985, and seem pleased to receive plant-workers' caps and, of course, ice cream.

with the Co-op. The lumber yard manager extended credit to Norseman without the guaranteed contracts that Kardash and Kostaniuk had assumed were be the basis of these sales. It was a complete surprise to the Co-op's senior managers when Norseman applied for bankruptcy protection. Surprise turned to shock when they were told that unless Norseman's unsecured creditors did not accept a repayment schedule of fifty cents on the dollar the company would suspend all operations and would only be able to pay pennies on each dollar of unsecured debt. Norseman owed the Co-op a total of $517,944, leaving the Co-op with the dubious distinction of being the largest unsecured creditor.

At best, the Co-op would lose over a quarter million dollars if it accepted the proposal. At worst, it could lose almost the entire amount and what had become one of its biggest sources of lumber sales, if it forced Norseman out of business. Reluctantly, the deal was accepted, and the Co-op agreed to five payments of slightly over $50,000 spread over two years. The final payment would not come until 1990, but, on the positive side, the Co-op did keep its

northern lumber business and shipped over a million dollars of lumber through Norseman beginning as early as December of 1983. This time the new lumber yard manager made sure the Co-op got its payment up front!

This loss, along with the other problems of the early 1980s, probably should have made the Co-op consider closing while it still had some equity. The creamery was still on a reduced workweek, was spending ever more on rebates and was still engaged in a ruinous price war it could never win. The lumber yard was not likely to show anything but a large deficit, and the garage branch was suffering because of the general economic malaise. So when Bill Kardash retired at the beginning of 1983 after thirty-five years as general manager, it was the end of an era. Perhaps then, a natural break point had arrived after fifty-five years of operation.

This, however, was not the view of Kardash's successor, Kosty Kostaniuk. Already past the usual retirement age of sixty-five, Kostaniuk was not ready to call it a day either for himself or the Co-op. There were, after all, still almost 150 people who relied upon the Co-op for their livelihoods and

thousands more who still had faith in it as an institution. Moreover, if the Co-op shut down, who would be left to counterbalance or to protest the dire impact of multinationals in the Winnipeg milk trade? Thus, the Co-op would soldier on, hoping as always for better days – or at least a stay of execution.

THE TURNAROUND

When it came, the Co-op's reprieve arrived in the guise of yet another crisis. The Milk Prices Review Commission announced early in 1984 that it would grant an increase of 4.67 cents per litre in the price paid to milk producers, effective February 20. The reaction of the large dairies and chain stores to this news was interesting: they declared an informal truce in the milk price war and suddenly allowed the price of milk to rise dramatically. By February 27 the price of milk in most Winnipeg supermarkets had risen by ten cents per litre, while prices at convenience stores rose by as much as eighteen cents per litre, and rural areas saw increases of up to twenty cents per litre. These dramatic increases, and the intimation that there might be some price col-

lusion behind it, forced the provincial government's hand. This time, however, it was a New Democratic Party government that responded to the crisis.

Within two days of the February 27 price hike, a new agency, the Manitoba Fluid Milk Commission, was established by order-in-council and charged with regulating milk prices at the wholesale level. One week later, this new agency rolled back maximum wholesale prices, and the MPRC reduced maximum retail prices. Studies were commissioned to examine the rebating systems for the express purpose of modifying those practices. On June 14, 1984, minimum price levels were re-established. In short, milk price control had returned, which helped Manitoba-owned dairies like the Co-op, Manco and Lakeland to stay in business.

For the Co-op the turnaround was almost miraculous. Creamery sales picked up, rebate levels fell and there was some hope that the creamery would go back to a five-day week. Business improved at the lumber yard, and once again there was talk of expanding it. With the overall position of the Co-op improving so quickly, patronage dividends were re-instituted early in 1985. Employees and former employees were also rewarded. For the financial year 1984 employees were granted a bonus equal to 3 percent of their salary (a third of which went into their pension funds), while retirees had $58,000 added to their cheques.

Campaigns in the mid-1980s brought in hundreds of new customers at a time. With the spread between home delivery and store prices greatly reduced because of government control, many consumers went back to the convenience of home delivery. The surviving small stores increased their volume sales now that their prices were much closer to the big stores. Finally, the recession of the early 1980s was lifting, which allowed the lumber yard, Minnedosa and garage departments to do

■ MIKE GIDORA ■

Mike Gidora, the Co-op's last general manager, grew up in a politically active family in the working-class community of New Westminster, British Columbia. As a child he participated in peace marches during the late 1950s when Cold War passions ran at their highest. After serving as the head of the Young Communist League, Gidora moved to Winnipeg in the early 1980s where, during the deep recession of that time, he organized unemployed workers and ran for Winnipeg City Council. Given his background and political experience it was not surprising he would end up working at the Co-op, eventually becoming its manager in the mid-1980s. He continued with the dairy after it was sold to the workers, leaving it in 1994 to work on a short-lived community newspaper. In 1995 Gidora returned to the west coast, where his work for the Victoria Cool Aid Society contributed to the development of low-cost housing in that community. Tragically, he was struck down by cancer in the summer of 1999 at the age of 46.

time when the institution was in the best financial condition of its almost sixty-year history. More to the point, he would be passing over direct management of an enterprise that was once again growing and was totally re-invigorated.

NEW LEADERSHIP

Transitions are rarely simple, and hardly ever completely popular. Thus, it is not too surprising that when Mike Gidora was appointed as the new general manager of the Co-op after only a year and a half on staff, there were some who were less than pleased to see this thirty-something political activist, who was originally from the west coast (not the North End!) leapfrog several internal candidates for the top job. However, it was a part of the Co-op's tradition that leadership should pass to a prominent and hopefully talented member of the left-wing community, a tradition begun with the

increasing volumes of business.

For the financial year 1985 the Co-op's operations generated a surplus of almost half-a-million dollars. Everyone, from employees to home-delivery customers, was rewarded: customers with patronage dividends of over a quarter-of-a-million dollars and the employees with another salary bonus of 3 percent. And a sizable contribution was made to the statutory reserve fund for the first time in several years. Truly an impressive turnaround.

When Kosty Kostaniuk announced his intention to retire at the beginning of 1986, he could do so with a feeling of considerable satisfaction. In his brief tenure he had helped the Co-op to weather some very difficult circumstances and he would be turning the Co-op over to a new generation of leaders at a

Employees and their families enjoyed fun and games at their picnic at the Workers Benevolent Association camp at Husavick in 1988.

appointment of Kolisnyk and maintained through the years by Bileski, Kardash and Kostaniuk. So Gidora, as the Labour Election Committee's candidate for Joe Zuken's old City Council seat, and a rising star within the Communist Party, was not all that unusual a choice. However, that was small consolation to some of those who now worked at the Co-op, especially among those who were less politically committed than the employees of the 1930s and 1940s (which meant the majority of the Co-op's workers in the mid 1980s).

The transition from the older generation to the new was eased by the presence of Kardash, Kostaniuk and Bileski on the Board of Directors and by their support for Gidora. Other changes in the Co-op's management, owing to retirements and the sudden death of the new lumber-yard manager, were not as devastating as might have been feared. Peter Stastook's retirement as plant supervisor saw Stephen Krall promoted to the job – the third generation of his family to hold that position. The garage department was being managed by Tim Kostaniuk, another third generation employee to serve the Co-op. Considerable continuity was provided by Harry Stefaniuk, who now held the recently reinstated position of creamery manager, while Eloise Popiel, who by 1986 had been working for the Co-op for the staggering total of fifty-four years, was showing no signs of retiring. Thus, there was a remarkable degree of continuity that balanced the arrival of a new generation of Co-op managers in the mid-1980s.

The energy of these younger managers, along with a much healthier economy and government control over the dairy industry, combined to produce an extremely positive situation for the Co-op. Its public garage service was again expanded in 1986, while the creamery received some much needed new equipment and a renewal of the delivery fleet. In all, $420,000 was put into capital expenditures in 1986, and all signs pointed to continuing increases in Co-op sales. The Co-op's gains in volume sales surpassed the dairy industry average in 1984 and 1985, and rose again in 1986. The financial report showed sales increases of 6 to 10 percent in every branch over the previous banner year, while fall campaigns were bringing in over one thousand new customers at a time – particularly important given that by the mid-1980s the Co-op was once again selling over half of its creamery products via home delivery. Once again, the Co-op's prosperity

was shared not only with its shareholders and patrons, but also with its workers, who received a bonus equal to 5 percent of their annual wage.

For the Co-op to continue to prosper Gidora and the Board knew that any attempt to deregulate the dairy industry had to be fought. This was not a self-serving position, because regulation had not only stabilized milk prices and preserved jobs, but provided Manitobans with some of the lowest milk prices in Canada. Far from making milk more expensive as some critics had predicted in 1984, the regulation of milk prices and rebating practices had produced the effect which the Co-op had always predicted: more people could get their milk at a reasonable cost – whether or not they had a car to get to one of the superstores; shut-ins and single-parent families, especially in the core area where there were no huge supermarkets, could afford to have milk delivered or to buy it at local stores; more small stores and small creameries could stay in business, saving hundreds of jobs; and, best of all, Manitoba's overall consumption of milk was on the rise, which was good for every part of the dairy industry and for the health of the province's population.

Gidora and representatives from Manco reiterated these points in presentations to the Legislature's Standing Committee on Agriculture and other bodies involved in regulating the milk industry. But change was inevitable, and by 1988 pressure was mounting on the provincial government to deregulate the dairy industry, as was being done with many other industries across North America. In Manitoba, the stage was set for de-control when the provincial Conservatives defeated the NDP in the May 1988 election.

Gidora and the Co-op's management team had continued building the lumber and garage businesses in the latter half of the 1980s and had worked to increase the creamery's sales volume. But business was increasingly expensive: replacing a Pure-Pak machine cost $139,700US in 1988; new pasteurization and clean-in-place systems cost $165,000; and renewing the fleet of trucks was a huge expense. Even more worrisome was the introduction of new forms of rebating within the dairy industry. As Gidora pointed out to the Milk Prices Review Commission early in 1989, there was a marked

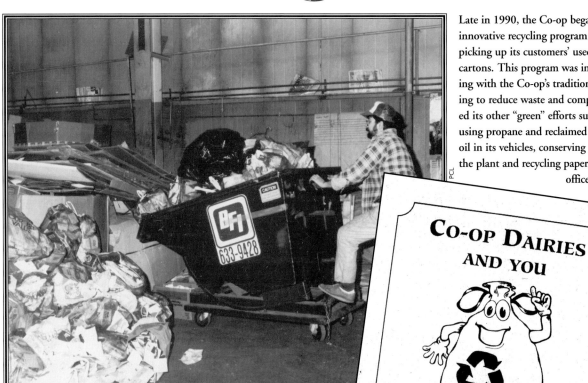

Late in 1990, the Co-op began an innovative recycling program by picking up its customers' used milk cartons. This program was in keeping with the Co-op's tradition of trying to reduce waste and complemented its other "green" efforts such as using propane and reclaimed motor oil in its vehicles, conserving water in the plant and recycling paper in the office.

CO-OP DAIRIES AND YOU

TOGETHER WE RECYCLE

trend towards rebate increases on unregulated dairy products, that is, on everything other than milk. As well, the provision of refrigeration and freezer units to stores at or below cost, in order to keep the store tied to one creamery, was an increasingly common practice. Gidora argued that both practices were linked to the regulated milk trade, as larger dairies were willing to lose money on by-products and the provision of refrigeration equipment in order to pressure store owners to handle only their milk. He admitted that the Co-op had been forced to follow such practices to stay in business, but he argued that the MPRC should ban them for the good of all dairies, especially the smaller ones.

However Gidora's argument met with an unsympathetic reception. In fact, the reason he was addressing the MPRC was to respond to their proposal to eliminate key portions of the existing regulations. In this proposal, limits on volume discounts would be discarded, minimum retail prices would be scrapped, and the MPRC-set prices that dairies charged to independent jobbers for milk they resold on home-delivery routes were also to be done away with.

This last category was important, not because it had independent jobbers but because these independents were becoming the Co-op's major competition in the home-delivery trade. From the 1970s onwards, dairies had been transforming their driver/salesmen into independent contractors. The savings to a dairy using such a system were considerable, as it eliminated the purchase and maintenance costs of delivery vehicles, and saved on UIC, CPP, pension plan and other employer contributions to a worker's compensation package. The Co-op had been an outspoken critic of such systems since the 1950s when one dairy had tried to introduce the independent jobber plan to Winnipeg, because they provided less security for the work force. If the various milk plants associated with the Modern/Beatrice chain could now provide their jobbers with

Music instruction
undergoes
metamorphosis/41

TEMPO /Food

DAVE JOHNSON/WINNIPEG FREE PRESS

Creme de la Creme

City firm's cream cheese sets national standard

By Alice Krueger

FORMER WINNIPEGGERS seldom, if ever, admit to missing anything about this city once they've moved away, except for certain foods, it seems.

Regardless of how green their new pastures are elsewhere, some people have difficulty weaning themselves from certain uniquely Winnipeg-style foods.

Some of these expatriots are easily recognized when they pay a return visit. They're the ones at the airport boarding flights for home with shopping bags stuffed full of bread, buns, sausages and other assorted foods.

Tulips in February may be heaven, but they're not enough to erase memories of Gunn's bagels, City rye bread, Winnipeg Old Country sausage or Co-op cream cheese.

Those who can't get back here often enough to load up on their own have been known to call or write letters to place special orders — even when the cost of shipping the special cargo far exceeds the value of the food product itself.

Just ask Mike Gidora.

The general manager of People's Co-operative Ltd. says hardly a month goes by when the north-end dairy doesn't hear from some former Winnipegger somewhere who has succumbed to the memories of cheesecake, Winnipeg-style.

That's not just any old cheesecake. We're talking here about the ultimate indulgence, made with what cheesecake fanciers insist is the smoothest and creamiest cream cheese to be found anywhere — Co-op brand, of course.

Sometimes, the orders are for as few as four packages — enough for one decent-size cheesecake — to whole cartons of the stuff.

"This summer I had to send 220 pounds of it for a big party in Vancouver," Gidora said.

Calls at Passover

"I'm not really sure what the occasion was, but somebody was having a big party."

Passover usually brings at least a couple of long-distance phone calls to Gidora's office.

"I sent four of these to Saskatoon," he said, holding up one of the 250-gram foil-covered packages.

"It was for Passover and somebody just wanted enough for a cheesecake, so I put it on Greyhound."

Another former Winnipegger, this one in London, Ont., was even more desperate.

"They wanted four pounds for a special occasion; they were willing to pay the air freight which was about $40," Gidora recalled, shaking his head in disbelief.

"Winnipeggers are really loyal when they are former Winnipeggers."

Then there was the elderly woman who called Gidora just a couple of weeks ago. She had just returned to take up residence in Winnipeg after more than 40 years away.

"She said, 'Are you the people who make the cream cheese, and if so, where can I buy it?'

"I find it incredible that she would remember after that long.

"She couldn't get out, so we delivered it to her door. Anybody who goes to that trouble, we'll make sure a milkman gets it to them."

Gidora said the special orders from outside Manitoba keep coming despite the fact that Co-op cream cheese has become available in just about every major Canadian city in the past year.

"Not in a big way, but we're in specialty, upscale shops. In most major centres now we can tell people where they can get it."

Even in Winnipeg, the much-sought-after product is found only in small delis or

independent food stores such as IGA and selected Food Fare outlets, and Gidora admits some retailers still refuse to list it because of the co-op's Communist connections. William Kardash, 77, a one-time Communist member of the Manitoba Legislature, still serves as president of People's board.

Gidora said the dairy co-op decided to go after markets outside the province last year after it was approached by Loblaws to put out the cream cheese under the President's Choice label.

He said that idea was rejected because it would have meant changing the packaging and stepping up production far beyond the dairy's capabilities.

Most consumed here

People's turns out only about 200,000 kilograms of the fresh cheese annually, with about 85 per cent of production consumed within the province.

The product, which comes in 250-gram bricks as other brands do, is not to be confused with Co-op's spreadable cream cheese, which comes in small tubs. Gidora said it's the block cream cheese, not the spread, that should be used for making cheesecake.

For best results, do not freeze cream cheese before using. Because of the high water content, it tends to crumble once it's defrosted, but baked cheesecakes can be frozen successfully.

Winnipeg cheesecake

Crust:
¾ cup graham wafer crumbs
½ cup brown sugar
Peel of 1 lemon, grated
¼ teaspoon cardamom
⅓ cup melted butter
Filling:
2 pounds (four 250g packages) cream cheese
¾ cup granulated sugar
Juice from ½ lemon
1 teaspoon vanilla

Preheat oven to 350°F.

To make crust, combine wafer crumbs, sugar, lemon rind, cardamom and melted butter; mix thoroughly. Press into the bottom of a buttered 10-inch springform pan.

In a large bowl, combine the cream cheese, eggs, granulated sugar, lemon juice and vanilla. Beat thoroughly and pour on top of the crust. Bake for 35 minutes.

When baking is complete, turn off oven, prop the oven door open with a

See YOU page 47

The Co-op's famous cream cheese was featured in the *Free Press* (Oct. 18, 1989). One former Winnipegger once described a "Winnipeg Care Package" as "A Jeannie's cake, Gunn's bagels, City rye bread, Old Country garlic sausage and Co-op cream cheese!"

lower-priced milk, the Co-op feared it would be squeezed out of the home-delivery trade.

Of course, the Co-op and Manco could protest the proposed changes all they wanted, but to little effect. Arguments that deregulation was inimical to the interests of the small-store owner, to the poorer residents of the North End and the core area, to the continued existence of any Manitoba-owned milk plants, and in the long-term, to milk consumers, fell on deaf ears. Arguments such as these, which had won the favourable attention of the NDP government and its appointees in 1984, had no impact in 1989. The proposals against which Gidora and officials of Manco had argued were put into place later in 1989, with the almost inevitable result.

Freed from any minimum price guidelines, the big stores could once again use milk as a loss-leader. Once again the competitive frenzy coincided with an economic downturn that made loss-leaders appealing to consumers, while making it even more difficult for small players. Although no one knew it at the time, there would be no reprieve for the People's Co-op this time round. The roller coaster ride was coming to an end.

THE BEGINNING OF THE END

When Mike Gidora was asked, at a June 1989 meeting of the Co-op's Board of Directors, what impact this partial deregulation of the milk industry would have on the Co-op, he gave a very cautious reply. In his estimation it was still too early to say, but he predicted that there would be some

Old-fashioned way gives cream cheese 'cleaner' taste

DAVE JOHNSON/WINNIPEG FREE PRESS

By Alice Krueger

People's Co-op cream cheese has been made the same old-fashioned way for 60 years.

Well, just about the same way. The co-op no longer uses giant boulders as weights to compress the cheese, explained production manager Steve Krall, whose grandfather, John, came here from Switzerland in the early '30s to become the co-op's first cheesemaker.

A mechanical press does the job now, but the stones still sit off to one side, just in case.

"We thought, this is stupid; somebody is going to get a hernia, so we designed the press about four years ago," general manager Mike Gidora explained.

The only other changes are new packaging, which was introduced about two years ago when the co-op decided to drop its use of the preservative potassium sorbate. Milk, cream, enzyme culture and salt are its only ingredients.

Co-op officials say it's the lack of preservatives, plus a "cold pack" production method, that sets their cream cheese apart from other brands and results in what Gidora describes as a "cleaner" taste.

Most other cream cheese products are made by what is known in the industry as the hot-pack method.

"It's a different process and it is a different product."

Ironically, noted Gidora, the dairy co-op has actually succeeded in extending the shelf life of the product to 90 days from the previous 35 by dropping the preservative.

Milk carton

Early packaging consisted of two sticks of cream cheese stuck inside a small milk carton to catch the whey, and stapled shut at the top.

To prevent the newer cardboard packages from becoming soggy, the updated version includes foil with a vacuum-sealed plastic overwrap.

Current cheesemaker is Luis Castro, a 25-year-old Chilean, whose presence has become the source of much good-natured banter in the Dufferin Avenue plant.

"We have a Chilean cheesemaker making a Swiss product that is loved by Jewish folks," joked Gidora.

People's Co-op production manager Steve Krall watches Mike Gidora hang bags of cream cheese to drain in bags.

You can't get cheesecake out of Winnipegger's soul

continued from page 35

folded tea towel and let the cake stand in the oven for about one hour.

Refrigerate for several hours before serving.

Serves 10 to 12.

(Recipe source: Heather Cram of Winnipeg, as published in *Across the Table* by Cynthia Wine)

Swedish tea ring

Filling:
1 package (250 g) cream cheese
¼ cup granulated sugar
½ teaspoon vanilla
Bread:
2 cups all-purpose flour
2 tablespoons granulated sugar
4 teaspoons baking powder
¾ teaspoon salt
¼ cup cold butter or margarine
1 cup cold milk
Nuts, raisins, chopped glaced cherries

Make filling first by beating cream cheese with sugar and vanilla

until smooth. Set aside.

To make dough, combine flour, sugar, baking powder and salt in bowl. Cut in butter until crumbly.

Add ¾ of milk first, adding the remaining ¼ cup if necessary to make a soft dough. Roll dough on lightly floured surface into rectangle about 8x12 inches.

Spread with cream cheese mixture. Sprinkle with nuts, raisins and chopped cherries. Beginning at long side, roll up into a roll; seal edge. Place on greased baking sheet, shaping into a circle. Seal ends together. Using scissors, cut over halfway through roll at 1-inch intervals. Turn each cut section on its side.

Bake in 425°F oven for about 15 to 20 minutes or until browned. If desired, brush with corn syrup to glaze while hot. May also be glazed with white icing, made by adding enough water to ½ cup icing sugar to make a barely pourable glaze. Drizzle over cooled tea ring.

(Recipe source: from Jean Pare's *Company's Coming* series)

The methods for preparing Co-op's cream cheese had not changed since John Krall's day, but the ethnic background of the cheese-makers had. The Co-op's cheese-maker in 1989 was a young Chilean, one of many new immigrants the Co-op employed.

decreased margins on milk, and some "reduced savings for the year."[3] This would prove to be the understatement of the year, for when the figures for 1989 were in, the Co-op showed an operating loss of $643,302. Nor was the Co-op alone in its plight. Selkirk's tiny Lakeland Dairy had already gone out of business and 1989 would see Manco – now a large multi-plant operation – sell out to a larger Saskatchewan-based co-op. Within months of deregulation the People's Co-op was the only Manitoba-owned dairy plant in Winnipeg. Even the giant dairy conglomerate Silverwoods (now known as Aults) sold its Manitoba operations to the new owners of Manco early in 1990, leading to a round of closures among the smaller and less profitable plants of the former Manco operation. If Manco and

Silverwoods could no longer compete in the Winnipeg market, the much smaller People's Co-operative had little chance.

This is not to say, however, that the Co-op was done fighting. A positive article in the *Winnipeg Free Press*, describing the virtues of Co-op cream cheese – and reminding readers that it was the essential ingredient for truly great cheese cake – sparked a 70 percent rise in Co-op cream cheese sales late in 1989. This prompted SuperValu's corporate parent to ask the Co-op to custom package "President's Choice Cream Cheese – Memories of Winnipeg" for its stores. This deal, however, was slow to reach fruition and was not enough to turn the Co-op around.

As losses on milk sales rose, the creamery could get no help from the Co-op's other departments. With the dismal economic situation of the late 1980s and early 1990s, Minnedosa, the lumber yard and the garage were lucky to break even or show only a small deficit, and most months, they too contributed to the Co-op's losses in 1990 and 1991. Everyone recognized that the Co-op could not continue to lose money at this pace, but it was running out of options. In the old days the Board would have turned to its shareholders and employees and asked for contributions. But the sad reality was that the vast majority of the Co-op's shareholders were now either pensioners or the absentee inheritors of Co-op shares, neither of whom were likely to put their life-savings on the line to help the Co-op. And although the Co-op still had some very dedicated and loyal employees, the sacrifices that its workers and shareholders had been willing to make in the 1920s, 1930s and 1940s were clearly a thing of the past. Nor could one blame them, for they were living through difficult financial times and earning less than the industry average. Moreover, only a handful shared the political and social vision that had motivated so many of the Co-op's early workers. The remaining plant and delivery workers felt that they were already making a great enough contribution to the Co-op and needed wage increases at least equal to the rate of inflation, not rollbacks or contributions.

Endings, of course, are never pleasant affairs and this was true for the Co-op. With losses mounting daily, negotiations for new contracts became nightmares for all concerned, and every negotiation from 1989 onwards was probably more difficult than at any other time in the Co-op's history. The enforced retrenchments of the winter of 1990–91 were extremely unpopular: routes were cut, plant positions eliminated, staff reduced at the lumber yard and garage, attempts were made to negotiate wage cuts at the lumber yard, pressure was put on people to take early retirement, a management position was cut and a wage reduction imposed on all remaining managers. But the anticipated quarter-million-dollar savings from these moves would barely scratch the surface of the Co-op's mounting deficit and would increase the division between the Co-op and its remaining employees. Most dramatic of all though, was the decision in the spring of 1991 to convert the Co-op's retail driver/salesmen into independent contractors.

The Co-op had long been the only dairy in Winnipeg to resist this trend. In 1990, the Co-op and Dairyland were the only two dairies which still

employed their own delivery personnel. However, so severe was the crisis that Gidora and the Board felt the Co-op had no choice but to make this change which it had long resisted as a matter of principle. Naturally, many drivers disliked this move. One told the *Winnipeg Sun* of his profound disappointment that the Co-op, a workers' institution, would adopt such a system.

As dramatic and controversial as this decision had been, there were more heart-wrenching changes. By May 1991, the Co-op was considering selling the lumber yard to Eskimo Point and at roughly the same time, Beatrice Foods expressed interest in the Co-op's dairy operations. The Co-op was still convinced that if it could get its bank overdraft down to a reason-

Cantor's, a small supermarket in the Weston area of the city, provoked a price war that sent milk prices so low that no small dairy could compete. (Ad, July 23, 1991)

John Sas recalled, "The milk price war in the 1980s was mean and ugly. It basically went after us because our customer-base was the home-delivery, what we lived and died with. But we just had to match it with our competitors and then we started looking at ways to save money. One of the ugliest things that I remember in my job as sales manager is telling a guy who's been there for twenty-five years that we're combining routes, saying, 'You might have 200 customers, but we're combining it to make it 350 customers and you're not going to be able to do it.'"

able level, sell the lumber yard and continue to effect economies in the creamery, then at least the creamery and the garage department might survive.

Unfortunately, this proved to be overly optimistic, primarily because of the latest price war. Ever since deregulation the major chain stores had kept milk at fairly low prices, and would occasionally put milk on sale, but no sustained undercutting took place – just a long slow battle of attrition. In the summer of 1991, Cantor's, a fairly large independent retailer, reopened the milk wars.

The last Board of Directors of the People's Co-op, 1992. Standing, left to right: Darcy Humeniuk, David Mackling, Gordon Billows, Hubert Ostermann, John Stefaniuk. Seated: Kosty Kostaniuk, Bill Kardash, Harry Stefaniuk. (Missing: Walter Weremiuk)

Located on Logan Avenue, Joe Cantor's store had long been a minor irritant to Winnipeg's larger stores, for it had consistently undersold them on milk prices since 1989. Because they had no stores in his immediate vicinity the big chains largely ignored Cantor, but this changed quite suddenly when Cantor launched his own price war in 1991, and in the process turned the Co-op into an unwilling combatant. The opening salvo came when Cantor announced that he planned to have the Co-op custom package milk for him, which he would sell at low prices. But before this deal was formalized, Cantor decided to drop the price of a two-litre container of 2 percent milk by eight cents, putting his price twenty-three cents lower than either Safeway or SuperValu. It also sparked a public fight between the Co-op and Cantor. Gidora, who knew that Cantor was selling the Co-op's milk for five cents less than he was paying for it, saw such blatant loss-leaders as a threat to the entire dairy industry.

The Co-op immediately withdrew from its deal with Cantor's, but the damage was already done. With all of the press coverage, and Cantor's advertising, the big chains could no longer ignore Cantor's price slashing. Within a week Safeway and SuperValu matched his price, so Cantor dropped his price even further. By August of 1991 milk prices in Winnipeg were lower than since 1984–85. No small dairy could compete.

Nothing was going the Co-op's way that summer. Negotiations with Eskimo Point over the purchase of the lumber yard were stalled, with the two sides hundreds of thousands of dollars apart. Contract talks with the Creamery Workers' Union were heading towards a strike vote. And Co-op deficits were on their way to a record loss of $702,000 for 1991.

Hope was not completely dashed. When the purchase agreement with Eskimo Point finally went through on November 1 there was a sense that the Co-op had turned the corner. Although it had received $200,000 less for the lumber yard and inventory than hoped for, and all the employees of the lumber yard had to be laid off as part of the deal, the sale did give the Co-op some breathing room. And with a truce of sorts in the milk price war, milk sales increased in the early months of 1992. Many environmentally conscious consumers seemed to be drawn to the innovative milk carton recycling program the Co-op had introduced in 1990 and the fact that the Co-op's trucks had been propane-powered for several years. A deal had finally been struck with Loblaws to package cream cheese for SuperValu, an arrangement which would yield the Co-op a guaranteed profit of $6,000 per month. Some on the Board of Directors still believed, early in 1992, that with further economies in the creamery and a turn-around at the garage, the Co-op had a future.

Members at a special Shareholders Meeting, October 20, 1992 at the Ukrainian Labour Temple, the birthplace of the Co-op. After hearing presentations from Board members **Kosty Kostaniuk** and **Bill Kardash** (seen below speaking), the vast majority of shareholders agreed to sell the Co-op to the employees.

AN ENDING AND
A NEW BEGINNING

This, however, was not the majority opinion. Having seen the Co-op amass deficits of well over half-a-million dollars for each of the past three years, many Board members believed that the Co-op should sell its remaining assets to protect shareholders and depositors. This was an obligation the Board took very seriously. Kardash, Kostaniuk and Bill Popowich had spent most of their lives in or around

the Co-op and knew that for many shareholders and depositors, the money they had in the Co-op was literally their life savings; money that these senior citizens could ill afford to lose. By the summer of 1992 it was clear to the Board that the Co-op would have to be sold to protect those people. The only question was to whom, for there were now two purchase offers on the table: one from Beatrice and the other from the Co-op's own workers.

The workers, keenly aware of the Co-op's problems, had started talking about forming their own employee-run co-operative as early as 1991. These discussions were motivated at least in part by rumours that Beatrice was interested in buying out the Co-op, but only for its equipment, client list and goodwill – not the actual land or buildings. Selling to Beatrice would probably cost all of the Co-op's remaining employees their jobs. Under the leadership of Rick Quinn, the Co-op's chief engineer, a plan was put together whereby the employees would purchase all of the Co-op's assets and run the dairy,

land at the old creamery. These could eventually be sold or converted into any other form of enterprise. Moreover, there was a strong feeling among Board members that this offer would be upped by another quarter- to half-million dollars. Even after deducting the costs of severance pay for the employees who would be let go under the terms of this deal, the Beatrice offer made the most sense in financial terms.

But the Co-op had never been just about money. True, there were times in the recent past it had been forced to make decisions based almost entirely upon financial considerations. But at its very core the Board of Directors knew that the way the People's Co-op came to a close could not be predicated on what was most profitable. However, the profound sense of responsibility the Board felt towards the shareholders had to be balanced with its desire to do the right thing for the employees. Thus, considerable time

Closing the deal. In October of 1992 the sale of the Co-op to its employees was finalized. Shown above, **Dave Mackling** and **Bill Kardash** signing for the People's Co-op, and right, **Rick Quinn** for the Dufferin Employment Co-operative.

the garage and the Minnedosa plant themselves – saving at least sixty-five to seventy jobs.

Over the course of late 1991 and 1992 this embryonic co-op within a co-op put together a business plan which they hoped would convince the provincial government to help finance their proposed purchase and to update the plant. By April of 1992 the Dufferin Employment Co-operative Limited (DECL) was ready to make a formal purchase offer – $845,000 for the Winnipeg and Minnedosa creameries, the garage and all other real assets.

By the time the Board had decided to sell the Co-op, though, Beatrice had made a firm offer, which was much better in financial terms. In August, Beatrice offered $2,250,000, which would have allowed the Co-op to continue butter-making operations at Minnedosa, keep the garage business in its entirety and retain possession of the buildings and

Historic dairy to draw last litre

By Treena Khan
City Hall Reporter

THE DAIRY that created Winnipeg cream cheese will close its doors at the end of the month.

The former Co-op Dairies on Dufferin Avenue will close April 26, owner Dairyworld announced yesterday, cutting 22 jobs. Operations will move to Dairyworld's more modern Brandon plant.

A Winnipeg distribution centre will remain open.

But Coun. Glen Murray said the company should reconsider before shutting down a piece of Winnipeg history — and part of the solution to the national unity problem.

"This is the solution, the perfect food — a bagel from Montreal, Winnipeg cream cheese and B.C. salmon," he said with laugh.

Dairyworld merged with Dairy Producers Co-operative Ltd. of Regina, Sask. in January. The closure of the plant was to increase efficiency, said Dairyworld's regional director Jeff Martin.

With tax breaks from the city on historic buildings or funding under the Winnipeg Development Agreement, the old dairy could be saved, he said.

He added Manitoba's Crocus Fund might be interested in supporting the project.

was spent examining the DECL's chances for success and crunching numbers to make certain that all of the depositors' loans and the shareholder's investments could be covered by the proposed deal with its workers. After much soul-searching, and several increases in the offer from Beatrice, the Board of Directors decided to call a special membership meeting on October 20, 1992 to recommend to the assembled shareholders the sale of all the Co-op's assets to its employees.

This was not an easy meeting to preside over or to attend, for it was pervaded by a sense of sadness and profound loss. It was conducted in the Ukrainian Labour Temple, the very same hall where the Co-op had been formed, and a sense of history haunted those in attendance. While the crowd was small – only seventy-two people cast votes that day – many there had dedicated large parts of their lives to the Co-op. Yet, there was almost a sense of joy as well, for at the end of the day – and despite a last minute offer from Beatrice of $3 million – the shareholders overwhelmingly voted to sell the Co-op to the workers for $1 million. This final act of altruism, of "doing the right thing", was perhaps the only way that the People's Co-op ever could have lived up to its own goals, and, in the final analysis, it did just that. It had secured enough from the DECL to ensure that, along with the Co-op's existing resources, every depositor and every shareholder would be well provided for. But it had also stood up to corporate capitalism one last time and proven that not everything – especially not the co-operative ideal – was subject to market forces. It was, in short, a magnificent and fitting end for "the little red dairy on the prairie."

This story has a more sombre coda. The Co-op members had done the right thing: but that did not guarantee the new worker-owned co-operative's future. Competition in the Winnipeg dairy business remained fierce. Within two years DECL was taken over by a British Columbia-based corporation, Dairyland. Two years later Dairyland decided it could meet its local demand from its other Winnipeg plant, and the old Co-op dairy building fell before the wrecking ball.

■ ■ ■

1   PCL, Box 1, Hearings-MCB, "Submission of the People's Co-op Ltd. to the MCB, May14, 1975."

2   Ibid., "Gordon Mackenzie, Acting Secretary of the Manitoba Milk Prices Review Commission to W.A. Kardash, Dec. 1, 1980."

3   PCL, Minute Book 4, "Minutes of the Board of Directors Meeting, June 25, 1989."

The People's Co-op had become a North End institution as unique in character as the North End itself. Its distinctive logo – "Co-op" rising over North America – was a familiar sight around Winnipeg and Manitoba for over sixty years and, given the Co-op's mandate, was a fitting trademark for this co-operative.

CHAPTER ELEVEN
A FITTING CONCLUSION

By now, most readers will have come to their own conclusions as to just how successful the People's Co-operative was. Some, of course, may wish to judge the Co-op harshly on political grounds, a choice that would hardly surprise the activists who founded and led it. Others will argue that the Co-op could have found a way to continue on in some modified form – the "what ifs" of history are always intriguing. Still others will see in the Co-op's struggle a pointless fight that went against the norms of Canadian society and which therefore never had any realistic chance of succeeding. Finally, there will be those who see in the rise and fall of the Co-op a simple barometer of the political and economic climate of the times.

I would argue, however, that none of these assessments do the Co-op justice, for its history is far more complex than that of a simple political or economic entity. It saw itself, from the moment of its founding, as an educational, political, economic and community institution for the working class in general and for the left-wing Ukrainian Canadian community of the North End in particular, and in those

terms of reference it succeeded. To take but one example, consider the countless young people from that community who got jobs at the Co-op. In the context of the 1930s, 1940s and 1950s it might have been almost impossible for some of these people to find decent jobs elsewhere, as the political activities of their families, their own political activities and, sometimes, merely their ethnicity excluded them from countless other opportunities, particularly during the worst days of the Depression and the Cold War.

Later, the Co-op provided jobs to a new generation of political activists, particularly those who had been forced to flee Chile after the assassination of Salvadore Allende. And hundreds of summer and part-time employment opportunities were provided for the young people of the North End as they attempted to work their way through school. The list of those who can claim the Co-op as one of their alma maters is indeed impressive: several luminaries of the Canadian left, such as Norman Penner, who would go on to become one of Canada's more distinguished and controversial political scientists,

The Wind-up Committee of the People's Co-operative with their legal counsel. Left to right, **Kosty Kostaniuk**, **Edward Chornous** (legal counsel), **Harry Stefaniuk** and **David Mackling** (insets, **Bill Popowich** and **Bill Kardash**, both deceased).

As it wound up the Co-op's affairs, the committee strove to locate every shareholder or their descendants in order to return share capital. Bill Kardash's son, **Ted Kardash**, recalled the way his father made sure that none of the people who had built and supported Co-op were overlooked in this process:

"Over the last years of his life, my dad was occupied with winding down the affairs of the Co-op which consisted mainly of disbursement of funds to shareholders. He worked, basically full time at that for quite some time. The minute, painstaking work that he and Kosty went through to trace people. They put ads in the paper, they found people spread around Canada and the United States and really went to a lot of effort to ensure that people received their due from the shares that had been in Co-op. In many instances, people didn't even know that they had this money and, in many instances, people were very grateful. I saw the joy that it brought Dad, that he could deliver, sometimes, fairly large sums of money to people. And even the small sums were often gratefully received. Often it was the children or even the grandchildren of the original shareholders, so there would be reminiscing and connecting, and that was really important to Dad."

and his brother, Roland Penner, who would become both a professor of law and Manitoba's Attorney General, worked at the Co-op just as their father, Alderman Jake Penner, had done before them. And the Co-op also provided employment to countless future teachers, university professors, doctors, lawyers and other professionals over the years – most of whom came from the North End community the Co-op so conscientiously served.

Nor did the Co-op limit its contributions to providing work or services to the people of the North End. The leaders of the Co-op were also community leaders: Kolisnyk, Bileski and Kardash in particular were indefatigable fighters for the rights of North Enders on City Council, the school board and in the provincial legislature. Nor did that role cease when they were out of office. On behalf of both the Co-op and the residents of the North End, Bill Kardash put hundreds of hours, from the late 1960s through to the early 1980s, into his role as a critic of the city's proposed Sherbrook-McGregor Overpass project. And these were not simple "it would hurt the Co-op" presentations – which such an overpass would certainly have done, either by forcing the Co-op to relocate its creamery or by limiting its working space through expropriation. By looking at the bigger picture, Kardash's arguments became finely honed critiques of the city's failure to implement plans that would truly revitalize the North End and the core area by enforcing rail line relocation and completely redeveloping the urban wasteland that was the CPR's main yard. As Kardash argued, it was this, not another bridge over those yards, which would have been an important first step in starting a renaissance in these once vital, but now decaying, neighbourhoods.

(left) Before the Co-op's books were officially closed, it made several donations to agencies and organizations throughout the city and province, in keeping with its tradition of community support. Shown here is a presentation to the Original Women's Network. (right) The Co-op always placed great importance on education: after its first year, it set aside 10 percent of its surplus for educational purposes. At its closing, it set up the People's Co-operative Education Fund. Here, **David Mackling** presents a cheque to **Rick Frost** of the Winnipeg Foundation to establish the fund.

And there were many other ways in which the Co-op sought to help the North End. In the 1980s it was an early and active corporate member of the Selkirk Avenue 100 Plus Group, a body whose goal was once again the revitalization of the North End. And the Co-op was always willing to put its money where its mouth was – at least when it had money. While it had started out with very small contributions in the 1930s, sometimes being able to afford nothing more than $1 worth of milk tickets to help support various community causes and events, over the years these contributions steadily increased until they amounted to hundreds of thousands of dollars that went to various North End institutions. The Mount Carmel Clinic, the Ukrainian Senior Citizens Club of Winnipeg, the Ukrainian Labour Temple, the Ivan Franko Manor (a senior's residence), the North End YMCA, the Shalom Aleichem Centre and the WBA's children's summer camp, to name but a few, were the beneficiaries of the Co-op's community spirit. Then there were the thousands upon thousands of dollars in direct contributions and indirect advertising contributions that helped to keep several progressive Ukrainian and English language papers alive. And this charitable tradition spilled over to other parts of the city, the

nation and even the world, as the Co-op provided donations to the University of Manitoba, to national, provincial and civic centennial projects, to the celebrations of the anniversaries of Ukrainian immigration to Canada, to various musical ensembles, to campaigns to provide milk for the children of El Salvador, to earthquake relief in Armenia, to the Tools For Peace program which aided impoverished Nicaraguans and to countless other such causes.

Beyond this, to the very end of its existence, the Co-op remained a strong voice for social change. It might have been in the fuel, lumber, garage and dairy businesses but that never stopped its annual shareholders' meetings from protesting against the way African Americans were treated in the southern United States in the 1950s and 1960s, against the war in Vietnam, against the murder of black South Africans by the apartheid regime or against nuclear testing. Nor was the Co-op afraid to add its voice to the protests against its own governments. The mistreatment of Canada's native peoples, the Goods and Service Tax, the Free Trade Agreement and a host of other harmful government policies – be they civic, provincial or national – all received scathing condemnations from the Co-op's shareholders over the years.

In short, as an institution, the People's Co-operative always had the courage of its convictions and
tried to live up to them – a rare commodity in any
time and place. That it was able to combine this
commitment to principle with the successful management of a set of economic enterprises which
employed thousands of people over the sixty-four
years of its existence – and served tens of thousands more in a variety of ways – was a remarkable
achievement by any standard. But, that this was all
accomplished on the basis of the dreams and life
savings of impoverished and often despised immigrants makes that achievement quite miraculous.

Perhaps it is true that only in a place such as
Winnipeg's North End could such an institution
really thrive. The North End's tradition of political
radicalism, its much broader political spectrum and
its sense of economic, ethnic and political alienation
from the rest of Winnipeg certainly provided fertile
soil for the Co-op. But it is also the case that the
Co-op nurtured those traditions. Along with other
agencies such as the Ukrainian Labour Farmer
Temple Association, the Association of United
Ukrainian Canadians, the Workers Benevolent
Association, the United Jewish People's Order, the
Federation of Russian Canadians and several other
such groups of eastern and central Europeans, it
very consciously helped to create a culture which
allowed and encouraged those who did not accept
the world as it was, to think and act differently. And,
because there is always a price to pay for thinking
differently, the Co-op provided a safe haven for
many of those who were activists for social change.

The Co-op consistently provided an example of
how things could be done in a different manner.
Co-operative rather than private ownership, service
at cost rather than for profit and standing up for the
rights of the common person – the worker, the
small storekeeper, the aged and the very young –
were all principles the Co-op fought for throughout
its history. And even though times and political fash-
ions changed considerably between 1928 and 1992,
the Co-op's commitment did not fade. Indeed, if one
considers the Co-op's final act of altruism – the sale
of its assets to its employees for one third of what
it could have received, so that these jobs could be
saved through a new co-operative endeavour – it

was the perfect conclusion to a tremendous record
of service and commitment.

Of course, no institution is perfect, and as the
preceding pages have shown, mistakes were made.
But on balance, and by its own very demanding standards, the Co-op was a success story. Indeed, even
in a strictly business sense it was a success, for as
the People's Co-op wound up its affairs in the years
following 1992, it was able to repay loans to every
depositor it could locate, plus huge amounts of
accrued interest, and to provide to every shareholder it could find a return several times their original investment – much to the surprise and joy of
many elderly shareholders who unexpectedly
received large cheques in the mail. Indeed, even after
all of these disbursements were made there was still
enough money left over for one final and sizable
round of charitable donations to North End,
Winnipeg and Manitoba institutions and to the
Winnipeg Foundation for the establishment of a
People's Co-op scholarship fund. Clearly, the faith
that the shareholders and dedicated long-serving
employees like Eloise Popiel, Albert Valleay, Peter
Kochan, Nick Mateychuck and many others had
invested in "the little red dairy on the prairie" had
not been misplaced.

At the end of the day, the Co-op's sixty-four-year
history strikes me as an inspiring story of what people of very little means and influence can do if they
put their minds and hearts into it. Dedication, hard
work, co-operation, commitment to principle and
attention to detail are not passé – or at least they
should not be. In my more hopeful moments, I
remain convinced that the success of the People's
Co-operative might yet be replicated by another
generation who harbour a view of the future that
does not accept the cold logic of the marketplace as
inevitable. As the new millennium unfolds, we need
more institutions like the People's Co-op that can
help to build communities and encourage people to
think in alternative, co-operative ways. We will need
these "havens in a heartless world" more than ever.

"I still meet guys on the street who say, 'Gee, I wish you guys still would have been around.' I still drive by that empty lot and take a look and think to myself what we could have done and what we could have achieved, but it's done, it's finished. Out of the 29 years there were 28 good years. Sure, there were a lot of problems and rocky roads, but everybody worked, everybody made a fair wage."
John Sas

"Many people you talk to express their sadness about the Co-op. Many of our children got their education, because in the summer holidays they hired these young people, they would earn money to further their education. Many of our retirees and the old employees, there wasn't a year that we didn't think about those employees at Christmas time. We would buy turkeys and wrap them and personally deliver them to these employees."
Harry Stefaniuk

"You could almost say it was a 'home away from home' feeling. The office staff was friendly, the sales staff was friendly, the employees that you worked with were friendly. It was a nice place to work for. I'd like to think I helped it build in its time and it was sad to see it go, but time moved on."
Tim Kostaniuk

"It was heartbreaking when we found out that they were actually breaking up. A lot of people were crying, me, number one. We always came to a resolution, everything always turned out okay, so you expect everything to go on and on the same way. You can have big arguments, but in the end, it comes out one way and the people are satisfied, at least most are satisfied. It's very hard to take, especially for people who had been there for so many years like me, and there was nobody there longer than me.

"When I go past the Co-op, now that they've broken down the building, I don't even want to look there. I have a brick that one of the girls who worked there got for me."
Eloise Popiel

"You'd almost think that the Co-op's legacy was that it helped raise a lot of generations. It helped me grow up. It was a like a counsellor, a big brother, an uncle. The Co-op helped a lot of people grow and live. Without the Co-op, a lot of people probably would not enjoy life today, a lot of people who retired from the Co-op wouldn't enjoy a nice retirement or the fact that they got there, because you have to have a decent job to get there, a job that provided a decent income and a pension. So there are a lot of people around today who are comfortable because of the jobs they had at Co-op. Whether it was hard or not, it still provided a good wage."
Bob Pawlyk

"When the Co-op was sold to the employees, I felt sorry. I liked everything from the Co-op. Now, it's not the same cheese, or cream, nothing. When I worked there, everything was good. Now, the butter is no good; it has no taste. They won prizes all the time because everything was the best."
Sophie Bilecki

"It's a sad situation for us [there being no Co-op]. I don't know at the time if we really appreciated as much as we do now the things that we had and what we lost when the Co-op finally ended up being sold to a big company and they took the place apart and now it's just an empty lot."
Arthur Gunn

"Co-op made me the person that I am – values, family values. We were all together. Everybody got treated the same and that showed you that one person was never better than the other. They showed how you could make a business run by investing which was, I think, 60 percent of their success, investing in something else besides milk. But the money they made, they gave it not to the Co-op but to the employees. When I left, they handled their money wisely, they looked after my little savings account wisely and it will help me in my retirement years."
Murphy Dola

A Brief Note on Sources

This book has been based largely upon the records of the People's Co-operative Limited. Although still held privatel, and housed in the Ukrainian Labour Temple in Winnipeg, this collection will eventually be transferred to the Provincial Archives of Manitoba where it, and the tape recordings from the still ongoing People's Co-op Oral History Project, will be available to all researchers. This is a particularly rich collection, consisting of an almost full run of minute books from 1928 to 1992[1] and hundreds of linear feet of correspondence files, financial records, personnel files, submissions to various government bodies, in-house publications and records of many activities related to the creamery, fuel yard, garage and lumber trades in Winnipeg and Minnedosa. Because the managers and office staff of the Co-op had a keen sense of history – and were what can only be described as "pack-rats" – documents that would have been removed by "records management specialists" as being irrelevant to the day-to-day functioning of the business, remain within the collection. Moreover, because these people were the original conservationists (no piece of paper was ever left with only one side written upon) wonderful surprises confront the researcher when he or she flips the page and finds an advertising flyer or some other Co-op publication thought to be long lost.

Still, while this is a fine collection, those interested in the political side of the Co-op will be somewhat disappointed. Given the obvious political orientation of the Co-op's founders and management collective, there are relatively few direct references to political matters. The Co-op's records, while they document a strong commitment to issues of social and economic justice, are nowhere near as politicized as one might expect; indeed, it turns out that the Co-op was just as likely to make contributions to local charities and institutions, including churches and religious societies, as to the Communist Party of Canada. There are, however, some very useful inklings concerning a handful of political matters, such as the Lobay affair of the mid-1930s, the Simonite Inquiry, the impact of the raids and internments of 1940 and the red-baiting of the Cold War era.

While the Co-op's internal records were crucial to this study, they were heavily supplemented by a number of collections held in the Provincial Archives of Manitoba (PAM), the City of Winnipeg Archives and the National Archives of Canada (NAC). Of these, by far the most important were the heretofore unexamined papers[2] of J.D. Cameron held at the PAM (GR 1528, Range 30). Cameron, a former manager with Crescent Creamery, came to occupy a unique vantage point on the Winnipeg milk trade. He served as the Secretary of the Municipal and Public Utilities Board when it was first empowered to regulate the milk trade in Winnipeg, and he served in that role, or similar ones, with each successor to the Board until the 1950s. In this collection one finds file upon file of commission reports, verbatim records of testimony heard at various milk inquiries, and Cameron's correspondence with his appointed/political superiors, and between him and various creameries, milk producers, and special investigators. As well, there are Cameron's remarkably frank and often insightful memos and background papers on the "milk situation" in Winnipeg. Cameron also kept the most amazing collection of clippings and assorted trade journals and public reports, covering virtually every aspect of developments within the "Winnipeg milk shed." All in all, for anyone with an interest in the Winnipeg dairy trade, or in the evolution of government regulation within an industry, this is the place to start.

Also of considerable use were the PAM's collection of records dealing with the Milk Prices Review Commission (GR 1672), the Manitoba Milk Producers' Co-operative Incorporated (P 5185 – P 5218) and the records of the Attorney-General of Manitoba (GR 1542 A or old series RG 3 C1 (41)). This last collection, particularly Box 4, Files 41–42, proved to be a rich mine of data on both the financial health of the Co-op and its political troubles in the difficult years of 1939–41, as it contains all the reports derived from the seized Co-op records, a forensic audit of its books and many police and government reports concerning the Co-op and its relationship with other parts of the Ukrainian left. One of the chief advantages of this provincial source is that it contains unedited RCMP reports on the Co-op, a true blessing for any researcher who has been confronted by the numerous "blacked out" sections of RCMP reports acquired under the access to information regulations of the NAC.

The City of Winnipeg Archives – a vastly under-utilized repository – provided much of the information pertinent to the Simonite Inquiry. File A 47 is a researcher's delight, as it contains not only lengthy and often verbatim accounts of the proceedings and testimony, but also includes a wide range of contemporary newspaper reports. Minute books of Winnipeg's City Council were also useful, particularly those pertaining to the Special Committee on Unemployment Relief. Files in the City's H-series record group, notably H 217, H 480, H 1372, H 1458 and H 1617, also provided invaluable data on the key role played by the City government in regulating and influencing the business practices of the Winnipeg milk industry from the 1920s onwards. Finally, File H-206 and a few less focused files are among the very few sources available on the Winnipeg coal and fuel wood trade.

The Legislative Library of Manitoba was yet another important source of information for published government reports, but especially for its political scrapbooks and its fine microfilm collection of Manitoba newspapers. Winnipeg's mainstream press, represented by the *Free Press* and the *Tribune*, provided considerable background information on most of the matters discussed in this work. The short-lived (and co-operatively owned) *Winnipeg Citizen* was also useful, as were a few community newspapers, but it was the Ukrainian-language press, particularly the *Ukrainian Labor News* and its successor publications, which gave the most fulsome coverage to everything the Co-op did from its founding. Other publications such as the *Financial Post*, and especially the *Minnedosa Tribune*, were heavily used in the course of this study, while a smattering of specifically anti-communist publications such as *The Ensign*, and a series of Ukrainian-language anti-communist publications were also consulted regarding particular issues.

The final source of primary materials used in the preparation of this book is the RCMP records housed in the Record of the Canadian Security Intelligence Service (RG 146 Vols. 4089–4091 and 4163) at the NAC. After a long and arduous vetting process, hundreds of pages of "confidential" records were finally copied and released, although far too many of these pages were blank, removed from the file altogether or heavily "blacked out" for reasons unstated, but somehow or other "pursuant to the provisions of the Access to Information Act." Still, despite the limitations of these censored documents, they illustrate just how closely the Mounties were watching the Co-op, right from 1928 until the 1970s. The records which pertained to the late 1920s through to the 1940s had far fewer blank spots than those for subsequent years, so the researcher is able to get a much better idea of the RCMP's view of the Co-op for that period. These records, when cross-referenced with the unedited copies of RCMP reports which ended up in the PAM, scattered throughout the files of the Attorney General of Manitoba and in the papers of political leaders such as Premier John Bracken, are of considerable interest and show the extent of police harassment of left-wing organizations such as the Co-op.

Space does not allow a full listing of all the works consulted in the preparation of this book. However, the work of a few authors must be mentioned. The literature on co-operatives in Canada is surprisingly limited, but Ian Macpherson's work, especially *Each For All: A History of the Co-operative Movement in English Canada, 1900–1945* (Toronto: The Macmillan Company, 1979) is an important exception to this rule, and provides an outstanding analysis of the mainstream co-operative movement in

Canada. Regarding Winnipeg, and its ethnic and class divisions, Allan Artibise's numerous articles and book length studies, including *Winnipeg: An Illustrated History* (Toronto: James Lorimer and Company, 1977) are the place to start. Meanwhile, Ruben Bellan has detailed many aspects of the city's economic history in several works, most notably *Winnipeg First Century: An Economic History* (Winnipeg: Queenston House Publishing, 1978). The unique nature of Winnipeg's political life has been examined by several political scientists and historians, but the best work is that of A. B. McKillop in *Citizen and Socialist: The Ethos of Political Winnipeg, 1919–1935*, (Winnipeg: unpublished Master's thesis, University of Manitoba) and J.E. Rea's work on civic politics from the time of the General Strike through to the 1970's, particularly *Parties and Power: An Analysis of Winnipeg's City Council, 1919–1975* (Winnipeg: The City of Winnipeg, 1976).

Ukrainians in Winnipeg, the West and in Canada have been covered in many different studies, ranging from J.S. Woodsworth's *Strangers Within Our Gates* (Toronto: University of Toronto, 1972 – reprint of the 1909 original), through Paul Yuzyk's *The Ukrainians in Manitoba* (Toronto: University of Toronto Press, 1953) up to Orest Martynowych's *Ukrainians in Canada: The Formative Years, 1891–1924* (Edmonton: Canadian Institute of Ukrainian Studies Press, 1991) – with many stops in between. The last of these works is the best balanced and most nuanced account of Ukrainians in Canada, although its usefulness is limited owing to the time span covered. More encyclopedic and covering far more ground is Michael Marunchak's *The Ukrainian Canadians: A History* (Winnipeg: Ukrainian Free Academy of Sciences, 1970), but it is seriously flawed by a poor translation and some poor editing. However, various works by Francis Swyripa, including both her fine analyses of the historiography of the Ukrainian experience in Canada, and her deeply researched work on Ukrainian Canadian women, *Wedded to the Cause: Ukrainian Canadian Women and Ethnic Identity, 1891–1991* (Toronto: University of Toronto Press, 1993) help to bring the history of Ukrainian Canadians up to date, both in terms of time and scholarship.

On the involvement of Ukrainian Canadians in left-wing political, social and cultural organizations there is a wide variety of sources. Most of the works dealing with the Canadian Communist Party or with Ukrainian Canadians have lengthy, and usually harsh, assessments of the political role played by radical Ukrainian Canadians. For example, readers familiar with Paul Yuzyk's work will be aware of how hard he worked to separate the majority of Ukrainian Canadians from what he saw as a noisy, troublesome (and to him) embarrassing minority of radicals. Meanwhile, former Communists have also had much to say in works such as John Kolasky's *The Shattered Illusion: The History of Ukrainian Pro-Communist Organizations in Canada* (Toronto: Peter Martin Associates, 1979). However, those on the left have not been shy about getting their own point of view across, and have a strong tradition of publishing their views to ensure that their message is not lost. The Workers' Benevolent Association, for example, has written its own history, *Friends in Need: The WBA Story, A Canadian Epic in Fraternalism* (Winnipeg: The WBA, 1972). And the works of Peter Krawchuk — both in Ukrainian and in English translation — takes this tradition a step further.

A long-time activist within the ULFTA and AUUC, and one of the left's leading Ukrainian-language journalists, Krawchuck produced a quite sizable body of work over the years. He wrote short biographies of important leaders of the early Ukrainian left (Popowich, Navis and Shatulsky), histories of Ukrainians in Winnipeg, of the early socialist movement among Ukrainian Canadians and of the internment of left-wing leaders during World War Two and on several other topics related to Ukrainian Canadian history, literature and politics. These works, written by a participant and/or observer of many of the events described, are somewhat akin to primary documents and must be handled accordingly, for they are very much shaped by the author's perceptions and passions. Krawchuck's most fascinating publication is undoubtedly *Our History: The Ukrainian Labour-Farmer Movement in Canada, 1907–1991* (Toronto: Lugus Publications, 1996). This is an extremely useful compendium of information on the Ukrainian Canadian left, and in some ways is the capstone of Krawchuck's lengthy writing career. It embodies much of the research (unfortunately most of this is badly documented, when documented at all) that had gone into his earlier works, but it also includes some new source materials which Krawchuck apparently had in his possession for several decades and never revealed. This material, which related to the often bitter relationship between leaders of the ULFTA and the Communist Party in the late 1920s and 1930s, was used by Krawchuck to craft a very positive interpretation of the left-wing Ukrainian organizations, yet one which came to an overtly anti-Soviet set of conclusions — a fascinating shift for a man who had been so closely associated with the pro-Soviet faction of the Ukrainian Canadian left from the 1920s until the early 1990s.

There are several other works written by former activists, such as William and Kathleen Repka's *Dangerous Patriots: Canada's Unknown Prisoners of War* (Vancouver: New Star Books, 1982), which are also useful, and more will certainly be forthcoming, at least if the plans of people like John Boyd (known as Boychuk when he worked at the Co-op) are realized. But the most promising work in this field is a recently launched research project designed to record the history of the AUUC and ULFTA. A multi-year oral history project, conducted under the auspices of the Canadian Society for Ukrainian Labour Research, this project holds phenomenal promise. Indeed, if the preliminary results are anything to go by, researchers will soon have yet another outstanding source of "new" oral documents to cull through as they examine the complex and fascinating history of the Ukrainian Canadian left.

Of course, many more theses, articles and books than the few mentioned above have been utilized in the course of writing this book, but it is hoped that this very brief listing of primary and secondary source materials will provide an entry point for those who would like conduct their own investigations into this intriguing field.

■ ■ ■

1   Eighteen months of minutes are missing for the period 1938–40. My assumption is that they were lost either when they were seized by the provincial government in the raid of 1940, or shortly after their return to the Co-op. The gap in the bound minute books is partially filled by handwritten draft notes located in another file, covering late 1939 to the summer of 1940. Minutes for the last few years of the Co-op's existence were never transcribed or put into bound minute books, but they do survive in rough, handwritten form.

2   The strings which had been used to bind the files when they were put away for storage literally had to be cut by Archives staff so that I could examine them.